MATERIALS OF THE SCENE

AN INTRODUCTION TO TECHNICAL THEATRE

WELBY B. WOLFE

Professor Emeritus, Theatre Arts Department
University of Northern Colorado at Greeley

HARPER & ROW, Publishers
New York   Hagerstown   San Francisco   London

FOR IRENE
for her endurance, encouragement, and criticism.

Sponsoring Editor: *James B. Smith*
Project Editor: *Richard T. Viggiano*
Designer: *Frances Torbert Tilley*
Production Supervisor: *Kewal K. Sharma*
Compositor: *Ruttle, Shaw & Wetherill, Inc.*
Printer and Binder: *Halliday Lithograph*
Illustrator: *Welby B. Wolfe*

MATERIALS OF THE SCENE: *An Introduction to Technical Theatre*

Library of Congress Cataloging in Publication Data

Wolfe, Welby B.
  Materials of the scene.

  Includes bibliographies and index.
  1. Stage management. I. Title.
PN2085.W6 792'.025 77-24252
ISBN 0-06-047184-0

CONTENTS

iii

BUILDING AND HANDLING SCENERY   117

5

PAINTING THE SET AND PREPARING SCENERY FOR PAINTING   199

DRESSING THE SET   **241**

PREFACE

Materials of the Scene was prepared to assist those wishing to learn the fundamentals of technical theatre. This is primarily a textbook for an introductory course in theatre technology and stagecraft. The reader who has only a casual acquaintance with technical terms and procedures will find that the book is written in a style that is understandable, explicit, and well illustrated, so it is a valuable source book of materials, scenery construction, scene painting, and properties as well.

The organization and content of the book follows the format that I used in teaching introductory technical courses at the University of Northern Colorado. As designer and technical director for the university theatre, I insisted that students become familiar with architectural characteristics of the stage and types of scenery, in addition to acquiring a working knowledge of materials, techniques of working with them, and technical responsibilities. Thus, this book urges the nonprofessional technician to enlarge his or her capacity for technical efficiency, artistic achievement, and enjoyment of the theatre.

I am deeply indebted to the students, colleagues, and friends who encouraged me to prepare this book, and to the publishers, photographers and theatre companies who granted me permission to use their materials. I am equally indebted to John Willcoxon, III, chairman, the Theatre Arts Department and director of the Little Theatre of the Rockies at the University of Northern Colorado; Virgil Purvis, teacher of English in the Denver Public Schools; and the editors of Harper & Row for their suggestions and editoral assistance.

WELBY B. WOLFE

AN INTRODUCTORY OVERVIEW

Theatre technology, as we know it today, is an accumulation of techniques gathered over a period of 2500 years. Within our span of historic credibility, the Greeks were the first to formalize drama and build theatres in which it could be performed. We still retain many terms in our theatre vocabulary that originated with them. The Romans modified the architectural form of the Greek theatre to suit their taste, but it was their alterations that later evolved into the proscenium theatre. There was a period following the Classic Period when theatre appeared to have dropped from sight. However, it reappeared during the Middle Ages, and staging techniques of that era are still in use today. Since the Renaissance, theatre technology has developed immeasurably. Thus, the brief overview that follows is to call attention to sequential developments contributing to our technical knowledge of the theatre.

The Greek theatres appeared first during the middle of the sixth century B.C. Taking advantage of the hilly terrain for their auditoriums, they leveled a circular area at the foot of the slope which they called an *orchestra*. This was the performance area for dance-chants, their earliest dramatic form. When these ceremonies assumed a verbal form featuring actor poets, a low structure was added behind the orchestra. This building was called the *skene*. In the beginning it probably served as a dressing room. A low porch along the front separated the skene from the orchestra. This porch was called the *proskene*. Three doorways led into the skene. Holes found in the floor of the proskene at some of the theatre ruins are believed to have been used for poles to support painted screens.[1]

---

[1] James H. Butler. *The Theatre and Drama of Greece and Rome* (San Francisco: Chandler, 1972), pp. 31–33.

Figure 1–1. *Drawing by the author, based on reconstruction conjecture of fifth century Theatre of Dionysus. (Allen,* Antiquities of the Greeks and Romans. *New York: 1927.)*

Figure 1–2. *Epidaurus.*

The Greeks must also be given credit for developing the first stage machines. One such device was a *pariaktos.* Pariaktoi were triangular screens which could be turned to show a change of scene. These could be placed in a doorway or near the wall of the skene. Another device was the *eccyclema,* a sliding platform that could be moved through the doorways of the skene. A third consisted of levers and pulleys set on the roof of the skene, a *mēchēne,* to lower the gods (*deux ex machina*).[2] These terms and the devices they describe are common stage language today: scene, proscenium, pariaktoi, orchestra, stage wagon, and auditorium.

While the Romans undoubtedly patterned their theatres after the Greeks, their theatres were architectural constructions. The auditorium was semicircular, rising steeply around a half-round orchestra. The skene was an elaborately decorated facade that rose to the full height of the auditorium and joined it structurally. The proskene was raised and widened. There were three main entrances at the back and one at either end to give

Figure 1–3. *A portion of a reconstruction of the Roman theatre at Ostia, as conceived by D'Espouy, Fragments d'Architecture Antique, Vol. I, 1901, redrawn by the author. The architectural elegance of the skene was typical of the Roman theatres.*

[2] Sheldon Cheney. *The Theatre—Three Thousand Years of Drama, Acting and Stagecraft* (London: Longmans, 1958), p. 64.

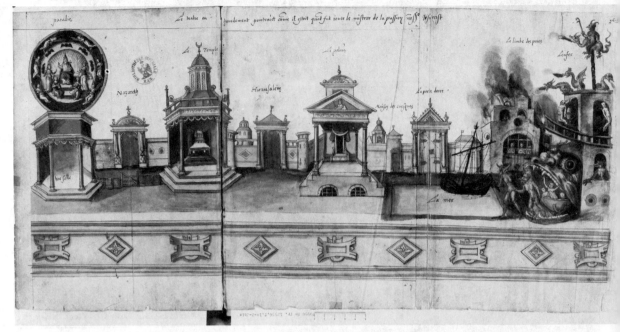

Figure 1–4. The stage for the Passion Play, Valenciennes, France, 1547. A simultaneous staging platform showing the symbolized mansions, with Paradise (heaven) at the left and the Hell's mouth on the right. (From a manuscript in the Bibliotheque Nationale; reproduced with their permission.)

Figure 1–5. Jo Mielziner's full set rendering for Summer and Smoke, by Tennessee Williams (1948). An example of contemporary adaptation of simultaneous staging. (Courtesy, Atheneum Publishers, New York. From Designing For The Theatre, by Jo Mielziner. Copyright 1948, by Jo Mielziner.)

access to the skene. Most of the Greek theatres were altered to conform during the Roman occupation, the one notable exception being the theatre at Epidaurus.

Painted scenery was used in staging Roman plays. In manuscripts written by Vitruvius, rediscovered long after the classic period, painted scenery was described as it was used for backgrounds for comedy, tragedy, and satyric plays.[3] Other sources indicate that the Romans utilized the mechanical devices of the Greeks, but also introduced stage traps and other paraphernalia to create spectacular staging.[4]

The fall of Rome as a political force marked the end of the Classic Period. Most of the theatres throughout the empire were pillaged or destroyed completely during the early Middle Ages. During this period, the cultural preoccupation was religion. No new theatres were built, but three forms of dramatic presentation and staging did appear in the later years that are technically significant.

The church, which was instrumental in banning the theatre in the late classical period was, ironically the institution that revived it. To enhance biblical teaching of the illiterate parishioners, dramatized versions of the scripture were acted out by the clerics. These plays were first performed in the church, but were later staged on a long platform in the churchyard. Symbolic scenery was set on this stage to depict scenes from the Bible, with Heaven at stage right and a large Hell's mouth on the left. This whole panorama of action was viewed simultaneously, hence the term "simultaneous staging." *Summer and Smoke* by Tennessee Williams, is an excellent example of this form of staging as adapted by a modern playwright.

A second form employed a temporary platform stage that could be set up in the streets or courtyards. Many drawings and old manuscripts remain which indicate that these temporary stages were often high enough so that the area below the stage could be used for a dressing room. The stage area was often enclosed on three sides with curtains. The Commedia dell' Arte

---

[3] Lee Simonson. *The Art of Scenic Design* (New York: Harper & Row, 1950), p. 3.
[4] Cheney, op. cit., p. 97.

Figure 1–6. A Pageant Car, etched by Jacques Callot, typifies the extravagant tableau stages on wagons used in both England and France. Similar wagons were used by the English trade guilds for religious festivals. (From The Theatre by Sheldon Cheney, published by Longmans, a division of David McKay Co.)

Figure 1–7. The New York Shakespeare Festival Mobile Theatre. The large trailer units transport the stage, lighting, scenery, dressing rooms, and other equipment anywhere. A show can be set up in under two hours. (Courtesy of The New York Shakespeare Festival. Photographer, George E. Joseph.)

players, popular throughout southern Europe, used similar improvised stages, though they were lower to the ground with a curtained-off area at the back. Temporary stages similar to these are still seen at fairs and festivals.

A third type of stage was mounted on a wagon drawn by horses. Wagon stages are usually associated with religious festivals for staging Miracle productions and morality plays. The pageant wagons and those sponsored by the trade guilds of Western Europe and England were elaborately decorated. Today's colorful parade floats are a carry-over from this period. Mobile theatres have been revived recently in several of the larger cities in the United States to bring theatre to smaller communities. These are mounted on large vans that are a self-contained theatre unit.

The Renaissance began in Italy. The lavish Italian courts brought about a renewed interest in classical plays, particularly those by Roman playwrights. New theatres were built which were either replicas of the classical Roman theatres with a roof added, or similar

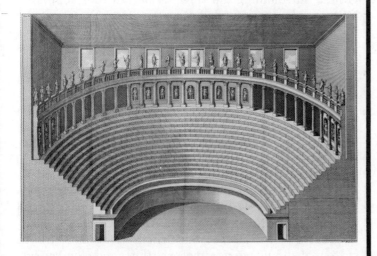

Figure 1–8. *The auditorium of the Renaissance theatre, The Theatre of the Olympian Academy, Vicenza, Italy (1580). The stage was similar, except in scale, to the Roman theatre at Ostia, see Fig. 1–3. Courtesy The Metropolitan Museum of Art, Harris Brisbane Dick Fund, 1942.*

to the court ballrooms which had been used for pageants and the production of plays. Thus, for the first time, the theatre was brought indoors.

A second innovation was the enlargement of the center doorway into the skene so that painted vistas (scenery) could be set back of the opening. The opening was soon enlarged further so that it could become a part of the acting stage, as well as a frame surrounding elaborately painted scenery in perspective. The proscenium arch and perspective scenery became known as the Italian style theatre.

During the last half of the Sixteenth Century, a theatre was developing in England that was architecturally unique. The best known of the Elizabethan theatres was the Globe Theatre because it was there that William Shakespeare acted and produced his plays. Elizabethan theatres utilized raised stages which thrust out from one side of a near circular enclosure that was open to the sky. The outer rim of the structure was roofed to cover stalls rising two or more tiers above the ground for spectators. Those unable to afford seats stood on the ground surrounding the stage. A partial roof supported by two columns extended over the stage. Portals at the back of the stage served as actors' entrances as well as "inner below" scenes. A second level over the stage was used for seating, or an "inner above" acting area. There can be little doubt that our persent-day "thrust" theatres were inspired by the Elizabethan theatre.

The excitement over the Italian style proscenium spread rapidly. The area back of the proscenium arch was enlarged to accommodate rigging to raise and lower borders and drops from above. Tracks and grooves were set in the floor of the stage so that scenery could be moved in from the sides. To enhance the visual spectacle of perspective scenery, the stage floor was sloped toward the audience. (Southern, in *Changeable Scenery*, in great detail describes the British Wing and Groove system of sliding wing frames, shutters, and cloud effects during the seventeenth century.)[5] The auditoriums were modeled after the Italian ballroom theatres with

---

[5] Richard Southern. *Changeable Scenery* (London: Faber and Faber, 1952).

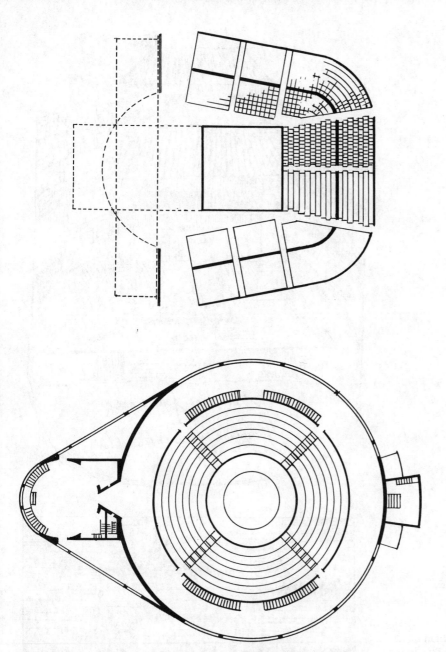

Figure 1–10. *Farkas Molnar's Design for a U-Theatre, 1924, and (below) Norman Bel Geddes' Intimate Theatre, 1924, were project designs that greatly influenced the trend toward arena and round theatres. (Redrawn in larger scale from Hannelore Schubert, The Modern Theatre: Architecture, Stage Design, Lighting, translated by J. C. Palmes. By Praeger Publishers, New York, 1971. Reproduced by permission of Karl Krämer Verlag, Copyright 1971, Stuttgart, Germany, p. 13.)*

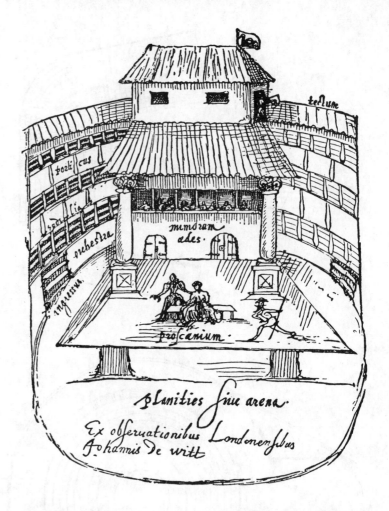

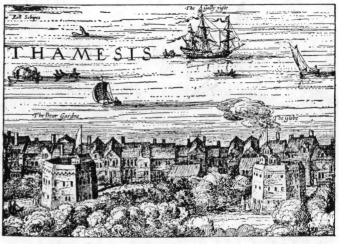

Figure 1-9. Johann De Witt's sketch of the Swan Theatre in London in 1596, verifies the form of the Elizabethan theatres. (Below) In 1616, Visscher's pictorial map of London included a portion showing the Globe Theatre and the Bear Garden Theatre near the bank of the Thames. (From The Theatre by Sheldon Cheney, published by Longmans, a division of David McKay Co.)

U-shaped galleries rising several tiers. The main floor was nearly flat. This style of theatre structure was predominant throughout Europe and the United States until the close of the nineteenth century.

The first signs of impending changes began with the rise of a movement opposing the picturesque, romantic, and presentational form that had pervaded the theatre. Adolph Appia, a Swiss painter and designer, and Gordon Craig, an English actor/designer, were among those influential in bringing about changes. Both were critical of the lack of artistic unity in the relationship of scenery to acting and dramatic theme. They also argued that the means to esthetic unification was to place production control in the hands of a single artistic director who had full authority to coordinate the creative arts of the theatre.[6] In the early years of the twentieth century these changes were being realized.

The development of the incandescent spotlight and the means to control it were possibly the greatest technical achievement of the twentieth century. The spotlight, which can be focused on specific areas of the stage and controlled in both intensity and color, was a manifestation of both Appia and Craig's ideas of stage lighting. By 1920, nearly every established theatre had converted from gas to electric stage lighting.

Among other revolutionary movements there was a growing demand for greater intimacy between the actor and the audience. The proscenium theatres were deemed by many to be unsuitable for the more realistic styles of playwrighting and acting. During the 1920s, architects were invited to submit proposals that would eliminate the proscenium barrier. Two concepts emerged that have affected our contemporary stages. One of these proposals extended the stage apron out into the auditorium, rearranging the seating so that it surrounded the projecting acting area on three sides. A second proposal suggested a circular arena with a stage area completely surrounded by the audience.

The extended apron has been developed further, in most instances eliminating any suggestion of a prosce-

---

[6] George R. Kernodle. *Invitation to the Theatre* (New York: Harcourt Brace Jovanovich, 1967), p. 336.

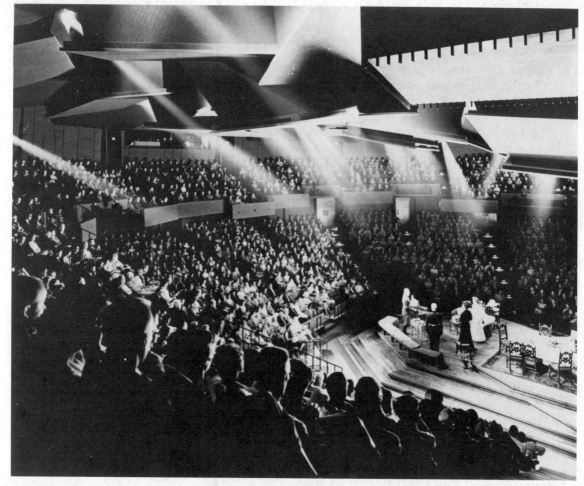

Figure 1-11. *The Guthrie Theater (1963). Note the extended thrust surrounded on three sides by steeply banked seating. No seat is more than 52 feet from the stage center. (Courtesy, The Guthrie Theater.)*

nium. This is today's "thrust" or "three-quarter" stage. The circular arena has also been widely adopted. While the round configuration is usually modified, the audience is seated on all sides of the acting arena. We refer to these as "theatre in the round" or "arena stages." Open stages of these types have minimized the need for massive scenic units since they would obstruct the audience's view of the stage. Where scenery may be required, it is suggestive or skeletal. Lighting and properties are the most vital scenic elements.

Proscenium theatres have by no means been abandoned. Many of the older ones have been modified. Most

Figure 1–12. The Pioneer Theatre in Palo Duro Canyon State Park near Canyon, Texas, is the site of "Texas," a regional musical drama presented during the summer months. Photograph by Bill Rhew. (Courtesy Mrs. Ples Harper, Founder.)

Figure 1–13. The Arena Stage, Washington, D. C., inaugurated in 1961; clearly depicts the arena concept. Great flexibility is achieved with movable platforming. Architect, Harry Weese. (Courtesy of the Arena Stage.)

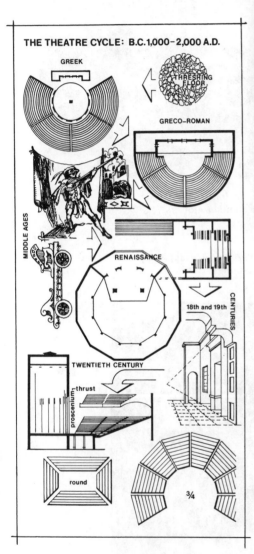

THE THEATRE CYCLE: B.C.1,000–2,000 A.D.

GREEK

THRESHING FLOOR

GRECO-ROMAN

MIDDLE AGES

RENAISSANCE

18th and 19th

CENTURIES

TWENTIETH CENTURY

thrust

proscenium

round

¾

Figure 1–15. *The theatre cycle. Drawing by the author.*

Figure 1–14. *The Nelke Experimental Theatre on the Brigham Young University campus, Provo, Utah, retains the proscenium, but provides intimacy by steeply banking the seating in a "continental" arrangement. (Courtesy of the Department of Theatre and Cinematic Arts.)*

new ones include permanent thrust or conversion capabilities that permit flexibility of staging. Auditoriums can now be steeply banked with seats partially surrounding the thrust to achieve intimacy.

Architecturally, the theatre has swung a full cycle to return to many of the characteristics of the classic theatres. The major difference is in the vast amount of theatre technology we have acquired. The text that follows deals only with an introduction to one phase of this technology: the stage, the materials, and the preparation of scenery. The art of scenic design, lighting and lighting design, and stage costuming and design have been omitted intentionally because they are too advanced in technical preparation.

Those with serious intentions of learning and practicing the technical arts of theatre should explore in detail the developments touched upon in this brief overview. Time will be well spent in perusing the books listed below and at the end of each chapter, if for no other reason than to acquire an appreciation of one of our oldest institutions, the theatre.

SUGGESTED READINGS

Brocket, Oscar G. *History of the Theatre*. Boston: Allyn & Bacon, 1968.

———— *The Theatre,* 2nd ed. New York: Holt, Rinehart & Winston, 1969.

Butler, James H. *The Theatre and Drama of Greece and Rome*. San Francisco: Chandler, 1972.

Cheney, Sheldon. *The Theatre—Three Thousand Years of Drama, Acting and Stagecraft*. London: Longmans, 1929, 1952, 1958. Copyright 1972 by David McKay Co.

Kernodle, George R. *Invitation to the Theatre*. New York: Harcourt Brace Jovanovich, 1967.

Mielziner, Jo. *Designing for the Theatre*. New York: Atheneum, 1965.

Schubert, Hannelore. *The Modern Theatre Architecture*. New York: Praeger, 1971.

Simonson, Lee. *The Art of Scenic Design*. New York: Harper & Row, 1950.

Southern, Richard. *Changeable Scenery*. London: Faber & Faber, 1952.

Whiting, Frank. *An Introduction to the Theatre,* 3rd ed. New York: Harper & Row, 1969.

THE PROSCENUIM
STAGE AND SCENERY

The major part of our scenic technology stems from the eighteenth and nineteenth centuries, with the exception of lighting, sound, and projections which are more recent additions. Even though newer theatres are requiring less scenery, there is little reason to believe that scenery will not continue to be an important part of the theatre. The spirit of experimentation has affected theatre architects, playwrights, directors and designers. Playwrights like Ionesco, Albee, Beckett and Pinter, and others like Baldwin, Williams, Saroyan, Giraudoux and Simon have covered the gamut of style and theme. Their words have resulted in dramatic forms that we refer to as the theatre of the absurd, the theatre of cruelty, as well as themes on ethnic injustices and comedic satire. The ultimate discovery is that new theatres with their open stages can be used effectively for both realistic and nonrealistic drama, but at the same time, the proscenium theatre in the hands of a good director and designer can be equally effective. True, realistic drama may suffer somewhat from the lack of realistic scenery, but audiences have become more imaginative and less dependent on full settings, which is good.

For the stage technician, the proscenium stage will always be of major importance because we have gained most of our stage jargon and staging techniques from it. Thus, to become familiar with the stage and its terminology, a familiarity with the proscenium theatre is a prerequisite to the study of scenery, even though those theatres that require less scenery may often present greater challenges to the stage technician.

Scenery used on the proscenium stage, and seen only from the front, is usually less complicated to construct because the back surface does not require finishing. Cleats, braces, and hardware can be attached where they are required without concern for their appearance. Scenery used on an open stage where it will be seen from many angles and at closer range, requires greater attention to structural detail and workmanship. Distorted, skeletal and structural styles of scenery are frequently used as a means of accentuating the expressive demands of the play. Therefore, the technician will benefit from a basic understanding of the various styles of scenery, as well as a knowledge of the functions of scenery as they relate to the production of the play.

THE PROSCENIUM STAGE

The proscenium stage evolved from the Greco-Roman skene, and as noted in the first chapter, consisted of a structural wall having three or more doorways. The projecting platform stage in front of the skene—the proskenion—prompted our present use of the term proscenium wall to describe the wall containing the openings. The center archway, first enlarged to reveal painted vistas behind it, and later to frame and to separate the acting area from the spectator, is now referred to as the proscenium arch or frame. The orchestra, originally the dance-chant circle of the Greek theatre, is a term we use to designate the sections of seats on the lower floor of the auditorium. A pit that separates the front row of seating from the stage is still referred to as the orchestra pit, but it was added during the eighteenth century to seat the musicians below the eye level of the audience. Because the orchestra pit is still a prominent feature in most proscenium theatres, the edge of the pit is a starting point in describing the general characteristics of the stage.

The Orchestra Pit

An orchestra pit may be 10 to 12 feet in width and extend the full length of the proscenium opening. If the pit is permanent, the depth is usually determined by the height of the stage floor above the auditorium floor and the eye level of the front rows of spectators. It is desirable that the pit be deep enough that the musicians or their instruments will not obstruct the view of the stage.

In theatres where only an occasional musical production is given, an orchestra pit creates a gaping void between the audience and the stage. Various ways have been devised to overcome the disadvantages of a pit when musicians are not needed for the production. One

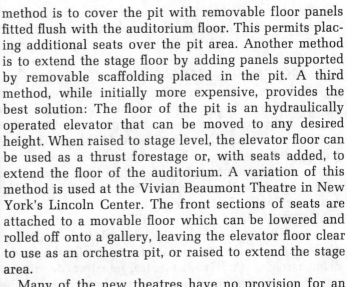

method is to cover the pit with removable floor panels fitted flush with the auditorium floor. This permits placing additional seats over the pit area. Another method is to extend the stage floor by adding panels supported by removable scaffolding placed in the pit. A third method, while initially more expensive, provides the best solution: The floor of the pit is an hydraulically operated elevator that can be moved to any desired height. When raised to stage level, the elevator floor can be used as a thrust forestage or, with seats added, to extend the floor of the auditorium. A variation of this method is used at the Vivian Beaumont Theatre in New York's Lincoln Center. The front sections of seats are attached to a movable floor which can be lowered and rolled off onto a gallery, leaving the elevator floor clear to use as an orchestra pit, or raised to extend the stage area.

Many of the new theatres have no provision for an orchestra pit, but various arrangements have been employed to seat an orchestra. In the musical production *Man of La Mancha*, produced on a thrust stage, the orchestra was divided with half on either side of the stage behind the performance area. A similar arrangement was used for the musical *I Do, I Do*, with the full orchestra situated back of a semitransparent curtain upstage. In such cases, a closed circuit television camera is often used to give the conductor visual contact with the performers.

The Apron

The stage apron is an extension of the acting floor beyond the proscenium frame. While we might consider the thrust of a wide forestage as a wide apron, the stage term "apron" is used in the context of the traditional proscenium theatre in which the apron extended out 3 to 5 feet in front of the curtain. This narrow space has little value as an acting area, but before electric lighting was introduced, the apron served as a base for footlights. When electric lights replaced the gas jets, light bulbs were strung along the front edge of the apron with a hood over each bulb to shield the light from the audience. Later a trough was set into the floor of the apron to hold the lights, and finally, a device was developed that would rotate to close the trough when it was not in use. Most of the older proscenium stages still have narrow aprons, and unless they have been floored over, footlights, but they are used primarily for "curtain warmers" (to illuminate the curtain between scenes).

The Proscenium Arch

The surface surrounding the proscenium opening has progressed through many decorative phases. The Romans decorated the front of the skene with niches, carvings and statuary, but those were nothing compared with the baroque sculptured ornamentation of the seventeenth century. One has to realize that dimming of the house lights during a performance did not start until late in the last century. Before that, the proscenium face was a part of the scenic spectacle. Today, the proscenium face is extremely plain, often finished in dark tones that will not reflect light.

The size of the proscenium opening is determined by the over-all scale of the auditorium. To improve the sightlines from the sides of the house, the side walls often terminate at the edges of the proscenium opening. If the auditorium contains balconies, the height of the opening must be greater than in one without balconies. The width of the proscenium is determined by the kinds of productions most frequently staged. An opera stage is usually large to accommodate big casts, whereas a play with a small cast would be better suited to a stage with a smaller proscenium. The average size of a proscenium opening is 36 feet wide by 18 feet high. If the house has a balcony, the height may range up to 20 feet. The proscenium opening for an opera stage may be anywhere from 45 feet to 70 feet wide. The shape of the opening may vary from rectangular to nearly semicircular, although the former is most common. Where a proscenium is used in conjunction with a thrust, the frame may extend only part of the way across

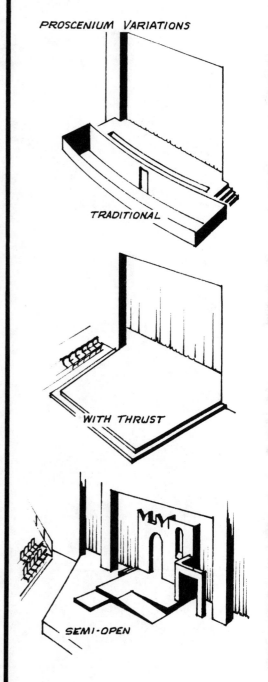

PROSCENIUM VARIATIONS

TRADITIONAL

WITH THRUST

SEMI-OPEN

the width of the playing area so that the sides of the thrust join the side walls of the auditorium.

The Stage House

The stage area back of the proscenium wall, extending from wall to wall and from the floor to the roof, is called the "stage house." The floor of the stage house, including both the playing area and the space at the sides and back, should be soft wood. Any floor surface that will have scenery, wagons, and platforms set and moved on it will soon become scarred and scratched. Even though a floor laid with the harder woods like oak or maple will be more beautiful, the stage floor is a working floor and it should be economical to maintain, refinish, or replace. It should be possible to drive a nail or set a stage screw in the floor of the stage without inflicting damage to the surface: This can be done with a soft floor, but not with a hardwood floor. Some architects have made the mistake of putting down concrete floors. Concrete makes an extremely hazardous surface for actors and dancers to work on, not only because it lacks resilience, but because it becomes very slick in a short time.

It is a common practice to lay a plywood or compressed wood fiber layer over the permanent stage floor when heavy wagons are to be used. Any grooves made by the casters are made in the paneling, rather than in the permanent floor, and this overlay also makes it possible to paint the stage floor. After the run of the show, the panels can be taken up, leaving the permanent floor virtually undamaged. A heavy canvas "ground cloth" is sometimes used on the playing area to protect the surface and dampen the sound of footsteps. This practice has been abandoned in many theatres in favor of the overlay, or inexpensive carpeting to deaden floor sounds.

Many stage floors have "traps" cut in the floor to make it possible to open sections for descending stairways, or to lower an actor or units of scenery below the stage. Elevator rigging, such as winches or hydraulic lift devices, make it possible to raise the trap floor above, as well as below the level of the stage safely. There are instances where the edges of a trap floor have been rimmed with metal to prevent the splintering of the wood; however, this usually results in ridges as the wood wears away, making it difficult to move wagons across the floor. To be totally effective, a greater part of the acting area of the stage should be trapped, but this would also require a "trap room" beneath the stage for elevators or landing areas.

A built-in turntable, or revolving stage, intended to speed up the shifting of scenery, is set in the floor of some stages. The Kalita Humphreys Theatre in Dallas, designed by Frank Lloyd Wright, Frasier Theatre on the campus of the University of Northern Colorado, and the Metropolitan Opera in New York City have such stages. The revolving stage was first introduced in Europe, but the idea for it is believed to have originated in Japan a century or more ago. The revolve is flush with the stage floor and the diameter varies. To attain the greatest efficiency, it should be possible to rotate the turntable for a complete change of scenery with a minimum of manual shifting.

The floor area at either side of the proscenium opening is called the "wings." For all practical purposes, there should be no less than 15 feet from the edge of the proscenium opening to the side walls. A multiscene production that may call for stage wagons, large set pieces and furniture storage offstage can cause so much congestion in the wings that there is barely passageway for performers to get on stage. Ideally, the width of the wing space should be slightly greater than the width of the proscenium opening and the area should be completely clear of all obstructions on the floor or walls that would affect the stacking of scenery and properties. Unfortunately, one rarely finds such ideal space.

The depth of the stage house, from the back side of the proscenium wall to the rear wall, may vary from less than 25 feet to as much as 45 feet. A working depth of 35 feet to 40 feet is considered average.

The height of a stage house is determined by the height of the proscenium opening. The area above the floor to the roof is called the "fly," and when a unit of

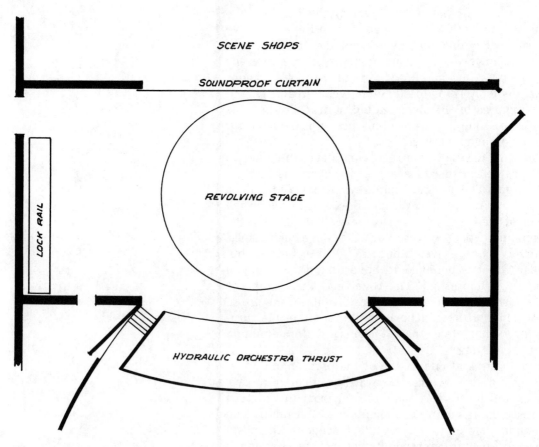

Figure 2–1. *Revolving stage and hydraulic orchestra thrust, Frasier Theatre, University of Northern Colorado. Will Ireland, Architect.*

scenery is to be raised, or "flown out," it should be possible to lift it high enough to be out of view of the spectators in the first row of the house. To fly a unit of scenery, it must be attached to ropes, or "lines" that pass through a set of pulleys that are either secured directly to the roof beams, or rest on a gridwork floor a few feet below the roof called a "gridiron." The height of the gridiron must be at least one and a half times the height of the proscenium opening. The distance from the gridiron floor to the roof of the stage house should be sufficient to permit a stage hand to stand upright.

Needless to say, the gridiron makes it much more convenient to add or adjust the placement of pulleys than where underslung pulleys are attached to the roof beams, which requires a scaffold when adjustments are necessary.

Before the use of structural steel, the gridiron was made of heavy wooden beams that spanned the space between the proscenium wall and the rear wall of the stage house. Wooden beams have been replaced by steel I-beams or channel iron at the main loadbearing points. These beams are floored over with channel iron spaced 3 inches apart, thus providing a safe walking floor, as well as a surface on which sheaves (pulleys) can be mounted so the lines pass between the channels at any desired location. Access to the "grid" is usually by means of a spiral stair or vertical ladder located in a back corner of the stage house.

At the side, and approximately 2 feet above the level of the grid floor, is a row of pulleys that are aligned with each set of sheaves. These are called "head blocks" and their purpose is to divert the direction of each set of lines downward to a counterweight carriage or pin rail.

Theatre building codes require that the roof of the stage house must have a "smoke trap" which rises above the level of the roof. The trap is actually a small steel houselike structure fitted with metal doors that open outward on all four sides. These doors are held shut with steel cables that extend to the stage floor for manual control, but the cables must also be fitted with fusible links that will melt apart at approximately 160° F. to release the doors automatically. It has been effectively demonstrated that the accumulation of hot gases generated during a fire will build up sufficient pressure to literally explode, blowing the roof and wall apart.

Many of the older proscenium theatres had a gallery set into the wall of the stage house called a "fly gallery." This was to provide working space above the stage floor for handling the sets of lines required for the "rigging" (rigging is the stage term to describe lines, sheaves and structure necessary for flying scenery). The fly gallery was usually 16 feet or more above the stage floor and extended from near the proscenium wall to the rear

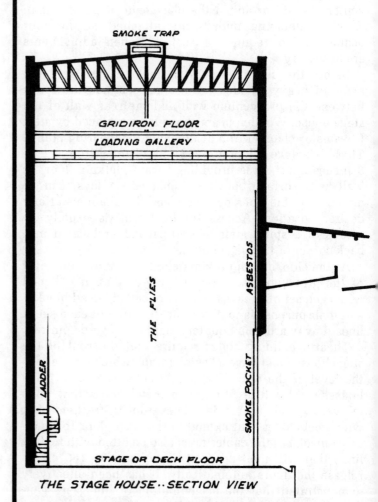

THE STAGE HOUSE ·· SECTION VIEW

of the stage house. The gallery was either set into the wall or projected out like a balcony. The floor of the gallery was 8 to 10 feet wide with a heavy wood or steel rail along the open side. Belaying pins were set into the rail at 12 inch intervals, very similar to the railing of a sailing ship, from which the term "pin rail" is derived. Hemp fly-lines from the gridiron were passed through a "head block" which converted the direction of pull downward to the pin rail where they were coiled around the pins and tied to secure them. A double pin

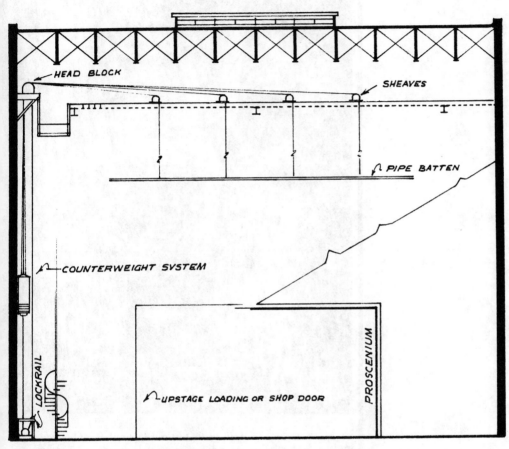

rail was often used: the lower railing for tying off at the set position, and the upper rail for the take-up or flown position. A stage equipped in this manner was called a "hemp house."

The pin rail with its seemingly endless coils of rope and "flymen" to handle the sets of lines have been replaced with "counterweighted rigging" in most theatres. Though a counterweight system reduces the manpower required to fly scenery, it is difficult to shift a set of lines up or down stage. Consequently, many theatres

Figure 2–2. *The fly gallery in the old Walnut Street Theatre, Philadelphia, before remodeling in 1970. (Courtesy of Theatre Design and Technology and Photographer, Jack E. Boucher, Linwood, New Jersey.)*

are equipped with a pin rail on the floor or in a gallery to supplement counterweighted systems.

The counterweight system utilizes a "carriage" or rack that is guided up and down a side wall of the stage house by tracks or cables. The carriage is loaded with cast-iron weights to counterbalance the flown weight of the scenery. Flexible steel cables, instead of hemp lines, are attached to the top of the carriage and run up through the head block, across the gridiron over the sheaves and down over the stage where they are secured to a "pipe batten." The carriage is raised and lowered by means of a "handline" which passes through a separate set of pulleys (one mounted just below the head block and the other on a rack attached to the floor) and a locking device that clamps the rope in any position. Each unit of this kind of rigging system is called a "set," and the sets are aligned on a long rack along the wall called the "lock rail." Sets are spaced 6 inches to 12 inches apart and the number of sets is determined by the depth of the stage house.

In passing, it should be noted that the pipe battens used with counterweight rigging are made up of two or more sections of 1¾ inch soft iron pipe joined with a sleeve inserted at each joint, and riveted in place. Soft iron pipe is recommended for this purpose rather than steel pipe. Iron pipe will bend if it is overloaded, whereas steel pipe is harder and will crimp or fold, making the likelihood of breaking much greater.

In order to add weights to balance that of the scenery to be flown, it is necessary to have the counterweight carriage in the high position. This necessitates a platform, called a "loading gallery," just below the gridiron where flymen can add weights to compensate for the new load. The front railing of this gallery may be fitted with belaying pins that can be used for tying off "spot lines," single lines added when flying small units, or when the advantage of counterweights is not required.

Access to the stage house from other backstage areas can very often affect the efficiency of operation. In commercial theatres one may find a large door opening directly onto an alley or side street where there is a loading dock, or in many cases an opening large enough to permit a van to drive onto the staging area for unloading scenery. Where the preparation of scenery is done in the theatre, openings into the stage house are complicated by their location, their size, and the sounds of backstage work during performances.

For obvious reasons, it is desirable to have construction areas as close to the stage as possible. Openings onto the stage should be large enough to permit the movement of scenery on or off without having to tip it over, and to permit passage of stage wagons on a floor free of obstructions. An opening at the side of the stage house has certain advantages, particularly for the movement of large wagons. However, a side opening prevents stacking scenery close to the stage area. If the opening is located in the rear wall of the stage house, it is often blocked by a cyclorama that must remain in fixed position, thereby making it inaccessible. In either case, an opening for the movement of scenery should be large enough, both in width and height, for the passage of large scenic units. Closing off this size opening, so that sounds of activity in the offstage areas will not reach the stage, is difficult. Attempts to solve this problem have been made in a variety of ways, including the installation of thick soundproof doors that can be lowered on tracks set in the wall or huge stage elevators that make it possible to lower an entire setting to a basement shop. Other doorways onto the stage are required to provide for access of actors, properties, and equipment, but such openings are usually kept to a minimum to avoid opening and closing doors during performances.

Prior to 1960, the New York theatre fire code stipulated that an asbestos fire curtain that could be lowered to separate the staging area from the auditorium must be installed. Although the code has been changed to permit the construction of theatres with open stages, similar statutes still remain in effect in many parts of the country specifying that a curtain made of heavy asbestos fiber, large enough to cover the entire proscenium opening, must be used. To prevent the passage of fire around the asbestos, the edges of the curtain extend into steel channels on each side of the proscenium opening. These channels form a *smoke pocket* that reaches from the floor to well above the opening. The asbestos is flown and counterweighted, with a safety line to hold it up in position. Fusible links placed at intervals in the safety line release the curtain automatically when temperatures exceed 160° F., but a fire axe or knife to cut the line is usually found in a case near the stage manager as an extra precaution. Automatic sprinkling systems and dry chemical fire extinguishers are considered most effective for controlling backstage fires.

The typical proscenium has been described; however, only in commercial theatres would one find a stage that is so completely barren. At the very least, there usually is a house curtain and a few stage curtains to dress the stage as well as some other basic operational equipment. The terminology and location of these pieces of equipment is important in the development of a stage vocabulary.

The Basic Equipment

The term "basic equipment" should be interpreted as those things added to the bare architectural structure of the proscenium stage which are generally considered essential operational elements. Some of these things fall into the category of stage dressing and, as such, may be considered scenery. Others are literally equipment, because they are devices introduced to aid in the operation of the theatre. In either case, the equipment and its functions may be considered standard on most proscenium stages.

A short panel of drapery called a "valance" or "grand drape" is a trim curtain at the top of the proscenium frame. It was introduced very early in the development of the proscenium frame as a means of softening the contour of the opening, and as an additional touch of elegance. In the modern proscenium theatre, a valance may not be used at all, but where it is used, it is more apt to be a simple pleated drape, 18 inches to 36 inches wide, attached directly to the back of the proscenium wall. The fabric usually matches the house curtain behind it.

The act curtain is directly upstage (toward the back of the stage) of the valance. The act curtain is the drape that is drawn, flown, or opened to announce the start of a performance. Because this curtain is in full view of the audience when it enters the theatre, the material is usually rich in color and made of velour, damask, or an

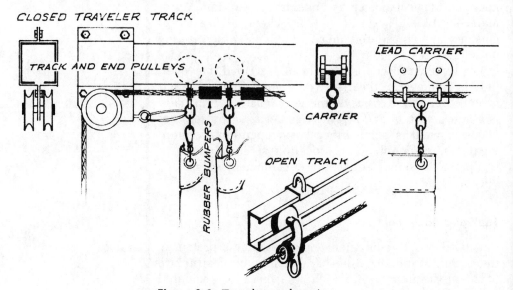

Figure 2–3. *Travelers and carriers.*

equally decorative fabric. An act curtain which parts in the center, with each section moving off behind the sides of the proscenium, is a "traveler curtain." It is attached at the top to carriers that move in a two-section track: one panel of the drape travels on each section. The track may be suspended from the gridiron, or it may be mounted on heavy brackets on the back of the proscenium wall. In either case, the curtains are drawn open by means of a handline which passes through a pulley attached to the floor, or by a motordriven winch controlled by the stage manager.

An act curtain may also be raised vertically, in which case it is hung on a pipe batten that is counterweighted so that it can be raised and lowered quickly and easily. A traveler curtain can also be flown out in this manner by removing the floor pulley. A "contour curtain" is another style seen in some theatres. It is raised by a series of lines that lift the curtain in billowy swags from the floor, giving the effect of huge scallops as it rises. A "tableau curtain" works in a similar fashion, except it requires a diagonal set of lines running through rings

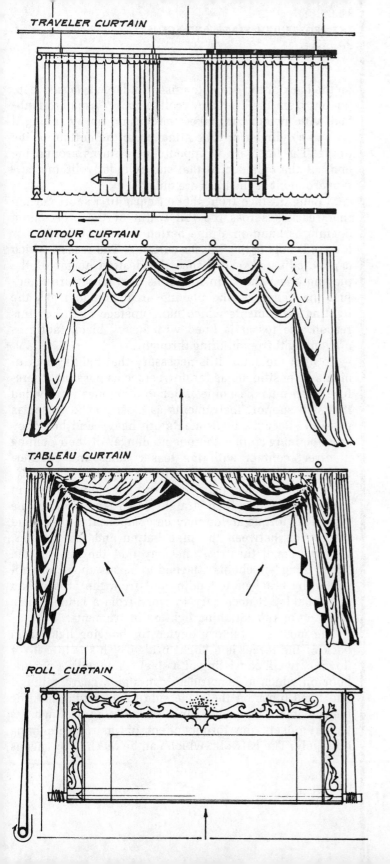

TRAVELER CURTAIN

CONTOUR CURTAIN

TABLEAU CURTAIN

ROLL CURTAIN

on the back of the drape to raise it in large swags sweeping out from the center. A "roll curtain," usually identified with melodrama, takes the curtain up by rolling it around a cylinder or tube attached to the bottom of the drape. The lines are wrapped several turns around the ends of the cylinder so that the cylinder rolls the curtain around it as the lines are pulled.

Moving upstage from the act curtain, a short curtain that reaches across the full width of the proscenium opening is hung on a pipe batten that can be raised or lowered. This is the "teaser curtain." The teaser, which can be adjusted, establishes the desired height of the playing area. The main functions of a teaser are to adjust the height of the playing area, and to mask the lighting instruments which hang upstage of it. For this reason, the teaser is lined with heavy black fabric to prevent light from filtering through.

To light the actor, it is necessary that lighting instruments be positioned as far downstage as possible; therefore, there must be a pipe batten or other means provided that will support instruments as close to the teaser as possible. Because instruments are heavy and hot, they must be hung so that there is no danger of their coming in direct contact with the teaser; lines and counterweights must be heavy enough to raise the load safely. An instrument clamped to an ordinary pipe batten in any position other than straight down tends to turn the pipe. This torque action may be compensated by a rigid connection between the pipe batten and the fly-lines. In some small theatres, one may find the light batten "dead hung" on chains attached to beams above, or supported by brackets extending out from the proscenium wall, making it necessary to work from a ladder when focusing or repositioning lighting instruments.

The most satisfactory device for hanging lighting in back of the teaser is a "light bridge." This is literally a flown catwalk consisting of a steel frame with a narrow floor on which an electrician can stand, guard railings, and fixed pipes on the stage side for clamping lighting instruments. The bridge can be dead hung or flown. Its weight offsets the torque effect of instruments hung obliquely. The catwalk, which can be reached by means

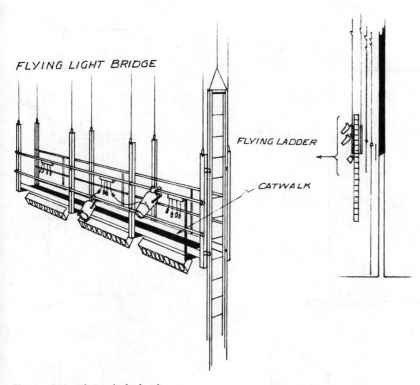

FLYING LIGHT BRIDGE

FLYING LADDER

CATWALK

Figure 2–4. *Flying light bridge.*

of an attached ladder, provides a working platform for the electrician to focus and adjust lights without scaffolds or high ladders. The mass and weight of the bridge are its chief disadvantages. The bridge should be at least the length of the proscenium opening. When instruments are attached, its width takes up a minimum of three feet.

The next units are regarded as the beginning of the scene because they extend to the floor on either side of the playing area, and define the width of the scene. These are the "tormentors." The tormentors are usually panels of drapery on a single batten flown parallel to the proscenium. Each panel can be adjusted to establish the width of the playing area, but each must also be wide enough to extend into the wings to mask the backstage area from the front rows of spectators. It is

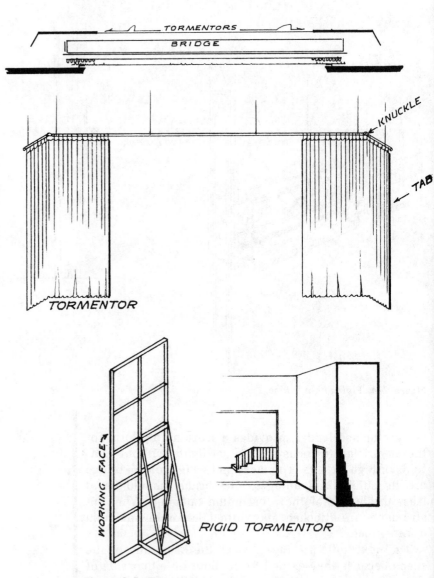

Figure 2–5. Tormentors.

desirable to have the tormentors located as closely to the act curtain as possible, but if a bridge is used for the lights, it may be necessary to fly them as much as 5 feet upstage of the curtain. To minimize this space, the tormentors can be made adjustable in height so they will telescope when the bridge is raised or lowered, thus allowing them to be hung in line with the bridge. The teaser may also be framed scenery attached to the downstage side of the bridge to move with it. To assure complete masking, a "tab" is often added to the offstage end of tormentors. A tab is a narrow panel that can be swung downstage.

The tormentors should be at least one or two feet higher than the edges of the proscenium frame. Although tormentors are most often flown drapes, solid panels, or frames faced with plywood and covered with fabric are also quite common. These hard panels are usually made to be free-standing pieces that can be adjusted more easily than flown panels. They also provide a rigid supporting frame to which other units of scenery can be attached, if necessary.

Educational theatres, as well as many private and community theatres, are often used for other kinds of activities besides the staging of plays. A neutral background is required that will be suitable for concerts, lectures, or assemblies that use the auditorium and the stage. Two methods of dressing the stage are usually employed. The stage may be enclosed in draperies that surround the performance area completely, or panels of draperies may be hung, one behind the other like tormentors to mask the sides of the stage. A full length backdrop is used to define the upstage limits. In either situation, this type of stage dressing is referred to as a cyclorama setting. The fly area above the stage is masked with a series of short drops called "border" curtains. Borders may be 3 to 10 feet wide, depending on the sightlines from the front rows of seats. The length is determined by the width of the stage area, but borders should extend far enough into the wings so the ends will not be visible.

A cyclorama, as the term implies, encloses the stage. The term defines a draped stage dressing; most cycs enclose a trapezoidal staging area with the narrow side of the parallel upstage. The angle of the raked sides is determined by the angle of sightlines from the sides of the auditorium. Where the cyc encloses the stage com-

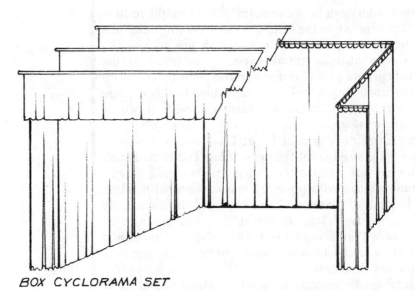

BOX CYCLORAMA SET

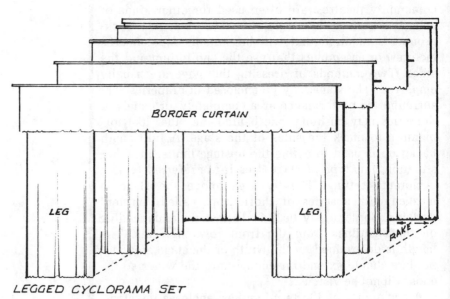

BORDER CURTAIN

LEG   LEG

RAKE

LEGGED CYCLORAMA SET

Figure 2–6. *Cyclorama settings.*

pletely, other battens cannot be lowered below the pipe supporting the cyc unless the cyc pipes are hung outside the regular battens. This type of "box cyc" is usually made up with two or more panels of drapery on either side and across the back. Each panel overlaps the other to prevent gaps. These overlaps also provide openings for entrances. The drape is attached to the cyc pipe by means of light tie-lines inserted through grommets set in the top hem of each panel. A "trim chain" is often used to link the fly-lines to the cyc pipe so the pipe can be trimmed easily. Where there is no fly space, one may find a cyc hung on a curved traveler track so that it can be drawn to stack in back of one or both tormentors.

More commonly, the side and back sections of a box cyc pipe are joined with a special pipe fitting called a "cyc knuckle." The knuckle can be slid along the back pipe to adjust the rake of the side sections. The knuckle also makes it possible to fold over the side sections on the back so the entire cyc can be flown out on a single batten. It is often necessary to add a "tab" that is parallel to the tormentor in order to mask the downstage end. The short tab pipe is attached to the side pipe with knuckles so that it, too, can be adjusted. (See illustration.)

If the stage is to be dressed with side panels that run more or less parallel to the tormentors, each set of legs (panels) is spaced to provide passage to the wing area. The height of each leg will depend on the maximum

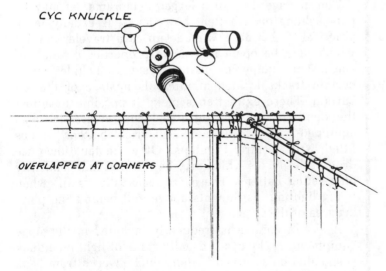

Figure 2–7. *Cyc knuckle and ties.*

height desired and the trim of the teaser above the floor.
The width of each leg may vary from 8 to 12 feet, but
the legs must extend far enough into the wings to mask
the offstage area. This is affected by the sightlines of
the house. Legs are usually flown in pairs, one on either
side of the acting area on a single batten. Each successive upstage pair is hung closer to the center of the
stage so they conform to the angle of sightlines from
the extreme side seats of the auditorium. The border
curtains are flown immediately in front of each leg batten to mask both the pipe and the fly area. (See
illustration.)

In some theatres, cyc legs are hung from channeled
tracks that make it possible to move the legs on and
off the stage. To avoid pull ropes, a long pole is used to
move the legs back and forth. Another device has been
designed to give greater flexibility to the arrangement
of stage draperies using a short batten, matching the
width of the leg, fitted with a rotary joint. The joint device is clamped to the flown batten, making it possible
to turn the legs to any desired angle, even straight up
and down stage, so that the legs overlap to form an enclosed cyc. A long pole with rakelike hooks on the end
is supplied by the manufacturer to manipulate the
rotary batten.

The upstage drop of a legged cyclorama set may be
panels hung on a batten; however, it is usually more
practical if this drop is made up as a traveler curtain
which may be opened to move properties on and off
stage. The equipment on many stages includes spare
curtain tracks located at intervals upstage of the act
curtain. These extra tracks make it possible to adjust
the depth of the staging area. Most stages are also
equipped with two or more "electrical battens": pipes
fitted with electrical outlets. Other installations use
drop outlet boxes which may be lowered independently
of existing battens. These are especially useful when
flying lighting instruments above and behind the playing area of the stage.

A sky cyclorama is frequently included in the stage
equipment. A sky cyc is usually made of light blue duck
suspended on a curved batten which sweeps from back
of the tormentors to deep stage to form a complete en-

closure. Unlike dress cycs, the sky cyc is stretched tightly giving the effect of an unbroken expanse of sky. A variety of techniques have been developed to stretch the wrinkles out of a huge drop of this size, but they are too complicated to discuss here.

The back stage area of some theatres may still contain the light control center. While this is the most inconvenient location for the switchboard and dimmer banks, older theatres and some of the smaller ones have no other provision for lighting control. In the more modern theatres, stage lighting control has been removed from the stage house to a booth or room located at the rear of the auditorium. The advantage of this location is that it gives the lighting technician a full view of the stage. However, controls for stage machinery must be back stage.

Other centers of activity are essential to the operation of a theatre, but they will be mentioned here in the context of what should be expected beyond the stage house. A large open area for assembling and painting scenery is of primary importance. Ideally, this area should be adjacent to the stage house with some provision for closing it off from the stage to prevent the transmission of sound. A property room for the preparation and storage of working properties is necessary for a smooth running production. A spacious scene shop for the construction of scenery should be close to the assembly area. A wardrobe and costume shop does not need to be next to the stage, but it should be close enough so that quick repairs can be made during performances. Actors' dressing rooms that have space for putting on makeup and costumes, in some degree of seclusion, as well as an offstage waiting room (greenroom) should be close to the stage. Lastly, accessible storage rooms for scenery, wagons, stage furniture and lighting equipment must be close at hand.

THE FUNCTIONS OF SCENERY

The visual relevance of scenery to the dramatic presentation has been a significant part of the theatre since the Greeks first used the skene as a representational object. When the spectators' understanding of the poet's words is enriched by the addition of visual elements, their empathy with the actor's interpretation is strengthened and they identify more with the theme. Yet modern scenography is not wholly dependent upon painted, representational units of scenery made of boards and cloth to achieve visual and emotional identification. The actors may speak their lines in an isolated pool of light on a blacked out stage and project greater impact upon the audience than if they were backed by a castle under full light. In other instances, scenery is often essential to carry out the business of the play and to give motivation for the performer's action. Thus, scenery, or lack of it, provides an environment in which the actor can act and the audience can react. In other words, it is not the province of scenery to dictate how each member of the audience shall respond; instead, it should create a climate that will stimulate members of the audience to identify in their own way, within his or her own frame of experience.

When units of scenery are set on the stage, they should be put there for a reason other than to decorate empty space. The primary function of scenic elements is to enhance the actors' capability to characterize and move effectively in the roles they are playing. A second function is to establish for the actors the locale in which their characterizations may be developed, one in which the audience may identify with the thematic content of the play. A third function is to assist both the actor and the audience in establishing the time or period as it relates significantly to the understanding and meaning of the play. A fourth function is to aid in the development of the tone, mood, and emotional environment of the play.

There may be set pieces arranged on the stage to form a partial room, rock and tree forms to suggest an exterior, or a stack of platforms and steps that have no particular identity: This is scenery, but only a part of the visual composition. One must be cognizant of the entire stage. For example, as the curtain opens on the interior scene we may be aware of sunlight through the window, shadows in the corners, and a general feeling of lived-in warmth suggested by the furniture, draperies, and pictures on the wall. The actors in the scene are costumed appropriately and appear to belong in the room before us. The exterior scene may show a fading sky with rays of the setting sun highlighting the trees and rocks, and the actors appear in dress suitable for the out-of-doors. The third scene may open in darkness except for one area where we can see a figure bent over a small table. As the lights gradually brighten, we may discover other actors on other levels of the platforms. What should be evident in these imagined scenes is that the total composition of each one is an organization of four theatrical design elements: scenery, lighting, properties, and costumes.

Scenes like the interior and exterior settings described above are representational and clearly establish the locale for the action to follow. This should not imply, however, that this degree of representation is always necessary. For example, in Arthur Miller's play, *Death of a Salesman,* the scene is a run-down house with a kitchen and bedroom on the lower floor and a second floor bedroom above. The setting is not realistic, since we are able to see all three rooms simultaneously, yet each playing area is clearly defined and furnished with plausible properties. The downstage area in front of the set is used alternately to represent the back yard, an office, a hotel room, and for the epilogue, the cemetery. To utilize the downstage area in this manner requires that a "convention" be established—in this case a manner of use that is acceptable to the actors and the audience. A swivel chair and desk are brought into this area early in the play to suggest an office, thereby establishing the convention. From this point on, any action in this area is accepted for what it is, and only a few simple properties are needed to establish the locale of other scenes that follow.

In the third scene the platforms and steps have no recognizable characteristics to establish the locale: They are merely acting areas. The director must block the actors' movement so that the audience will be able to associate areas with incidents or characters, otherwise the shift of action from one platform to another can become confusing and distracting. Another of Miller's plays, *After the Fall,* exemplifies how locale can be established in this manner. The play is a series of fragmented scenes which flow from one to the other like flashbacks in memory. No scenery is essential except the platforms. These are arranged in different levels with steps or ramps between so the actors can move from one to the other. The audience soon discovers that each level is identified with certain characters or places, and the actors may remain in these established positions in the darkness until the lights fade on one area and come up on theirs.

Scenery that relates period and time, like locale, can be stated directly or subtly. If we use the same imaginary interior setting, the time of day is clearly evident by the light from the sun, but the description does not go far enough. If the window in the set is narrow and tall and the curtains are lace with swagged over drapes edged in ball fringe, the furniture rounded, low and ornate, and the costumes of the women are full-length dresses with bustles at the back, the period is probably late Victorian. Thus, period and time can be established through the movement of light, the introduction of symbols that associate with events or periods, or through the use of stage dressing and costumes.

Units of scenery by themselves, without lighting or the presence of the actor, seldom convey emotional feeling to the audience. It is quite true, however, that light and shadow, color, and form can affect and stimulate responses. Massive units with deep shadows and dark hues can arouse a sense of foreboding and mystery, while bright gay colors immediately suggest a light happy mood. Distorted shapes are often used to suggest conflict, distress, and terror, but barren space can often be equally effective. A degree of caution should be exercised in using such devices so that they do not become decoration for the sake of "effect." They should be used only as they are consistent with the requirements of the actor and the play. It would be a mistake, for example, to stage Beckett's *Waiting for Godot* in a grassy meadow with bright flowers on either side of the path. The mood and tone of the play is one of desperation and solitude. A vast expanse of space and a withered tree are the only scenic requirements and the audience should sense the mood of the play the moment the lights come on.

STYLES OF SETTINGS

A single piece of scenery, apart from the stage, is nothing more than a piece of construction. Not until it is combined with other units of scenery and set on the stage, can it be assumed to be a stage setting. Many changes have occurred, both structural and philosophical, in the past hundred years which have affected the use of scenery. The outcome has been the development of scenic styles that are far more expressive, and therefore more compatible with our contemporary concepts of good theatre than those that preceded them. The style in which a setting will be rendered is ordinarily the result of decisions reached between the director and set designer. The stage technicians, who have the responsibility of building, painting and assembling the set, will work more effectively if they have a basic understanding of the styles. Too often the technician follows the set of plans given him, with no conception of what his work is to produce.

At the outset, there is apt to be some confusion because few designers hold to any one style consistently, and few authors who attempt to describe the style of settings agree completely in their definitions. This is due, at least in part, to the overlapping and mergence of the various movements which set the styles in the beginning, as well as to the influence of playwrights seeking new forms of expression. Therefore, the definitions that follow are for the purpose of identifying the styles literally, even though they are no longer under the direct influence of any active movement, and are often combined in actual practice.

Naturalism

Not to be confused with Realism which began as a writing style, Naturalism tried to bring Nature to the stage in protest of the use of painted canvas and cardboard. This style was first introduced late in the last century, but both audiences and critics were loud in their disapproval. In the first place, the sight of hard, plastered walls, growing trees, and actual rocks on the stage was incongruous. In the second place, audiences were so awe struck at seeing nature reproduced on stage that they became preoccupied with searching for flaws. Although the cinema still relies heavily on location photography for authenticity, naturalistic settings on the stage are rarely seen. However, natural forms do provide the starting point from which other styles emerge.

Restricted Realism

The frequent need for settings that reflect a lifelike environment has forced set designers to seek a compromise between naturalism and plausible theatricalness. A suggestion of nature on the stage was found to be much more acceptable because it permitted the deletion of nonessential details that were most often the very ones which made the naturalistic setting distracting. As an example, a window in a naturalistic setting would be cased in complete detail: surfaces varnished or painted, and glass, stops, and moldings authentic. The fact that most of these details were not visible beyond the apron meant that many could be eliminated.

Restricted realism (we often hear the term limited or suggested realism used) is a style which stops short of nature and emphasizes only those essential details that are required to establish the effect of reality. Like vocal projection, which the actor must exercise so that every nuance of his characterization will reach the back row of the audience, scenery must project to be effective. Exaggeration of important scenic elements is necessary, but those having no visual significance can be omitted. Even natural forms occasionally need assistance. Howard Wicks, who was technical director for the Theatre Guild in New York during the early thirties, related an incident that occurred while he was working with the distinguished designer, Robert Edmund Jones. Jones had requested a live rubber plant for the set, but

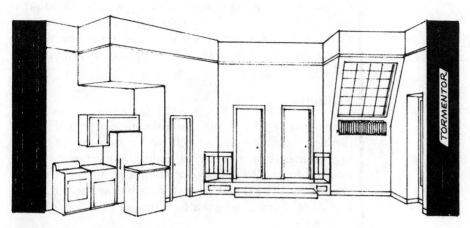

BOX SET - REALISTIC STYLE

EXTERIOR SET - REALISTIC STYLE

Figure 2-8. *Realistic styles.*

discovered that under stage lights the plant appeared lifeless and artificial. He solved the problem by having the scene painter spatter the leaves with bright red scene paint. The droplets of red on the deep green leaves created a high color vibrancy which accentuated their natural luster, even to the back of the auditorium. Painted shadows, moldings, and paneling are acceptable shortcuts as long as they are rendered with skill and are not distracting.

Stylization

Stylization extracts the realistic elements and either through exaggeration, simplification, or conventionalizing, utilizes them as a design, rather than a replica of the original form. The free use of color and the repetition of shapes for the sake of pattern may be carried out in the structural forms, or created through the use of light and shadow.

It might appear that this style would only lend itself to whimsical plays where decoration was the main function of the setting. However, it can be employed as a highly expressive form, but the play must be considered to determine whether the style is suitable. The settings for *A Midsummer Night's Dream* can be done stylistically because it is a fantasy, while *The Man Who Came to Dinner* would be more appropriately set in a more realistic style. Jo Mielziner's skeletal setting for Tennessee Williams' *Summer and Smoke* is an excellent illustration of stylized selectivity in which the architectural period provides the design motif. The oval windows, shaped shingles, and the curved lines of the roof appear to hang in space like a line drawing, yet there is never any doubt about the representational objective. (See Figure 1–5, p. 4.)

Expressionistic Style

In a literal sense, and expressionistic setting aims to convey the emotional environment which may, or may not, be based on reality. Distortion, nonobjective forms, color, and lighting may be used as expressive elements rather than representational devices. However, the expressionistic style may also be used for the setting for a play like *The Glass Menagerie* by Tennessee Williams, in which each segment can be set realistically, but each seems to emerge out of the darkness as the thoughts and memories of the characters in the play shift from one episode to another.

Specifically, expressionistic scenery may be characterized as having heavy jagged forms, with coarse, and unusual textures set against a dark or almost surrealistic background. As a further departure from realism, unusual lighting and sound are often used to augment the expressionistic theme. Projections may also be used as a means of showing inner conflicts, flashbacks, or abstract symbols that are expressive of the characters in the play.

Constructivist Style

Constructivism, as a revolutionary movement, lasted only a few years, but it inspired a scenic style that is used extensively today. It can best be described as the furthest departure from realism. It may consist of simple boxes stacked on top of one another, or austere structural scaffolding made of steel or wood on which actors can perform. No attempt is made to suggest locale, period, or mood: It is a "machine for acting."

Because raw structural forms tend to be cold and disassociated with the actor, designers often digress by combining the constructivist concept with stylized forms suggested by the natural environment of the play. This produces a skeletonized form of setting in which the structural elements are the motif for the design. Thus, instead of a setting composed of heavy platformed masses, or spidery with crisscross structural bracing of the scaffolds, the skeletal forms are more delicate and theatrical.

Suggestivism and Symbolism

Suggestivism, as a single style of stage setting, refers to any form in which a fragment or brief statement is considered sufficient to establish the locale. The scenery may be a mere abbreviation of a full set, and is often referred to as a "fragmentary" style. The scenic units may be two or three dimensional, rendered in a cartoon style or in a realistic manner using actual objects. Since suggestive scenery does not fill the entire stage, the ef-

STYLIZATION – ARCHITECTURAL

STYLIZATION – NATURAL FORMS

Figure 2–9. Stylization.

fectiveness is highly dependent upon good lighting control in order to isolate the scene of action.

The staging of *Our Town* by Thornton Wilder, is an excellent example of how one may use suggestive setting. A board supported across the backs of two chairs suggests the soda fountain, and two stepladders give George and Emilie the proper elevation to suggest their second floor bedrooms. Where a suggestion of realism is desired, a park bench and a trash container connote a scene in the park, just as the desk and swivel chair suggested the office in *Death of a Salesman*. This style of setting is commonly employed where scenes are short and follow in rapid succession, or where offstage space for scene storage is so cramped that full settings would be impractical.

Symbolism, like suggestivism, is more likely to be used in a fragmentary form than as a full stage setting. The chief difference lies in the use of a symbolic motif that is related to the theme of the play, as opposed to the representational characteristics of suggestivism. An Inca sunburst dominates the stage throughout Peter Shaffer's epic play, *The Royal Hunt of the Sun*, symbolizing the devotion of the Incas to their Sun King. A gigantic monument stands center stage in Peter Ustinov's satiric play, *The Unknown Soldier and His Wife*, as a stark memorial to those who lost their lives in futile wars.

In conclusion, there are other stylistic distinctions that might be drawn, but most of these are composites of, or extreme departures from, those already described. It should be relatively easy to discern how these styles can be combined in actual application: stylized realism, stylized constructivism and expressionistic fragmentation, as examples. It should also be obvious that all of these styles, with the possible exception of restricted realism, can be used on open, as well as proscenium stages. The fragmented form of suggestive settings adapt well to open stages, and constructive platforming and skeletal framing can be used on the arena stage.

An examination of the proscenium stage is relevant because much of our present technology of the theatre,

EXPRESSIONISTIC STYLE

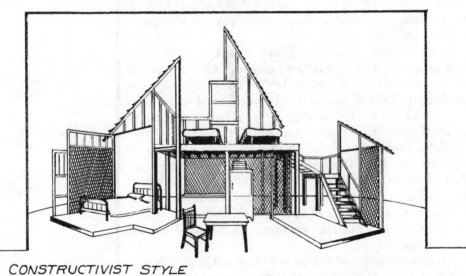

CONSTRUCTIVIST STYLE

Figure 2–10. Expressionistic and constructivist styles.

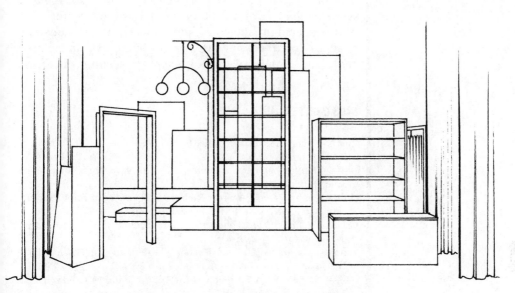

SUGGESTIVISM - FRAGMENTARY STYLE

SYMBOLISM

Figure 2–11. Suggestivism and symbolism.

including machines, staging methods and vocabulary was developed from it. Even though the characteristics of a proscenium stage are quite varied, due to constant changes and developments in our technology, those presented are typical of those in most proscenium theatres.

SUGGESTED READINGS

Burris-Meyer, Harold and Cole, Edward. *Scenery for the Theatre.* Boston: Little, Brown, 1972.
———*Theatres and Auditoriums,* 2nd ed. New York: Van Nostrand Reinhold, 1964.
Dolman, John, Jr. and Knaub, Richard K. *The Art of Play Production,* 3rd ed. New York: Harper & Row, 1973.
Gillette, A. S. *Stage Scenery: Its Construction and Rigging,* 2nd ed. New York: Harper & Row, 1972.
Hainaux, Rene (ed.). *Stage Design Throughout the World Since 1935.* New York: Theatre Arts Books, 1956.
——— *Stage Design Throughout the World Since 1950.* New York: Theatre Arts Books, 1969.
Kernodle, George R. *Invitation to the Theatre.* New York: Harcourt Brace Jovanovich, 1967.
Parker, W. Oren and Smith, Harvey K. *Scene Design and Stage Lighting.* New York: Holt, Rinehart & Winston, 1963.
Seldon, Samuel and Sellman, Hunton. *Stage Scenery and Lighting.* Englewood Cliffs, N.J. Prentice-Hall, 1959.
Whiting, Frank. *An Introduction to the Theatre,* 3rd ed. New York: Harper & Row, 1969.

MATERIALS
OF THE SCENE

From the outset, the playwright is the initial creator in the theatre, but a play is written to be performed. A skillful director with creative imagination and interpretive insight, actors who are fully in command of their skills, and designers and technicians who have the sensitivity and creative skill to stage the play in its most effective manner, are all essential before the playwright's work can achieve fruition.

If the technical staging of a production is well executed, the focus of attention must be entirely on the play. The actors, scenic effects or any other technical assistance must not stand apart. When all aspects of the production are merged, the production becomes an artistic whole. Any facet of technical achievement that fails to provide this level of support for the actor, or exceeds its functional requirements, will inevitably stand out as a distraction. A platform covered and painted to look like a stone parapet that shakes and quivers when the actor moves not only destroys the illusion it was intended to create, but is an indication that bad judgment may have been exercised in the method of construction, and that the materials used were not adequate for the job. The best assurance a stage technician can offer the actor and the director is a thorough knowledge of his craft, and an understanding of materials and how to use them most effectively.

STRUCTURAL MATERIALS

Because of its availability and workability, wood is the most common scenic construction material. The scarcity of wood resulting from extensive building has forced the cost upward, but compared to other kinds of structural materials, wood remains the least expensive to use. In addition to the natural woods available in a variety of sizes, modern manufacturing methods have produced a number of processed and wood by-products that have many uses in scenic construction. Fabrics, both natural and man-made, are used extensively in construction, set decoration and upholstery. Metals are used where strength and durability are needed, and because of their patina and natural color. Plastics, such as styrofoam and other higher density urethane foam derivatives, fiber glass, Celastic, and other synthetic material are found in many scene shops. Modeling and casting materials, adhesives and glue, and hardware must all be considered materials used in the construction of scenery.

Many structural materials are available through local hardware, lumber and material suppliers, although it will be necessary to get some from dealers who specialize in scenic materials. It is always wise to do some comparative pricing, particularly if orders must be shipped from great distances at high freight rates. One should not overlook the availability of used materials that can be purchased at a fraction of the cost of new stock. Theatre people have a standing reputation for being scavengers: remarkable bargains can often be found at the junk yards; old houses that are being demolished can produce such items as newel posts, stair spindles, mantle pieces, and hardware that are next to impossible to find elsewhere.

Wood and Wood Products

Among the wide varieties of wood to be found at the lumber yards, Northern white pine and Douglas fir are the most practicable for general scenic construction. White pine ranges in color from a creamy white to tan, with a pale yellow to light brown grain pattern. It is relatively soft, which makes it easy to saw by hand, and it can be nailed with little likelihood of splitting. It is strong, lightweight, and available in sizes that adapt well to most construction problems.

Douglas fir may be slightly darker in color than pine, depending on the part of the country where it is grown, and its grain heavier and darker. It is a harder wood than pine and tends to be splintery, but is less brittle. Primarily, fir is stocked in 2 inch thicknesses to be used for heavy construction for wall studding, rafters, beams and joists where structural weight bearing is a major concern. Fir is also used extensively for making laminated (plywood) sheets, which will be described later.

In selecting wood for scenic construction, one must keep in mind the function of the finished form, as well as the fact that stage hands must handle and move the set pieces on and off stage. Weight that workmen can handle easily and quietly is as important as the strength and durability. Flats, for example, are built as small individual units that must often be fitted together. If the wood used in framing the flats is warped and twisted, it becomes extremely difficult to fit units together snugly. If the lumber is marked with knots, there is a greater likelihood of breaking the framework because the grain swirls around the knots and weakens the wood. Pockets of pitch or sap in the surface of the wood will inevitably result in brown stains which will penetrate through painted muslin or canvas coverings.

Any wood will split or separate along the grain if sufficient stress is exerted. All woods have a breaking point that will occur if the load exceeds their weight bearing capability. Even though wood has a certain degree of flexibility, and the breaking point will vary considerably depending on the moisture content and grain characteristics, government standards have been established to regulate quality and load bearing limits. A familiarity with the grading and sizing of lumber can help the stage technician avoid many construction problems.

The grading of lumber is done at the sawmill before the boards have been surfaced. The wood is dried in a kiln—a large oven—to remove excess moisture to prevent shrinkage, then graded according to uniformity of grain and surface quality. It is then planed on all four surfaces to uniform thicknesses and widths essential for the building trades. The choice grades are classified as *Select* and the less desirable grades as *Common*. Since select grades are less prevalent than common, the price of better grades is considerably higher. Each grade is broken down into subgroups, according to the degree of surface perfection.

Select grades are divided into four groups. *A Select* is clear of all knots, pitch marks, blemishes or erratic grain and is free of warp, twist, or split ends. Grade *B or Better* is similar, but the pitch content of the wood is often higher which makes it heavier, and the grain is less uniform. C Select grade will have a few small tight knots, that is, the knots will not exceed ½ inch in diameter and they will not fall out leaving a hole. The lowest select grade is D Select in which there is a greater number of knots, an occasional pitch pocket, and some warping. The scarcity of A Select and B or Better grades has forced many lumber yards to discontinue them in their stock, but a good building carpenter can usually choose enough clear C and D grades so that by trimming out sections to avoid knots, he can get by very economically with the lower grades of lumber.

Common grades of lumber are classified by a number system. Number 1 Common differs from D Select in the size of knots which may be 1½ inches or more in diameter, with no assurance that they will not fall out. The probability of warping and twisting is also greater since common stock is cut nearer the heart of the tree. Number 2 Common will contain larger knots and the edges may show an occasional strip of underbark, even though the stock is planed on all edges. Lower grades are seldom usable. Common grades of lumber are satisfactory for bracing, flooring of platforms or construction where irregularities are not crucial to appearance or safety.

In addition to selecting the proper grades of lumber for the job, the carpenter should be aware of the standard dimensions. Both Select and Common grades are sized in accordance with standards of thickness, width, and length established by the U.S. Department of Agriculture. Sizing is done at the mill before the boards have been surfaced, so the dimensions of each board are nominal, rather than actual. Board lengths are standardized to accommodate the building trades and may be purchased in 8′, 10′, 12′, 14′ and 16′ lengths. One should not presume that the given length is exact, because a slight allowance is usually made for possible shrinkage, which makes it a good practice to measure each piece of stock before using it. The thickness of graded lumber is supposed to be uniform, although slight variations may occur. The following chart, based on the U.S. Department of Agriculture booklet *The Wood Handbook,* shows the standard sizes of graded lumber.

Nominal Dimensions (Thickness × Width*)	Actual Dimensions (Thickness × Width)
1″ × 2″	$^{25}\!/_{32}$″ × 1⅝″
1″ × 3″	$^{25}\!/_{32}$″ × 2⅝″
1″ × 4″	$^{25}\!/_{32}$″ × 3½″
1″ × 6″	$^{25}\!/_{32}$″ × 5½″
1″ × 8″	$^{25}\!/_{32}$″ × 7¼″
1″ × 10″	$^{25}\!/_{32}$″ × 9¼″
1″ × 12″	$^{25}\!/_{32}$″ × 11½″
2″ × 2″	1⅝″ × 1⅝″
2″ × 4″	1⅝″ × 3½″
2″ × 6″	1⅝″ × 5½″
2″ × 8″	1⅝″ × 7¼″
2″ × 10″	1⅝″ × 9¼″
2″ × 12″	1⅝″ × 11½″

* For metric conversion, 1″ = 2.540 centimeters.

Dimensioned lumber, as described above, is priced in one of three ways: by the linear foot, by the board foot, or by the piece. Linear measurement refers to the length of a piece of stock at a given price per foot of length. Board foot measurement is computed by converting the dimensions of the lumber to equal that of a comparable piece of stock that is 12″ × 12″ × 1″ thick. Piece pricing is usually done for the convenience of the customer who is not familiar with the method of converting the dimensions of stock to board feet. For example, 1″ × 2″ and 1″ × 3″ stock is sold by the linear foot, but all stock wider than 3″ is sold by the board foot. A piece of 1″ × 3″, 14′ long, grade B or Better, may be quoted at 15¢ per foot, or 14′ @ .15 = $2.10 per piece. On the other hand, the price for a 1″ × 4″, 14′ is often quoted at the price per thousand board feet.

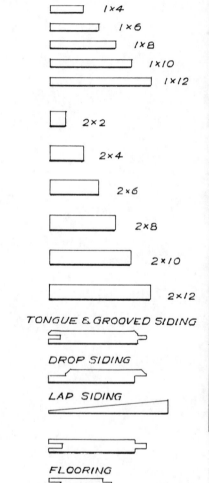

STANDARD DIMENSION LUMBER

1×2
1×3
1×4
1×6
1×8
1×10
1×12

2×2
2×4
2×6
2×8
2×10
2×12

TONGUE & GROOVED SIDING

DROP SIDING

LAP SIDING

FLOORING

Figure 3–1.
Standard dimension lumber.

Let us assume that six pieces of 1″ × 4″, 12′ long are required to brace a platform, and since the bracing will not show, we can use Number 2 common stock. The lumber yard quotes a price of $160 per thousand board feet. How many board feet are there in the order, and what will the cost be? First, the number of board feet can be determined by applying a simple mathematical equation: The number of pieces multiplied by the thickness, times the width, times the length in feet, and divided by 12, can determine the number of board feet, or

$$\frac{6 \times 1'' \times 4'' \times 12'}{12} = \frac{288}{12} = 24 \text{ Bd. Ft.}$$

The cost per board foot is determined by moving the decimal three places to the left, or 16¢, and .16 × 24 = $3.84, the cost of the material.

There are several kinds of flat dimension stock that have specially milled edges and surfaces for particular uses for wall siding and flooring. Such pieces are designed so that the edges overlap or fit together with a tongue and groove joint. Aside from tongue and grooved flooring, which may be used for permanent platforms, these materials are used for their decorative surface, rather than for standard construction.

In addition to the dimension stock, a wide variety of moldings and trim strips are carried by most lumber yards. Because of their interesting shapes, moldings are used extensively as trimming and edging, as well as for other uses in construction. Most moldings are available in white pine and are sold by the linear foot. Lengths may be standard, but random lengths are not uncommon. The following list will identify those moldings and trims most commonly used for scenic construction:

a. PARTING STOP

   ½″ × ¾″, lengths up to 14′

   Intended use: guide strips for sliding sash windows

   Stage uses: same, stop strips for stage doors around jams and header, simulated iron bars, spindles for iron stair railing, muntins for window panes, etc.

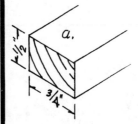

b. LATTICE

> ¼″ × 1″ and 1¼″, lengths to 14′
>
> Intended use: crisscross and flat woven lattice work
>
> Stage uses: same, arbors, slat blinds, decorative screens, fluting, balustrades, pilasters, flat panel trim, platform edging, etc.

c. BARN BATTEN

> ⅜″ × 2¾″, lengths to 14′
>
> Intended use: batten over joints of vertical barn siding
>
> Stage use: similar to lattice, curved ribbing, base board, and door trim, etc.

d. QUARTER ROUND MOLDING

> ½″ × ½″ to ¾″ × ¾″, lengths to 14′
>
> Intended use: inside corner trim
>
> Stage use: same, rounded edging on tables, steps, platforms, door, and window facing, etc.

e. HALF ROUND MOLDING

> ½″ to ¾″ diameter, lengths to 14′
>
> Intended use: screen and panel trim
>
> Stage use: same, rounded step and platform edging, reeding on pilasters, door, and window facing trim, etc.

f. COVE MOLDING

> ½″ × ½″ to 6″ × 6″, lengths to 14′
>
> Intended use: inside corner trim, cabinet and case trim
>
> Stage use: same, fluted detail, picture and wall panel trim, handrail trim, pilaster and wainscot detail, cornices, etc.

g. BED MOLDING

> 1¼″ to 1½″ × ¾″, lengths to 14′
>
> Intended use: inside corner trim for mantle and cabinets
>
> Stage use: same, wall paneling and framing, wainscot, pilaster, handrailings, etc.

h. CROWN MOLDING

    2¾" to 6" wide, lengths to 14'

    Intended use: interior trim, paneling and cabinetry

    Stage use: same, base and cap of pilasters, mantle
       pieces, etc.

i. PICTURE MOLDING

    1½" × ¾", lengths to 14'

    Intended use: picture molding

    Stage use: same, wainscot, panelings, trim, etc.

j. CASING

    2" to 5½" wide × ¾" thick, lengths to 16'

    Intended use: face molding for doors, windows and
      baseboards

    Stage use: same

k. FULL ROUND RODS AND POLES

    Doweling: ⅛" to ¾" diameter, length 36", hard-
      wood, maple or birch

    Intended use: dowel rods, cabinetry

    Stage use: flag sticks, scroll rods, wall pegs, etc.

    Poles: 1³⁄₁₆" to 1½" diameter, lengths to 16'

    Intended use: closet and curtain rods

    Stage use: same, cell bars, banner poles, shafts for
      spears and halberds, pipes, etc.

    Handrailings: 1½" to 2" diameter, lengths to 14',
      slightly flat on one side for brackets

    Intended use: stair handrailings

    Stage use: same, poles, pipes, small colonades, etc.

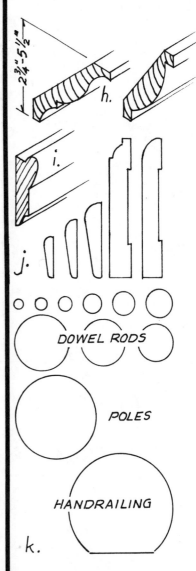

DOWEL RODS

POLES

HANDRAILING

Lamination is a process of gluing several thin layers of wood together. Douglas fir plywood is made in this manner by bonding together three or more layers, the grain of each running in the opposite direction. The wood is shaved from around the log in wide strips which makes it possible to form large sheets of stock. Lamination increases the strength relative to equivalent thicknesses of natural wood, and produces large sheets that are highly resistant to splitting.

Douglas fir plywood is manufactured in standard

sheets that are 4' × 8', and in thicknesses from 1/8" to 1 1/4". Plywood is quality graded according to surface finish. *CD Grade* is the lower grade. The front and back surfaces are rough sanded and may have many surface imperfections. It is used mainly for sheathing and sub-flooring where the surface is to be covered by another finish. Its strength is not reduced, however, and it may be used for platform tops and other construction where appearance of the rough surface is of no concern. CD grade is available in 3/8", 1/2", 5/8", and 3/4" thicknesses.

AD Grade plywood is smooth sanded on both sides, but only one of the surfaces is clear of imperfections: the back side may have patches and irregularities in grain pattern. This grade is ideal for most scenic work, although the prominent grain pattern makes it necessary to cover the surface with lightweight muslin before it is painted to prevent the grain ridges from showing through. AD grade is available in 1/4", 5/16", 3/8", 1/2", 5/8" and 3/4" thicknesses at most lumber yards.

AA Grade plywood is clear on both sides and is intended to be used where both surfaces will be exposed. Unless the surfaces are to be stained and varnished, AA grade is generally too expensive to use for most construction.

Plywood is also prepared for both interior and exterior use. The difference is in the bonding agent used in the lamination. Exterior plywood is bonded with a moisture resistant phenol resin glue. Interior plywood is bonded with either soybean glue or extended (diluted) phenol resin which is not moisture resistant and will separate if the wood becomes soaked through. The exterior type is more expensive, but if scenery is to be used out-of-doors, the difference in cost is worth considering.

Plywood is priced by the square foot and the cost will depend upon the grade, thickness, and type. The thinner plywoods can be used to cover curved forms if the radii are not too extreme. Plywood is more flexible parallel to the surface grain; this fact must be considered when using it as a reinforcing plate in scenery construction. Where special construction may call for finer woods, plywood is available in a wide variety of unfinished and prefinished stock, including walnut, mahogany and fruitwood.

In addition to plywood, there are two forms of sheet stock made that are by-products of wood. One is called *particle board* which is composed of wood chips and sawdust combined with a bonding agent and compressed into 4′ × 8′ sheets. Particle board is available at all lumber suppliers in thicknesses of ⅜″ to ¾″. Its uses include core stock for laminated hardwood paneling, cabinet shelving and partitions, sub-flooring and a variety of other applications similar to plywood. Due to its granular composition, the edges crumble easily unless they are protected and it should not be used as a substitute for plywood for reinforcement. It is sold by cost per square foot, and is less expensive than plywood.

The other sheet stock is best known by the trade name of *Masonite,* although there are other brand names for similar material. Masonite is composed of wood pulp compressed into 4′ × 8′ sheets in ⅛″, ¼″ and ⅜″ thicknesses. It is available in two degrees of hardness, tempered and untempered. Untempered Masonite is a light brown color and softer than tempered, which is dark brown and extremely hard. Both are quite brittle, but excellent for cabinet backing, door paneling, and facing on curved forms that will not be subjected to sharp blows which would break the surface. The ⅜″ tempered Masonite is often used as an overlay for the stage floor because it is highly resistant to compression and will withstand the pressure of heavy stage wagons without damage to the surface.

Metal and Metal Products

Until quite recently, metals had rarely been considered as structural substitutes for wood. The spiraling cost of wood and the reduced reliance upon frames covered with cloth for scenery has resulted in greater attention to metal as a structural material. Iron and steel are considered best in terms of strength and durability, but aluminum, when formed into the proper shape to give it strength, is not only strong enough for most scenic

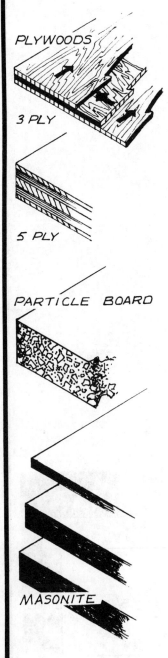

PLYWOODS

3 PLY

5 PLY

PARTICLE BOARD

MASONITE

requirements, but is lightweight and easier to handle. Copper and brass have fewer uses, although their color and workability gives them importance in the construction of costume jewelry and trinkets for properties and costumes.

Most metals are available in a variety of forms including sheet, bar, rod, pipe, mesh, and screen, as well as cable and wire. Most structural forms are sold by the pound. Mesh and screen are sold by the foot, and cable and wire may be sold by the spool or by the running foot. The thickness of sheet metal is indicated by gauge or in thousandths of an inch as determined by the U.S. Bureau of Standards. Wire size is determined by diameter, stated by wire gauge or in thousandths of an inch. Cable is purchased by the diameter given in fractions of an inch and the number of strands. Rods and bars are dimensioned by size, while pipe dimensions are given by inside and/or outside diameter. The following list describes those metal products that are used most frequently and notes some of the ways they can be used.

a. SHEET METALS

Black Iron

Sheet size: 30″ to 36″ × 96″ long
Thickness: 18 ga. to 28 ga.
Color: Blue-black to brown
Metal to metal joint: Rivets, sheet metal screws, bolts, folded seam, welding
Forming: Can be hammered, folded, crimped or stamped
Uses: Lanterns, ornamental iron, medallions, armor, reinforcing plates, thunder sheets, etc.

Galvanized Iron (zinc coated to rustproof)

Sheet size: 30″ to 36″ × 96″ long
Thickness: 18 ga. to 28 ga.
Color: Silver gray and mottled
Metal to metal joint: Rivets, sheet metal screws, folded seams, soft solder
Metal to wood: Round head screws, bolts, or nails if holes predrilled, rivets

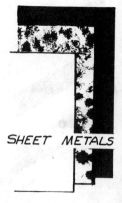

SHEET METALS

Forming: Can be hammered, folded, crimped or stamped

Uses: Splash pans, reinforcing plates, armor, etc.

Aluminum (sheet aluminum is available in hard and soft)

Sheet size: 24″ to 36″ × 96″ long

Thickness: 18 ga. to 30 ga.

Color: Aluminum

Metal to metal joint: Aluminum solder, rivets, sheet metal screws

Forming: Can be hammered, annealed, folded, spun on spinning lathe

Uses: Armor, jewelry ornaments, reflectors, etc. (A modeling aluminum that is extremely soft can be purchased at hobby and art suppliers)

Tin Plate (tin plated steel sheet)

Tin plate is noted here because it is available in sheets 24″ × 30″ at metal dealers. Small quantities can be obtained by cutting up metal containers. It cuts and solders easily, making it useful for small jewelry items.

b. STRAP IRON, CHANNEL AND PIPE[1]

Strap Iron (mild and cold rolled steel)

Sizes: $\frac{1}{8}$″, $\frac{3}{16}$″ and $\frac{1}{4}$″ thickness; widths $\frac{1}{4}$″, $\frac{3}{8}$″, $\frac{1}{2}$″, $\frac{5}{8}$″, $\frac{3}{4}$″ and wider

Color: Mild steel, black; cold rolled, silver gray

Joints: Bolts, rivets or welded

Forming: Bent by hand, in vise or with bending jigs

Uses: Sill irons, brackets, hooks, straps, ornamental iron, swords, and daggers

Perforated Strap

Size: 20 ga. × $\frac{3}{4}$″ wide with $\frac{1}{4}$″ holes spaced $\frac{1}{2}$″ o.c.

Color: Galvanized or black

Joints: Bolt

Forming: Hand bent or with pliers

Uses: A reinforcing band around joints, etc.

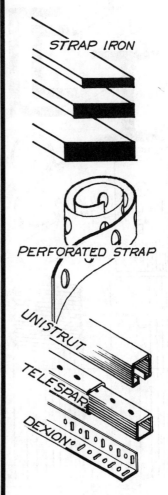

STRAP IRON

PERFORATED STRAP

UNISTRUT

TELESPAR

DEXION

---

[1] Other steel shapes are available—bars and rods—but their use does not warrant their inclusion.

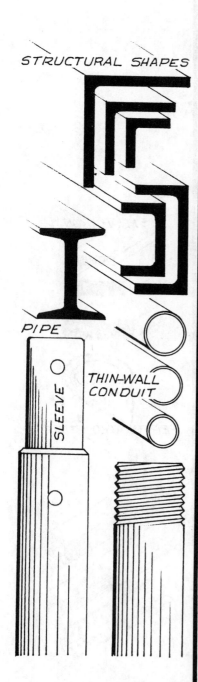

STRUCTURAL SHAPES

PIPE

SLEEVE

THIN-WALL CONDUIT

Channels and Tubes (Unistrut, Telespar and Dexion)
Sizes: 1″ to 2″ angle and square
Color: Painted or black
Joints: Bolts
Forming: Preformed
Uses: Steel platform legs, scaffolds and braces

Angle and Channel (mild steel)
Sizes: 1/8″ and 3/16″ thickness × 3/4″ to 1 3/4″ wide
Color: Black
Joints: Bolts, rivets or weld
Forming: After miter cut, may be bent
Uses: Platform legs, bracing, platform edging, wagon guide, jacks, and braces

Aluminum Channel and I Beam
Sizes: 1/8″ to 1/4″ thickness, face widths to 4″
Color: Aluminum
Joints: Rivet, bolt or weld
Forming: Preformed
Uses: Structural platforming, understructure for stage wagons, scenic construction

Pipe (thin wall electrical conduit tubing)
Sizes: 1/2″ to 1″ diameter in 10′ lengths
Color: Silver gray
Joints: Special joint fittings or gas weld
Forming: May be bent with bending jig
Uses: Light skeletal construction, non-weight bearing

Black Iron Pipe
Sizes: 1″ to 1 3/4″ diameter, lengths to 18′
Color: Black
Joints: Sleeve joints, weld
Uses: Pipe battens, structural set pieces

Steel Pipe (black and galvanized, zinc coated)
Sizes: 1/4″ to 1 3/4″ inside diameter, lengths to 21′
Color: Black or mottled silver gray
Joints: Threaded fittings, weld, or bolted to wood
Uses: Scaffolds, railings, platform legs, pipe battens

c. MESH AND SCREEN

Steel Mesh

Size: 6″ mesh in rolls 6′ wide, $\frac{5}{32}$″ to $\frac{3}{16}$″ strands

Color: Black

Joints: Wiring or weld, stapled to wood

Forming: Bent or folded

Uses: Textural mesh, leaded glass effect, etc.

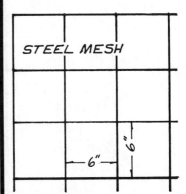

Rabbit Wire (hardware cloth)

Size: ¼″ to ½″ mesh, 24″ to 36″ wide in rolls

Color: Galvanized

Joining: Lap soldered, wired, or stapled

Forming: Can be bent and shaped by hand

Uses: Mesh grillwork, screens, rigid modeling

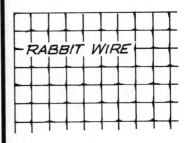

Chicken or Poultry Wire

Size: Large and small mesh, 18″ to 60″ widths by roll

Color: Galvanized

Joining: Wiring or stapled to wood

Forming: Can be bent and shaped by hand

Uses: For irregular shaping for rock and tree forms

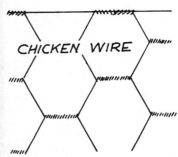

Window screen (steel and aluminum)

Size: 24″ to 48″ wide, $\frac{1}{16}$″ mesh, by roll

Color: Gray

Joining: Staple

Forming: Can be bent and shaped by hand

Uses: To simulate glass, for irregular shaping for rocks and tree forms, straining paint and sifting plaster

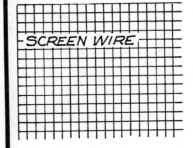

d. CABLE AND WIRE (See table.)

Flexible Steel Cable (copper clad, 6 × 19, fiber core)

Sizes: ¼″ to ½″ diameter, by spool

Color: Copper plated to rustproof, or uncoated steel

Joining: Cable clamps, clove hitch to pipe

Uses: Fly lines that must run over pulleys

Table: Safe Load Bearing Range for Cable and Wire*

Galvanized Aircraft Cable or Cord

Dia. in.	6 x 7 strand lbs	7 x 7 strand lbs	7 x 19 strand lbs	Safe Load— 7 x 19 lbs
1/16	400	480	480	90 to 100
1/8	1,440	1,700	2,000	350 to 400
3/16	3,150	3,700	4,200	800 to 900
1/4	5,200	6,100	7,000	1,400
5/16	8,000	9,200	9,800	2,000
3/8	11,500	13,100	14,400	2,800

Music Spring Steel Wire—ASTM Designation A 228

Number	Approx. standard gauge	Diameter in.	Safe working load lbs
10	24 ga.	0.024	Under 100
11	23 ga.	0.026	Under 150
12	22 ga.	0.029	Under 200
13	20 ga.	0.031	Under 250
14		0.033	Under 300
15	19 ga.	0.035	Under 300
16		0.037	Under 350
17		0.039	Under 350
18		0.041	Under 400
19		0.043	Under 500
20	18 ga.	0.045	Under 500
26	16 ga.	0.063	Under 900

* The above data has been supplied and verified by the American Society for Testing Materials, Philadelphia, Pa.; the Wire Rope Technical Board, Washington, D.C.; and the Wire Rope Corporation of America, Inc., St. Joseph, Mo.

Aircraft Cable (cord or rope) (Galvanized)
   Sizes: 1/16″, 1/8″, 3/16″, 1/4″, 5/16″ and 3/8″ diameter
   Color: Silver gray
   Joining: Compression (Nicropress) sleeve or cable
      clamp with spool in loop
   Uses: Flying scenery

Stove Pipe Wire

    Sizes: 18 to 22 gauge, by roll or spool
    Color: Black
    Joining: Wrapping around itself
    Uses: Property construction, hanging small objects, and guying where no great stress is required

Bailing Wire

    Sizes: 12 and 14 gauge, by roll or foot
    Color: Black
    Joining: Wrapping around itself
    Uses: Property construction, hanging small objects, and guying where moderate support is required

Miscellaneous Structural Wire

    Sizes: 9 to 12 gauge, by roll or foot
    Color: Black, galvanized iron and aluminum
    Joining: Wrapping around itself
    Uses: Property construction, vines, and inner structure for clay models

Music Spring Steel Wire (Piano Wire)

    Sizes: #13, #20 and #26 most common sizes (Note: Music wire is often numbered and does not conform to Standard Wire Gauge). Sold by pound in boxed coils.
    Color: Bright steel or black
    Joining: Tightly coiled around itself
    Uses: Because of its great tensile strength, it may be used for flying scenery or persons where invisibility of fly-line is desired. Caution: kinks or surface blemishes can cause wire to break.

Fiber and Paper Products

Many of the fiber and paper products used by the building trades have been adopted for scenic construction because they are less expensive than woods and are lighter in weight and easier to cut with simple hand tools. Most can be found at local lumber suppliers. The strength of these products does not compare with that of compressed wood products or plywood, so they should not be used as substitutes where strength is a factor. Never-

CABLE

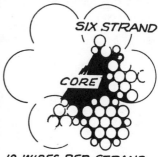

SIX STRAND

CORE

19 WIRES PER STRAND

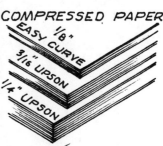

COMPRESSED PAPER

1/8" EASY CURVE

3/16" UPSON

1/4" UPSON

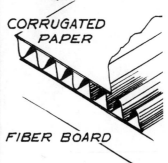

CORRUGATED PAPER

FIBER BOARD

(CELOTEX)

theless, they are most useful where intricate cut-out patterns are needed, or where curved surfaces need covering.

a. COMPRESSED PAPER PRODUCTS

Easy Curve Upson Board
  Size: Sheets 4′ × 8′, ⅛″ thickness
  Color: Creamy white, pebble texture one side
  Joining: Staples, nails, glue to wood; gummed tape over joints
  Cutting: Saw, Cut-Awl or utility knife
  Uses: Hard surface flat covering, cut-out contours for groundrows, curved thicknesses for arches, curved facing where strength is not a factor

Upson Board
  Size: Sheets 4′ × 8′, 3/16″ and ¼″ thicknesses
  Color: Creamy white, pebble texture one side
  Joining: 3d nails, gummed tape over joints
  Cutting: Saw, Cut-Awl, utility knife
  Uses: Hard surface flat covering, groundrows and cut-out work where great rigidity is needed, properties, etc.

b. CORRUGATED PAPER

Corrugated Paper (corrugated layer between heavy kraft paper)
  Sizes: Single and double strength; sheet sizes vary depending on manufacturing source; thicknesses 5/32″ and 7/32″
  Color: Kraft paper brown or white
  Joining: Staples, 3d nails, gummed paper tape over joints
  Cutting: Utility knife, Cut-Awl, fine tooth saw
  Uses: Flat covering, cut-out shapes, curved forms, armor base, properties, etc.
  Source: Salvage from cartons or purchased directly from paper box manufacturer and paper supplier by the bale—20 sheets

c. COMPRESSED FIBER BOARD

Celotex and Similar Products of Vegetable Fibers

Sizes: 4′ × 8′ sheets, ⅜″, ½″, ⅝″, ¾″ thickness

Color: Buff to brown with one surface prefinished white

Joining: Celotex nail or 3d nails

Cutting: Fine tooth saw, band saw, utility knife

Characteristics: Soft, spongy, tends to flake and crumble unless edges are framed

Uses: Break-away wall sections, platform padding if covered with canvas, bulletin boards, cutting surface for using Cut-Awl

Plastics

The most recent addition to the materials of the scene is a group of synthetic products classified under the general heading of plastics. Initially, these were developed for industrial uses; however, many are now available on the open market and the cost has dropped to a level where they can be used in the construction of scenery. Most nonprofessional scene shops are still not equipped to work with many of the plastics which require controlled conditions and special equipment, particularly for casting. Yet, several of these synthetic materials require very little special equipment. The more common and readily available plastics are described, along with some suggestions for their uses.

a. STYROFOAM

Sheet Styrofoam (medium density urethane)

Size: 4′ × 8′ in thicknesses of ½″, ¾″, 1″ and up to 3″; also available in blocks

Color: White

Joining: Built-up layers with contact cement, Elmer's glue, spray adhesive, or adhesive recommended by manufacturer

Cutting: Can be cut with saw, shaping may be done with files, rasps, sandpaper, or hot wire

Uses: Sculpture, architectural detail, special properties, carved surface detail

Sources: Carried by many lumber suppliers for insulation material, plastic suppliers, and manufacturers

High Density Styrofoam

Sizes: Sheets and blocks up to 2″ thickness
Color: White
Joining: Contact cement, liquid latex, Elmer's glue, or cement recommended by supplier
Cutting: Saw, files and rasps, hot wire, or turned on lathe
Uses: Sculptured forms and architectural detail where greater rigidity or weight bearing is essential
Sources: Plastic suppliers and manufacturers

b. POLYURETHANE

Polyurethane (foam mattress stock)

Sizes: Widths from 37″ to 76″, lengths to 80″, thicknesses 1″ to 5″; also available in smaller cushion sizes
Color: Off white
Joining: Contact cement
Cutting: Knife or shears; surface carving with electric knife and hot wire
Uses: Upholstery, pillows, bolsters, texture surfaces on scenery
Sources: Furniture suppliers, surplus stores, department stores, etc.

c. POLYETHYLENE

Clear and Black Plastic Sheeting

Sizes: 36″ to 20′ wide $\times$ 50′ to 100′ lengths, 2 to 10 mil
Color: Opalescent clear and/or black
Joining: Clear polyethylene tape, staple or tack to wood
Cutting: Scissors
Uses: Drop cloth for painting, stage drops, layered for opalescent projection screen
Sources: Paint suppliers, farm and irrigation suppliers, hardware or lumber supplier

d. VINYL

Clear Vinyl Sheet
Sizes: 36″ and 48″ widths in rolls to 100′, 4 mil
Color: Clear
Joining: Clear tape, staple, or tack to wood
Cutting: Scissors
Uses: Glass substitute
Sources: Hardware or lumber supplier

e. ACETATE

Clear
Sizes: 40″ × 12′ rolls, 3 to 10 mil, and in single
sheets 40″ × 24″
Color: Clear
Joining: Clear tape, staple, or tack to wood
Cutting: Scissors
Uses: Glass substitute, heavier weights for stencils
Sources: Hardware, artists' suppliers

f. FIBER GLASS

Fiber Glass Cloth
Sizes: 44″ to 60″ widths in lengths to 5 yards
Color: Gray
Joining: Polyester resin and finishing resin
Uses: Hard surface forming and modeling
Sources: Marine and auto body shops, hardware,
theatrical supply

g. POLY-FOAM

Poly-Foam—Two Part Kit
Size: Quarts
Produces: 3 cu. ft. of foam
Uses: Properties, textural and three-dimensional
forms
Source: Theatrical suppliers

Scenic Fabrics

There are multitudes of fabrics on the market that can
be used for scenic work at one time or another. Some
are most suitable for draperies and upholstery, while
others are more serviceable and can be used in covering

scenery that will be textured and painted. In general, fabrics can be divided into four categories: service fabrics, pile fabrics, sheen fabrics, and nets and scrims.

The service fabrics are usually woven from cotton, linen or jute fibers. Pile fabrics, those that have a nap surface, include cotton flannel, velvet, velour, and plush. The sheen fabrics are those that have a shiny surface like satin, silks, and taffetas. Nets and scrims include those fabrics with an open weave and may be made of cotton, nylon, or linen fibers.

Those fabrics described in the following list include only the ones that have scenic uses, including drapery materials, but it excludes reference to their possible uses for costuming.

a. SERVICE FABRICS

Canvas (cotton)

Weight and widths: 36" to 69" widths in weights ranging from 9 oz. to 16 oz. (the weight of canvas is rated according to the weight per square yard)

Color: Natural or off white, black, olive drab, and light blue on special order from stage drapery supplier

Characteristics: Coarse woven, usually some flecks of dark fiber, very durable, available flameproofed upon request, adequate shrinkage (10%+)

Uses: Covering flats, floor cloths, canvas sky cyclorama, painted drops

Sources: Hardware and tent and awning suppliers, scenic supply houses, fabric suppliers

Duck (cotton)

Weight and widths: 36" to 69" widths in weights 5 oz. to 8 oz.

Colors: White, sky blue

Characteristics: Finer woven and lighter weight than canvas, flameproofed on request, adequate shrinkage (10%+)

Uses: Covering scenery, cycloramas, painted drops

Sources: Tent and awning suppliers, scenic supply houses

Scene Linen (flax)

Weight and width: 69" wide × approximately 50 yard bolt

Color: Natural tan

Characteristics: Coarse woven, very durable, less shrinkage than canvas, quite expensive

Uses: Covering flats, painted drops

Sources: Scenic supply houses and fabric suppliers

Unbleached Muslin (cotton sheeting)

Weight and width: 72", 81", 90", 108" in #114, #128 and #140 weights (numbers indicate the weft threads per inch), in approximately 50 yard bolts. Seamless muslin for painted drops is also available in 30' widths and sold by the running foot in height

Color: Off white and sky blue

Characteristics: Finer and lighter weight than duck, moderate price, adequate shrinkage (10%+)

Uses: Scenery covering, painted drops, small cycloramas, drapery, mâché, and textural effects

Sources: Widths to 81" at dry goods stores, scenic fabric suppliers, fabric supply houses

b. PILE FABRICS

Velour

Weight and Widths: 45" to 54" wide × yard or bolt; 12 oz. to 16 oz.

Color: Wide variety of colors and shades

Characteristics: Heavy cotton back with nylon, cotton or rayon pile that is quite deep, like a heavy velvet

Uses: Stage curtains, upholstery

Sources: Scene fabric suppliers, upholstery and drapery shops

Velveteen

Weight and Widths: 45" to 48" wide × yard or bolt

Color: Wide variety of colors and shades

Characteristics: cotton or cotton and rayon with short nap giving velvety pile; serviceable and about half the cost of velour

Uses: Upholstery and draperies, for scenery where light absorbing surface is needed
Sources: Scenic fabric suppliers, upholstery, and drapery shops

Duvetyne
Weight and Width: Lightweight 36″ wide; heavyweight 48″ wide
Colors: Wide variety
Characteristics: Cotton with short pile, lighter weight and less serviceable than velveteen
Uses: Light drops or cycloramas
Source: Scenic fabric suppliers

Plush
Weight and Width: 45″ to 54″ wide × yard or bolt
Color: Wide variety of colors and shades
Characteristics: Softer and longer pile than velour; usually rayon with silky luster
Uses: Drapery and upholstery
Sources: Stage fabric supplier, local fabric shops

Corduroy
Weight and Width: 45″ to 48″ wide × yard or bolt
Color: Wide variety of colors and shades
Characteristics: Heavy cotton with pile woven in ribs or ridges, called the wale, running length of material
Uses: Substitute for velvet or velveteen for drapery or upholstery
Source: Local fabric suppliers

Cotton Flannel (outing flannel)
Weight and Width: 36″ width × yard or bolt 30 yards
Color: Light sky blue
Characteristics: Thin soft cotton with fleecy nap; fades under lights
Uses: Excellent for small inexpensive sky cyclorama
Source: Local fabric suppliers

C. SHEEN FABRICS

Damask

 Weight and Width: 45" to 54" wide × yard or bolt
 Color: Single or multicolor
 Characteristics: Heavy, with pattern woven in high luster yarn in contrast to nonluster background, often raised pattern, rayon, and cotton
 Uses: Stage curtains, draperies, and upholstery
 Sources: Stage fabric suppliers, upholstery, and fabric shops

Taffeta

 Weight and Width: 45" to 48" wide × yard or bolt
 Colors: Wide variety of colors and shades, solid colors
 Characteristics: Smooth, silky luster, rayon fabric
 Uses: Banners and flags, satinlike drops, draperies
 Sources: Stage fabric suppliers, local fabric shops

Sateen

 Weight and Width: 36" to 45" width × yard
 Colors: Black, white, and ivory
 Characteristics: Cotton and rayon with low sheen on one side
 Uses: Primary use, drapery lining. Black can be used for effective stage mirror by flashing lightly with aluminum spray
 Sources: Local fabric and drapery shops

d. NET AND SCRIM (gauze)

Bobbinet

 Sizes: 30' × height desired
 Colors: Natural, white, black
 Characteristics: Cotton, hexagonal weave net $\frac{1}{8}$" to $\frac{3}{16}$" opening, can be dyed or painted, washable, seamless, flameproofed
 Uses: Diffusion effect by lighting from back and/or front, transparent drops, netting back for cut-out drops, etc.
 Source: Scenic fabric suppliers

Sharkstooth

Size: 30′ × height desired

Colors: Natural, black, or white

Characteristics: Cotton, ladder weave netting with opening approximately $\frac{1}{16}$″ × $\frac{1}{4}$″, can be painted or dyed, washable, seamless, flameproof

Uses: Semitransparent drops, appears opaque when lit only from front

Source: Scenic fabric suppliers

Theatrical Gauze

Size: 72″ × yardage required

Colors: Natural and limited colors

Characteristics: A fine meshed linen gauze resembling cheese cloth, but heavier; usually sized, which makes it wiry; can be painted, has some opacity but can be used as transparency; stretchy and soft after washing; flameproof

Uses: Transparent traveler curtains, transparencies where kept within size limitation or where seams are not objectionable, draperies

Source: Scenic fabric suppliers

Nylon Netting

Sizes: 60″ and 72″ wide × yardage desired

Color: Many colors including black and white

Characteristics: Very fine hexagonal mesh, heat formed rather than woven, fragile, and tears easily

Uses: Where extreme invisibility is desired; can be used for drops, window covering where signs or patterns are required, skeletal scenery requiring hanging, unattached forms (latex cement must be used to adhere objects: other glues will either not stick or will dissolve fabric)

Source: Local fabric shops

Cheesecloth

Size: 36″ wide × yardage desired

Color: White

Characteristics: Very soft flimsy, fine meshed cotton; stretchy, but can be dyed or painted

Uses: After painting, can be tightly stretched over

frame to simulate screen; flat pleated, stretched, and tacked top and bottom for French window curtains

Source: Local fabric shops

e. MISCELLANEOUS FABRICS

Repp

Size: 48" wide × yardage desired

Color: Wide range

Characteristics: Heavy cotton or cotton and rayon fabric with woven pattern in diagonal cording, chevron, herringbone, or bark texture

Uses: Cyclorama setting, draperies, or upholstery

Source: Local fabric shops

Monk's Cloth

Sizes: 45" to 54" wide × yardage desired

Color: Natural or limited color range

Characteristics: Coarse basket weave cotton, heavy, but soft; may be washed and dyed

Uses: Stage curtains, draperies, upholstery

Sources: Scenic fabric supplier, drapery shops

Brocades

Sizes: 45" to 54" wide × yardage desired

Colors: Wide range

Characteristics: Lightweight damask weave, rayon, and cotton; pattern defined by contrasting shiny and dull warp

Uses: Draperies, upholstery

Sources: Drapery and fabric shops

Antique Satin

Sizes: 45" to 54" wide × yardage desired

Colors: Wide range of plain and printed material

Characteristics: Heavy satin back with duller face; if patterned, design printed rather than woven

Uses: Draperies, cushions, pillows, upholstery

Sources: Drapery and fabric shops

Upholstery fabrics

Sizes: 48" to 54" wide × yardage desired

Color: Wide range of plain, printed, and woven textures

Characteristics: Very heavy, often backed with rubberized coating, too heavy to drape

Uses: Upholstery of chairs, sofas, benches, etc.

Source: Upholstery shops

Burlap

Size: 36" to 60" wide × yardage desired

Color: Natural and in some colors

Characteristics: Coarse, loosely woven jute fiber as in gunny sacks; finer quality in colors

Use: Coarse texturing on flats, tree, and rock forms; also for coarse draperies and upholstery

Source: Scenic fabric supplier, salvaged sacks

Modeling and Casting Materials

Many scenic details, as well as many properties, call for built-up or three-dimensional forms that cannot be created economically from the materials thus far presented. Although wood, chicken wire, and styrofoam may be used in the construction of the basic forms, the finished surfaces of scenic units often require additional modeling that must be achieved by other means. Several objects of the same shape are often required, especially where they may have to be broken during performance. Masks and sculptured forms must be modeled in clay and a plaster cast made so the finished forms can be made of papier-mâché or Celastic.

The theatre technician must have a working knowledge of the materials and techniques required for modeling, casting, and the mâché processes. The technical procedures will be presented in sections pertaining to construction of scenery and properties, but the following descriptions of the materials will familiarize the technician with their characteristics, uses, and possible sources.

a. CLAY

Moist Modeling Clay

Color: Gray or terra cotta red

Characteristics: Available in plastic wrapped 50 pound chunk that is ready-mixed, or as dry powder to which water must be added; additional moisture may be added to maintain modeling consistency; if too wet, moisture can be removed by kneading clay on a plaster bat to absorb water; while work is in progress, clay is kept moist by wrapping in damp cloths or polyethylene; work that will be cast in plaster does not have to be dry: If clay is to be fired as for pottery, it must be completely dry; biscuit firing in kiln at 1700° F.; unfired clay can be resoftened by soaking in water

Uses: Modeling of architectural detail, masks and properties for mâché or plaster castings

Sources: Artist and ceramic suppliers

Plasticine Modeling Clay

Colors: Gray or gray green

Characteristics: Clay mixed with an oil so that it retains its plasticity; nondrying; may be reused indefinitely; requires no attention to preserve except that it be kept free of impurities

Uses: Modeling for mâché or casting in plaster

Sources: Ceramic and art suppliers

b. PLASTER

Plaster of Paris (dental plaster)

Color: White powder

Characteristics: Calcium sulphate powder that sets or hardens when it is added to water; excellent for casting or making molds; sets hard in about 20 minutes but three or four days required to dry completely; must be coated with shellac before painting

Uses: Casting of modeled shapes; molds for duplicate forms; plaques, architectural detail

Sources: Artist and ceramic supplier; medical and dental suppliers

Plaster Gauze (surgical gauze)

Color: White

Characteristics: A gauze impregnated with plaster of Paris, 3″ wide in rolls; immersed quickly in water, it will harden in a few minutes to any shape

Uses: Mask making, life masks, plaster casts, or sculptured mâché

Sources: Medical supplier, drug store

Quick-Set Gauging Plaster

Color: White powder

Characteristics: Less refined, quick-setting plaster used by plasterers; all characteristics of plaster of Paris, but slightly grainier; available in 100 pound bags; inexpensive and adequate for most scenic work

Uses: Casting, molding, etc.

Sources: Lumber and cement suppliers

c. LIQUID LATEX (liquid rubber)

Liquid Latex Rubber

Color: Red or natural

Characteristics: A liquid rubber; several layers painted over a casting or inside a mold acts as an elastic parting agent for two or more piece mold

Uses: Parting agent for plaster casting

Sources: Ceramic, art, and craft suppliers

d. CELASTIC

Celastic or Sculpt-o-Fab

Color: Off white

Characteristics: A commercial fabric, flannel or cheese cloth in light, medium, and heavyweight which has been impregnated with cellulose nitrate making material stiff and heavy; to use, the Celastic is dipped in a solvent or acetone making it very soft so that it can be formed over any shape (the Celastic solvent contains a fire retardant, while the acetone does not. Both solutions are quite volatile and should be used where there is good ventilation); the solvent evaporates, leaving the Celastic very hard, water repellent and quite durable; hardens in a few minutes, ready to paint the next day; layers are built up; will adhere to most anything, so aluminum foil is used over forms if Celastic is to be removed

Uses: Armor, rock forms, properties, leaves, masks, etc.

Source: Scenic supply houses

e. MÂCHÉ

Papier-Mâché

Material: Any soft paper that absorbs water and paste

Characteristics: A process of building up layers of paper or pulp paper mixed with paste over a form and allowed to dry; paper may be soaked until pulpy consistency then mixed with paste, or paper can be cut in strips which are dipped in paste and applied in layers

Uses: Masks, rock and tree forms, properties, etc.

Cloth-Mâché

Material: Strips or large pieces of muslin, canvas, or burlap

Characteristics: Processed as papier-mâché except cloth is used for toughness; adhesive: scene glue, latex or diluted Elmer's glue

Uses: Tree bark, rock texture, sculpture, etc.

Adhesives and Glue

There is not an all-purpose glue to satisfy all the needs of the stage technician. Actually, most scenic carpentry does not rely on glue for bonding joints because much of the construction is temporary. The greatest quantities of glue are used for adhering cloth coverings on flats and in the preparation of scene paints. Where glue is needed for construction, a fast-drying adhesive, causing a minimum of fuss and bother, is the most practical. The adhesives described are those that meet most of the criteria for theatre usage.

a. ANIMAL OR HIDE GLUE

Animal or Hide Glue

Color: Amber

Characteristics: Available in flake or ground form; flake is in thin rectangular cakes, ground is granulated; must be dissolved in cold water which usually requires 8 to 12 hours; after soaking it is placed in double boiler or electric glue pot and heated to near boiling when it becomes a syrupy solution and ready to use; must be used hot; jells when cold, but will be reusable when reheated; do not scorch or set directly over heat; inexpensive

Use: Wood glue requiring six to eight hours to dry; mixed with whiting to make scene glue or dope; diluted with water to make sizing for mixing paint and priming flats before painting

Sources: Hardware or paint store, scenic paint suppliers, or through major meat packing companies who manufacture animal glue

b. WHEAT PASTE

Wheat Paste

Color: Off white powder

Characteristics: An unrefined flour paste used mainly for applying wallpaper; available in bags; mixed by sifting slowly in cold water and stirring to a smooth, thick paste consistency

Uses: Paste for papier-mâché; used in preparation of dutchman paste

Sources: Paint store, wallpaper supplier

c. WHITE GLUE

Elmer's Glue-All

Color: White

Characteristics: A commercially prepared glue available in plastic containers in quantities to 5 gallons; quick-drying and very strong; can be diluted with water (¼) where great adhesive quality is not required

Uses: Gluing wood, paper, cloth, styrofoam; diluted as a glaze coating on styrofoam; to stiffen felt, etc.

Sources: Hardware and lumber suppliers

d. LATEX CEMENT

Latex (Rug-Sealz or similar trade products)

Color: Milky white

Characteristics: A commercially prepared liquid latex used as a flexible cement for edging and joining carpets; water soluble until applied when it sets to latex rubber and remains pliable

Uses: Cementing cloth to cloth; patching canvas floor cloth; flexible adhesive for cloth-mâche; gluing net to cut-out drops

Sources: Furniture or carpet dealers

e. CONTACT CEMENT

Contact Cement

Color: Amber to clear

Characteristics: A highly volatile cement used to adhere nonporous materials; each surface is spread with light coating and allowed to dry; adhesion is immediate so care must be taken to position material before surface contact is made; if porous materials are used, two light coats are recommended

Uses: Adhering Formica or Masonite to wood; plastics to plastics; styrofoam requires very light coat and care must be used to avoid puddling of cement which would dissolve the styrofoam

Sources: Hardware, lumber supplier or Formica supplier

f. FLEXIBLE GLUE

Flexible Glue

Color: Amber

Characteristics: Animal glue prepared with glycerin to plasticize the preparation so it retains its flexibility; prepared for use by heating in double boiler or electric glue pot and applied while hot

Uses: A binder for paint pigments to be used for painting drops that are to be stored by folding or rolling

Source: Scenic paint suppliers

g. DEXTRINE

Dextrine

Color: Ivory powder

Characteristics: A starchy adhesive prepared by

dissolving in water to syrupy consistency and heated in double boiler

Use: Added to scenic aniline dyes to prevent spread of dye when applied to absorbent fabrics; mixed with bronzing powder for scenic gilt

Sources: Scenic paint and dye suppliers

h. GLUE AND PASTE PREPARED IN THE SCENE SHOP

Scene Glue or Dope

Color: White

Characteristics: A preparation composed of water, Danish whiting, and hot animal glue; cold water is added to whiting to mix to a smooth heavy paste and hot animal glue is added in proportion of two parts whiting mixture to one part glue by volume; mixture must be heated over double boiler and applied while hot; may be reheated and diluted with water

Uses: Gluing covering on flats; dope for cloth-mâché

Dutchman Paste

Color: White

Characteristics: A paste preparation combining four parts dry Danish whiting with one part dry wheat paste—this mixture is sprinkled into enough water to make a very thick paste—to which one part hot animal glue is added; must be heated in double boiler and applied while hot

Use: Applied to cloth dutchman strips to be adhered to flats to cover joints; applied with glue brush; after strips are in place, any excess must be removed from surface with damp sponge

HARDWARE

Hardware is a general term that describes everything from nails and screws to the more specialized pieces used only in the theatre in constructing, assembling and handling of scenery. Theatre technicians have developed many methods of adapting ordinary hardware in ways that are unique to theatre technology. The technician must acquire a knowledge of what hardware is available, the terminology that will describe it, and its functional characteristics and applications.

In order to introduce hardware in a logical order, those items which can usually be obtained through local hardware sources will be described first; those found through sources specializing in stage hardware will follow.

Fastening Devices

All hardware items, particularly fasteners, are standardized to assure uniformity of size. This proves to be a great convenience, providing the technician is knowledgeable about these standards and possesses the proper vocabulary to obtain them.

The most common fastener is the nail. Nevertheless, its descriptive terminology is complicated because sizes are still based on a system that originated long ago. The length of a nail is designated according to an old English system of pricing nails by the hundred. Since the penny was the base monetary unit, a sixpenny nail, for example, was one that cost six pennies per hundred. We now use the terms onepenny through twentypenny to describe the length of nails, but we still use the archaic penny abbreviation d (denarius) in writing the description, that is, 1d, 6d, 8d, 10d, etc.

To complicate matters further, regular flat head nails are sold in two shank sizes. The common nail has a shank drawn from heavier wire; the box nail is drawn from wire one to two gauges smaller in diameter. Since most scenic construction is with light lumber, box nails are used more often because they are less apt to split the stock. Common nails are used on heavy platform construction.

Other types of fasteners, such as screws and bolts, are described either by number or dimensions designated in inches and length. The following descriptive listing of the common fastening devices will indicate some of the uses of each type of hardware in construction.

a. NAILS, BRADS, AND TACKS

Common Nails

Sizes: 1d to 16d (shank size varies in accordance with length: 6d, 11½ ga.; 8d, 10¼ ga.; 10d, 9 ga., etc.)

Description: Heavy shanked, flat head nail, cold-drawn steel with cut point

Uses: Nailing soft wood where shank will not split stock; longer sizes used for nailing 2″ × 4″ and larger materials

Priced: By pound

Double Headed Nails

Sizes: 6d to 16d, common nail size only

Description: Formed with two heads, one above the other so that top head extends above surface for easy removal

Uses: Nailing scaffolding or temporary construction

Priced: By pound

Box Nails

Sizes: 1d to 16d (shank size varies in accordance with length)

Description: Slimmer shank than common nail; flat head nail; cold-drawn steel with cut point

Uses: General construction involving ¾″ stock; 4d, 6d, 8d, 10d, and 16d used most frequently

Priced: By pound

Cement Coated Nails

Sizes: 3d to 10d

Description: Flat head nail drawn from wire one or more gauges smaller than box nail; coated with resin which is heated by friction of driving to form a bond with wood; coating gives slight amber color

Uses: Nailing where tight fastening required; coating makes nails difficult to remove; may be used for flat construction in lieu of clout nails

Priced: By pound; slightly more expensive than uncoated

Finishing Nails

Sizes: 3d to 16d; shank same as box nail
Description: Small head that will imbed in wood
Uses: Nailing were visibility of nail head would be objectionable; nailing moldings and trim; furniture construction
Priced: By pound

Cut Nails

Sizes: 4d to 6d
Characteristics: Flat square nail tapering from head to point; stamped from flat stock; harder steel
Uses: Nailing tongue and grooved flooring
Priced: By pound

Wire Nails

Sizes: ¼″ to 1″ long, 18 ga. to 20 ga. wire diameter
Characteristics: Small wire nail with flat head
Uses: Nailing thin moldings and trim; small frames
Priced: By box

Brads

Sizes: ¼″ to 1″ long, 18 ga. to 22 ga. wire diameter
Characteristics: Small wire nail with small head similar to finishing nail
Uses: Nailing thin moldings and trim
Priced: By box

Carpet Tacks—Cut Tacks

Sizes: No. 4: ⁷⁄₁₆″, No. 6: ½″, No. 8: ⁹⁄₁₆″, No. 10: ⅝″, and No. 12: ¹¹⁄₁₆″
Characteristics: Flat head blue steel with tapered cut point
Uses: Tacking drapery, carpets, floor cloth, upholstery
Priced: By box or by pound in bulk

Brass Upholstery and Stud Tacks

Size: ⅜″ to ⅝″
Characteristics: Round head brass with straight round wire shank; polished or hammered finish
Uses: Decorative upholstery tack
Priced: By box

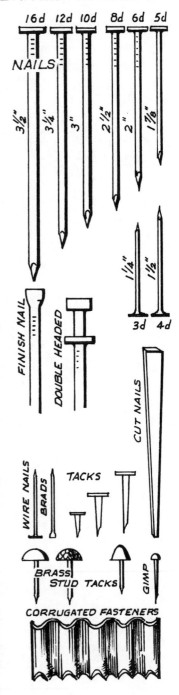

DRIVEN FASTENERS

Gimp Tacks

Sizes: ½″ to ⅝″

Characteristics: Small tapered shank with tiny round bead head; blue steel

Uses: Upholstery for blind tacking and gimp braid trim

Priced: By box

Corrugated Fasteners

Sizes: ½″ deep, 5 corrugations; ⅝″ deep, 5 corrugations; ⅜″ deep, 6 corrugations

Characteristics: Narrow corrugated steel band with one edge sharpened

Uses: Driven across flat butt joint so that corrugations hold joint together; for light framing; often used in flat construction to hold joint before corner block is attached

Priced: By box

b. STAPLES

Fence Staples

Sizes: ⅜″ across loop, ⅝″ to ¾″ long

Characteristics: U-shaped galvanized wire with sharpened points

Uses: Nailing chicken wire, small cording

Priced: By pound

Tacker Staples

Sizes: ¼″, 5⁄16″, ⅜″, ½″

Characteristics: Clips of steel, flat wire staples for staple tacker

Uses: For tacking muslin on flats, cardboard, cording

Priced: By box of 5000

c. SCREWS

Flat Head Wood Screws

Sizes: No. 8 (5⁄32″ diameter), No. 9 (3⁄16″ diameter); ¾″, 1¼″, and 1½″ lengths; sizes range from No. 4 to No. 12, in lengths from ½″ to 2½″

Characteristics: Flat beveled head with slot for flat blade screwdriver; tapered augerlike thread running partway up the shank ending in small point

Uses: Joining two pieces of wood; to attach hardware, hinges, or cleats; Nos. 8-9 most common

Priced: By box of 100

Round Head Wood Screws[2]

Sizes: Same range as flat head screws

Characteristics: Round head with slot for flat blade screwdriver; blue or bright steel

Uses: Used with wood or attaching metals to wood where head is not countersunk flush with surface

Priced: By box

Sheet Metal Screws

Sizes: 1/8" to 1/4" diameter, lengths from 1/4"

Characteristics: Threaded entire length of shank, heads round or pan shape; slotted for screwdriver

Uses: Joining sheet metal

Priced: By box

Phillips Screws

Sizes: In all sizes described above; flat, round, pan heads

Characteristics: Patented head design with four-pointed indentation; requires Phillips screwdriver

Uses: For all wood or metal applications

Priced: By box

Screw Eyes

Sizes: 1/16" to 3/8" shank

Characteristics: Steel eye with wood screw shank

Uses: Attachment of wire, cord, rope, or chain to walls or scenic units not subjected to great weight or stress; flying light objects

Priced: By piece

Screw Hooks

Sizes: 1/8" to 3/8" shank

Characteristics: Steel hooks with wood screw shank

Uses: General purpose hook with screw eyes, or in combination with S-hooks with cord or chain permitting quick removal

Priced: By piece

---

[2] Both flat and round head screws are available in brass.

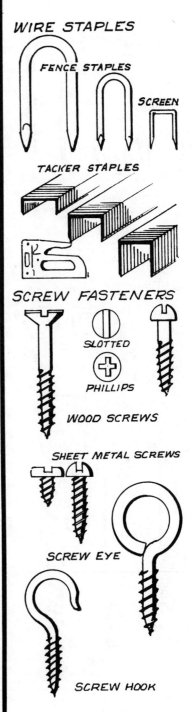

WIRE STAPLES

FENCE STAPLES

SCREEN

TACKER STAPLES

SCREW FASTENERS

SLOTTED

PHILLIPS

WOOD SCREWS

SHEET METAL SCREWS

SCREW EYE

SCREW HOOK

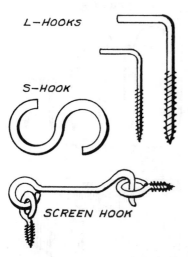

L-HOOKS

S-HOOK

SCREEN HOOK

BOLTS

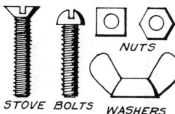

STOVE BOLTS

NUTS

WASHERS

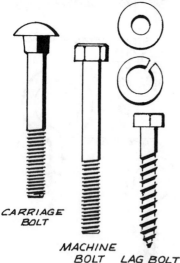

CARRIAGE
BOLT

MACHINE
BOLT   LAG BOLT

L-Hooks

Sizes: ⅛″ to ¼″ shank; lengths from 1¼″ to 3″
Characteristics: L-shaped screw shank
Uses: Set in wall for hanging screens, panels, or units of scenery with screw eyes
Priced: By piece

S-Hooks

Sizes: 1″ to 3″ long; wire size ⅛″ to ⅜″
Characteristics: S-shaped hook used in conjunction with cord, rope, or chain as linkage with eyes or hooks
Uses: As open or closed link with turnbuckle or rope
Priced: By piece

Screen Door and Gate Hook and Eye

Sizes: 1″ to 6″ hook length
Characteristics: Combination hook and eye with wood screw thread
Uses: To hook doors or hinged units while being shifted; to join light steps to platforms or units where stability is not a factor
Priced: By piece

d. BOLTS AND NUTS

Stove Bolts

Sizes: ³⁄₁₆″, ¼″ and ⁵⁄₁₆ diameter; lengths 1″ to 6″
Characteristics: Flat or round head slotted for screwdriver; shank threaded entire length; requires nut
Uses: To attach cleats, hinges, or hangers; joining metal to metal or wood to wood
Priced: By box

Nuts

Sizes: To fit all standard bolt sizes, ⅛″ to ¾″
Characteristics: Available in square, hexagonal or wing nut; standard thread
Uses: Attached to end of threaded bolts; square and hex shapes require wrench; wing nut for hand tightening
Priced: By box or piece

Washers

Sizes: To fit all standard bolts

Characteristics: Flat washers are flat steel disc with center bolt hole; lock washers stamped from spring steel, cut and spread to form spring tension against nut

Uses: Placed beneath nut to prevent nut from turning into wood and create bearing surface; may be used on stove, carriage, and machine bolts

Priced: By piece or box

Carriage Bolts

Sizes: ¼″ to ¾″ shank; lengths from 1″ to 24″

Characteristics: Round head steel with square collar formed beneath head; threaded ¾″ to 1¼″ up the shank

Uses: To bolt wood to wood or wood to metal; hole predrilled the size of shank and bolt set with hammer to embed collar; washer and nut required

Priced: By piece or box

Machine Bolts

Sizes: ¼″ to ¾″ shank; lengths from 1″ to 6″

Characteristics: Square or hex head; threaded ¾″ to 1¼″ up the shank

Uses: To bolt heavy iron; wood to wood if washers used under head and nut; joining platforms, scaffolding; wrench required for tightening

Priced: By piece or box

Lag Bolts

Sizes: ¼″, ⁵⁄₁₆″, ⅜″ and ½″ diameter; lengths from 1″ to 6″

Characteristics: A heavy wood screw with square or hexhead; threads run three quarters up shank; predrilled hole ³⁄₁₆″ to ⅛″ smaller than shank required to avoid splitting wood; tightened with wrench; washer beneath head recommended

Uses: Fastening wood to wood or metal to wood where access makes it impossible to use bolt; attaching hardware to wall or floor

Priced: By piece or box

Eye Bolts

Sizes: ¾₆″, ¼″ and ⅜″ shank; lengths to 6″
Characteristics: Eye with shank threaded for nut
Uses: Flying light scenery; platform pull ring, or numerous operations requiring attachment of lines or snaps
Priced: By piece or box

U-Bolts

Sizes: ⅛″ to ⅜″ rod; diameter of U, ¾″ to 2″
Characteristics: U-shaped rod threaded on both ends
Uses: To secure rod or pipe to flat surface
Priced: By piece

Threaded Rod

Sizes: ¾₆″ to ½″ diameter, length 36″
Characteristics: Continuous threaded rod
Uses: Extra long bolt fastener; can be bent to large U-bolt
Priced: By single length

e. RIVETS

Round Head Black Iron Rivets

Sizes: ⅛″ to ¼″ diameter; lengths ¼″ to 2″
Characteristics: Soft iron; round head with straight shank
Uses: To joint strap, angle, or channel iron; inserted through predrilled hole ¹⁄₆₄″ larger than shank; head formed with ball pien hammer
Priced: By box

Tinners Rivets

Sizes: ⅛″ to ¾₆″ diameter; lengths ⁵⁄₃₂″ to ¾₆″
Characteristics: Flat head iron, tinned; round head aluminum rivets also available
Uses: For joining sheet metals; predrilled hole required
Priced: By box

Harness or Split Rivets

Sizes: ⅛″ to ¾₆″ diameter; lengths ¼″ to ⅜″
Characteristics: Brass or copper; split shank to be spread over washer

EYE BOLTS

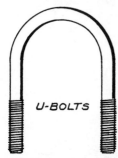

U-BOLTS

THREADED ROD

RIVETS

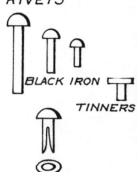

BLACK IRON

TINNERS

HARNESS SPLIT

Uses: For joining leather to leather, or leather to
   canvas

Priced: By box

Snaps and Catches

Operations involving shifting and handling of stage
scenery usually must be done rapidly. Fly-lines must be
attached to a unit so that it can be flown out, or ropes
attached to a wagon so stage hands can pull it on or off
stage. A heavy snap secured to the end of a rope or line
that can be hooked on a scenic unit often provides the
most effective means of readying it for movement in a
matter of seconds.

In this same general area, wire rope and aircraft cable
cannot be attached to a piece of hardware or batten by
tying a knot, as with manila or cotton rope. Clamps and
clips have been designed specifically for this purpose.
If a unit of scenery requires more than a single line
to fly it, manual adjustments in trim are usually necessary so the unit will hang even with the floor. A great
deal of time can be wasted making such adjustments by
tying and untying lines and shifting clamps by trial and
error until the unit is in trim. Turnbuckles, which can
be loosened or tightened to vary the length of a line, are
convenient devices for adjusting trim without changing the length of lines.

Latches and catches are required for stage doors, windows, cabinets, and cupboards. With few exceptions,
stock pieces of hardware are available, but improvisation is not to be ruled out in the manner in which these
pieces may be used. Realistic settings often demand authenticity in the sound of a closing door, or in the snap
of a cupboard latch. The hardware to accomplish this,
as well as some suggested ways of employing latches
for other purposes are noted in the section which follows.

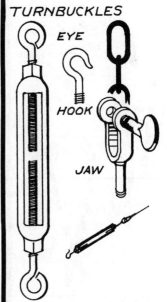

TURNBUCKLES

EYE

HOOK

JAW

a. TURNBUCKLES

Turnbuckles

Sizes:	Bolt Diameter	Take-Up	Working Load
	1/4″	4″	400 lbs
	5/16″	4½″	700 lbs
	3/8″	6″	1,000 lbs

SNAPS

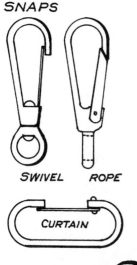

SWIVEL   ROPE

CURTAIN

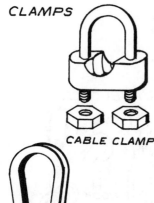
STRAP

CLAMPS

CABLE CLAMP

THIMBLE

Characteristics: Drop forged body of steel or heavy cast aluminum; bolt on either end threaded opposite hand to tighten in or out simultaneously; end of bolt formed with hook, eye, jaw, or combination

Uses: Attached between line and flown load to permit adjustment of trim; on cable guidelines to adjust tautness

Priced: By piece

b. SNAPS

Snap Buckles

Sizes: 3″ to 4½″ long; eye ¼″ to ¾″

Characteristics: Either steel hook with spring catch or spring bolt; stationary or swivel eye

Uses: Attached to rope or cable to clip into ring on flown scenery; a means of quick snap hook attachment

Priced: By piece

c. CLAMPS

Cable Clamps or Clips

Sizes: ⅛″, ³⁄₁₆″, ¼″, ⁵⁄₁₆″ and ½″ cable sizes

Characteristics: U-bolt with metal fitting grooved to conform to specific sizes of stranded wire rope

Uses: After cable is looped around pipe batten or through ring in snap, hanger iron, or ceiling plate, cable clamp is attached to join cable to standing end

Priced: By piece

Wire Rope Thimble

Sizes: To fit ⅛″ to ½″ cable

Characteristics: Teardrop shaped, grooved loop around which cable is looped to avoid sharp bend where used through ring

Uses: For forming loop in cable

Priced: By piece

Nicropress Sleeve

Sizes: Sizes for each cable size

Characteristics: Copper band ½″ to ¾″ long

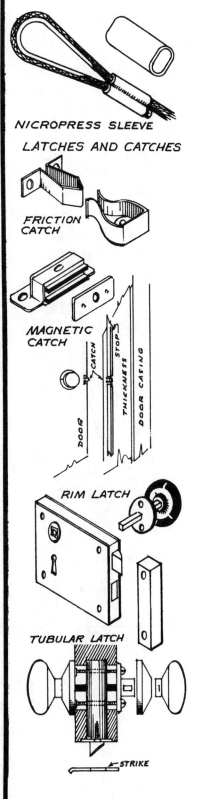

NICROPRESS SLEEVE

Uses: Permanent cable fastener to form loop around thimble; must be pressed on cable with Nicropress tool designed for each cable size

Priced: By box

LATCHES AND CATCHES

d. LATCHES AND CATCHES

Friction Catches

Sizes: $1\frac{1}{2}'' \times \frac{3}{8}''$

Characteristics: Two part catch of spring steel; clip or housing designed for shelf mounting; matching strike mounts on cabinet door

Uses: Cupboard door catch; may be used for stage door catch or casement window latch

Priced: By set, packet, or box

FRICTION CATCH

Magnetic Catches

Sizes: $1\frac{1}{2}'' \times \frac{3}{4}''$

Characteristics: Two parts consisting of magnet housing and a flat steel strike; designed for cabinet catch

Uses: Cupboard catch; can be used for door catch if alignment is true

Priced: By set, packet or box

MAGNETIC CATCH

Rim Latch

Sizes: $3\frac{3}{4}'' \times 3''$

Characteristics: Iron case lock-set mounted on back of door surface; knobs and strike

Uses: Used offstage side of stage doors mounted inside thickness frame; produces efficient latch and sound

Priced: By set

RIM LATCH

Tubular Latch

Sizes: For $1\frac{1}{4}''$ and $1\frac{3}{4}''$ door thickness

Characteristics: Brass tubular latch inserted in holes drilled through face and edge of door; face plate, knobs, and strike plate included in set

Uses: Door latch set

Priced: By set

TUBULAR LATCH

Closet or Dummy Latch

Sizes: $2''$ knob

Characteristics: Brass knob and face plate; no catch

STRIKE

CLOSET OR DUMMY LATCH

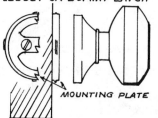

MOUNTING PLATE

ANTIQUE LATCHES - KNOBS

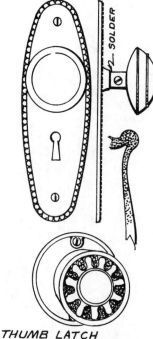

½ SOLDER

THUMB LATCH

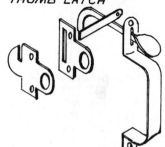

Uses: Door knob where catch not required, or in combination with friction catch

Priced: By set

Antique Latch

Sizes: Variable

Characteristics: Salvaged knob and face plate, sweat soldered or tack welded together; mounted with brass or round head screws through face plate

Uses: Knob and face plate; used with friction catch

Priced: Salvage

Thumb Latch

Size: 6″ strap handle, ¾″ wide

Characteristics: Black enameled with thumb lever extending through door; lever bar falls into slotted catch mounted on jamb

Uses: Rustic doors no thicker than ¾″

Priced: By set

Barrel Bolts

Sizes: 1⅛″ wide; lengths 3″ to 6″

Characteristics: Long narrow face plate with tubular channel encasing sliding rod; locks in open or closed position by ¼ turn of rod

Uses: To fasten door or windows shut during shift; mounted on edge face of stage wagons to latch into floor to prevent movement

Priced: By piece

Hinges

A hinge is two metal plates joined with a pivoting pin to swing a gate or door shutter. While several types of hinges are used in this way in the theatre, theatre technicians have devised methods of using hinges for fastening devices as well. Hinges are described by type, usually connoting shape or function, dimensions, and existence of a fast or loose pin.

a. STRAP AND T HINGES

Strap Hinges

Sizes: Length, 3″ to 8″ each leaf; width at pin varies

with length and light or heavy pattern (metal gauge)

Characteristics: Two elongated steel leaves joined with fast or loose pin; each leaf triangular; pre-drilled and countersunk for flat head wood screws or stove bolts; surface mount

Uses: Gate hinge; as hinged straps to join platform units, or step units to platforms; a device to lock insert window and door frames in place; by bending one leaf, may be used for hinging door and window shutters

Priced: By pair or dozen pairs

T-Strap Hinges

Sizes: By length of strap and width of T; light and heavy pattern

Characteristics: One leaf a triangular strap, the other a narrow rectangular leaf; fast pin unless special ordered; each leaf is drilled and counter-sunk for screws or stove bolts

Uses: As surface hinge; to hang doors that swing off stage; awning type lids on boxes or chests

Priced: By pair or dozen pair

b. BUTT HINGES

Cabinet Butt Hinges

Sizes: $2\frac{1}{2}''$ to $3''$ long; $1\frac{7}{8}''$ to $2\frac{3}{16}''$ across the combined width of the two leaves

Characteristics: Each leaf rectangular steel; avail-able with fast or loose pin; drilled and counter-sunk for No. 8 flat head screws

Uses: Hinge to fit between edge of door and jamb so that only pin revealed at joint; wood must be rabbeted out to receive each leaf for tight hinge joint; can be used as small surface hinge

Priced: By pair or dozen pairs

Broad Door Butt Hinges

Sizes: $2\frac{1}{2}'' \times 2\frac{1}{2}''$ and $3'' \times 3''$, for $1\frac{1}{4}''$ or $1\frac{3}{4}''$ factory made doors

Characteristics: Brass or steel leaf with loose pin

Uses: Hanging heavy doors

Priced: By pair

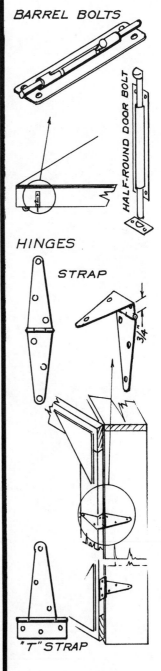

BARREL BOLTS

HALF-ROUND DOOR BOLT

HINGES

STRAP

"T" STRAP

Single Acting Spring Hinges

Sizes: 4" for 1¼" doors; 6" for 1¾" doors

Characteristics: Spring loaded pin housing with tension adjustment enabling door to swing shut; mounts to jamb and edge of shutter

Uses: Restaurant, bar, or kitchen doors

Priced: By pair

Double Acting Spring Hinges

Sizes: 4" for 1¼"; 6" for 1¾" doors

Characteristics: Double spring-loaded housing with tension adjustment for full swinging doors

Uses: Restaurant, bar, or kitchen doors

Priced: By pair

Light Swinging Door Hardware

Size: For mounting top and bottom of ¾" louvered door

Characteristics: Light brackets with stationary pins that allow shutter to pivot and return to closed position by gravity

Uses: Light barroom doors

Priced: By set

Double Acting Screen Hinges

Sizes: For wood thicknesses ¾" to 1¼"

Characteristics: Light double action hinge mounted on edges of screen frames to permit folding flat either direction; steel or brass plated

Uses: For screens; for flats that are reversible

Priced: By set

Piano Hinges

Sizes: 1¹⁄₁₆", 1¼", 1½" and 2" wide when opened flat; lengths up to 72"

Characteristics: Thin steel or brass, continuous strip hinge with holes for screws approximately 2" apart; may be cut to desired length

Uses: Hinging for light cabinet doors or chest lids where alignment or stock thickness is a problem

Priced: By piece

Casters

Casters fall into three general categories: stationary, swivel, and furniture. Sizes are indicated by the diame-

BUTT HINGES

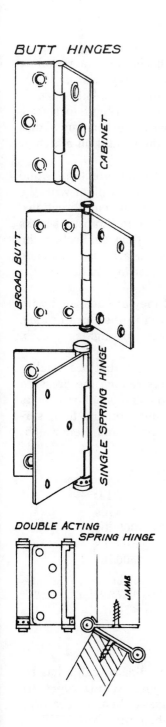

CABINET

BROAD BUTT

SINGLE SPRING HINGE

DOUBLE ACTING
SPRING HINGE

JAMB

SWINGING DOOR HARDWARE

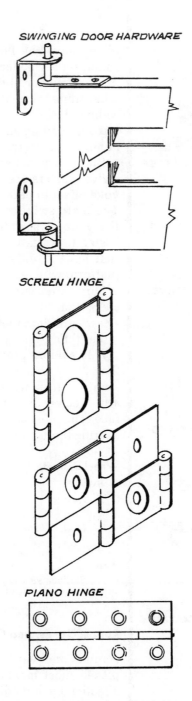

SCREEN HINGE

PIANO HINGE

CASTERS

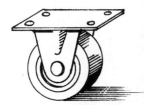

STATIONARY CASTER

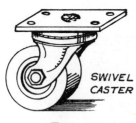

SWIVEL CASTER

FURNITURE CASTER

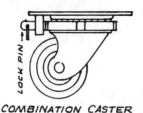

LOCK PIN →

COMBINATION CASTER

ter of the wheel, and the height of the caster mounting plate above the floor. Caster wheels cause a rumbling sound on a wooden floor unless the outer rim or tire is made of rubber. Rubber tires do, of course, flatten somewhat under weight, which makes it difficult to start a rolling platform: This can be largely overcome by avoiding overloading and distributing the weight on a greater number of casters.

Stationary casters move only in one direction, while swivel casters are mounted on a bearing plate with the yoke offset to permit the caster to move in all directions. There are swivel casters available with a pin that locks the yoke in a stationary position, thus converting the caster to a stationary type. Casters are also available that have a brake to lock the wheel in position so the platform will not roll.

Furniture casters differ in that they are designed with stems that fit into a socket inserted in the furniture leg. These are intended for movement of lighter pieces, rather than bearing weight.

It is seldom practical to use casters that are smaller than 2″ in diameter. Larger casters reduce the pressure required to start a rolling wagon and smaller casters are affected by small dents or debris on the floor surface. The most common sizes of casters and their weight bearing limits are:

Wheel Diameter*	Overall Height	Working Load
2″ swivel	3″	150 lbs
2½″ swivel	3⅝″	150 lbs
3″ swivel	4⁷⁄₁₆″	300 lbs
4″ swivel	5⁷⁄₁₆″	300 lbs
5″ swivel	6⁷⁄₁₆″	500 lbs

* Some variance will be noted among casters of different manufacturers. Stationary casters used in conjunction with swivel casters should match in over-all height.

Ropes, Cords, and Chains

As indicated earlier, flexible wire rope or cable has replaced most manila rope for rigging. Manila ropes are affected by humidity, which causes them to draw up when damp and stretch out when dry. Nevertheless, manila is still used extensively where a strong, flexible line that can be managed by hand is desirable.

Cotton ropes are used for handlines on curtain travelers, for lashlines, and for drapery ties because the fibers are soft and braided forming a compact, flexible rope that is comfortable to handle. Sisal rope has the appearance of manila, but the fibers are stiff and wiry, causing it to wear out when subjected to the friction of pulleys. Ropes made of synthetic fibers such as nylon and polypropylene have great tensile strength, but are more difficult to tie securely and the ends must be melted to prevent the fibers from unraveling.

Drops and cycloramas that are dead hung because of a low ceiling over the stage are usually suspended on chains. Chain will not stretch and it can be attached easily to eye bolts set in the drapery batten. Light chain is placed in the bottom hem of most floor length stage draperies to give the drape weight, but still allow for flexible draping. Heavy chains are attached to the top of asbestos curtains or large close off doors that move vertically in tracks. The chains extend to the gridiron, but they are not involved in the lifting operation: They are safety chains to prevent the unit from falling onto the stage in the event the track should pull loose.

The following descriptions of the sizes and comparative strengths of manila rope, cotton rope and chain are critical data for the theatre technician. Safety must be the primary concern when raising any unit of scenery or people above the floor of the stage. *A good rule to*

Manila Rope

Diam. In.	Gross Weight per Coil	Feet Coil	Feet per Pound	Breaking Strength	Working Strength
1/4"	50 lbs	2500	50.0	600 lbs	120 lbs
3/8"	50 lbs	1220	24.4	1325 lbs	270 lbs
7/16"	63 lbs	1200	19.0	1725 lbs	350 lbs
1/2"	90 lbs	1200	13.3	2650 lbs	530 lbs
9/16"	125 lbs	1200	9.6	3450 lbs	690 lbs
5/8"	160 lbs	1200	7.5	4400 lbs	880 lbs
3/4"	200 lbs	1200	6.0	5400 lbs	1080 lbs

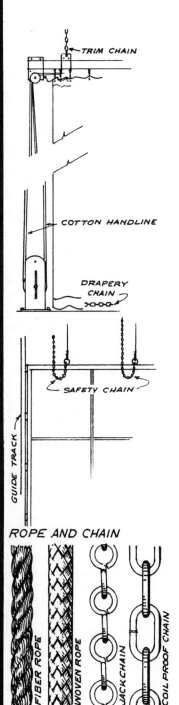

ROPE AND CHAIN

TRIM CHAIN

COTTON HANDLINE

DRAPERY CHAIN

SAFETY CHAIN

GUIDE TRACK

FIBER ROPE

WOVEN ROPE

JACKCHAIN

COIL PROOF CHAIN

follow: As a minimum margin of safety, any type line must be capable of bearing five times the weight of the actual load placed on it.

Braided White Cotton And Nylon Cord And Rope

Number	Feet per Hank	Diam. In.
4	48	$1/8$"
$4\frac{1}{2}$	48	$9/64$"
5	48	$5/32$"
6	100	$3/16$"
8	100	$1/4$"
10	100	$5/16$"
12	100	$3/8$"

($1/2$" and $5/8$" braided cotton rope for curtain tracks is sold by the foot or by the spool)

Steel Jack Chain

Number	Tensile Strength Pounds per Foot	Links per Foot	Length of Link
6	435 lbs	10	$1 9/16$"
8	268 lbs	11	$1 5/16$"
10	195 lbs	12	$1 1/4$"
12	145 lbs	16	1"
14	66 lbs	19	$13/16$"
16	55 lbs	25	$1 1/16$"
18	40 lbs	31	$1/2$"

Steel Coilproof Chain

Size	Links per Foot	Proof Test	Work Load
$3/16$"	$12\frac{1}{2}$	1045 lbs	520 lbs
$1/4$"	12	1800 lbs	900 lbs
$5/16$"	$10 3/4$	2720 lbs	1300 lbs
$3/8$"	$9 3/4$	3720 lbs	1860 lbs

(The above descriptive data courtesy of Mutual Hardware Corp., Long Island City, New York.)

STAGE HARDWARE

There are several pieces of hardware that are unique to theatre technology. While there are a few items like back flap hinges and clout nails manufactured for the general trade, their use in the theatre warrants their inclusion among stage hardware because they are rarely carried in the stock of general hardware suppliers.

Lash Hardware

Lashing is a technique of literally lacing flats together as one method of joining them to form a setting. A "lash-line" of No. 8 or No. 10 braided cotton rope is attached to the top right-hand corner on the back of one of the flats by means of a "lashline eye" or by inserting the rope through a ⅜" hole drilled in the corner block. The lashline is then cast around "lash cleats" located alternately along the inner edges of the adjoining stiles of the two flats, to a point a few inches above the floor, where it is tied off. By drawing the lashline taut, the two flats are drawn tightly together.

It is important that lash hardware lies flat so there are no protruding points to gouge or rip the cloth covering of the flats when they are stacked in the wings. Improvised substitutes are seldom practical. A "Wise lashline eye," cast in malleable iron, is designed with a spur that is driven into the edge of the stile just below the corner block. A small flat plate extends over the surface of the stile with a countersunk hole for a No. 9 flat head screw. There are three styles of lash cleats: The "Wise lash cleat," which has the spur and requires a single screw; a "flat cleat," 2" wide × 4" long, which requires four flat head screws; and a "round cleat" which is fastened to a stile with two screws. The cleats at the point of tie-off should be 30" above the floor, and directly opposite one another. Tie-off cleats may be regular lash cleats, or a flat tie-off cleat may be used. A "tie-off cleat" is stamped from ⅛" × ¾" strap iron with a ¾" rounded appendage.

There are times when there is insufficient clearance for a lashline to pass around a regular lash cleat. A

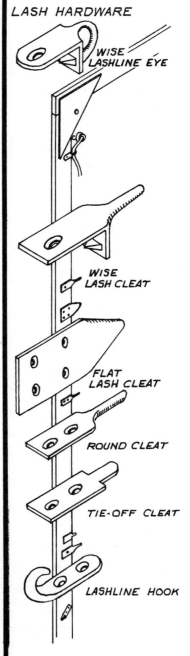

LASH HARDWARE

WISE
LASHLINE EYE

WISE
LASH CLEAT

FLAT
LASH CLEAT

ROUND CLEAT

TIE-OFF CLEAT

LASHLINE HOOK

LASHING DETAIL

LASHING DETAIL

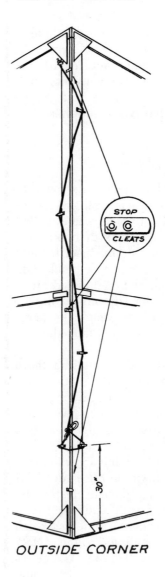

STOP
CLEATS

STOP
BLOCK

30"

OUTSIDE CORNER

INSIDE CORNER

"Towel lashline hook" has been devised that mounts on the surface of the stile. Lashline hooks may also be used for picture hooks or heavy frames.

Lashing scenery places extreme pressure on the joints, so there is a tendency for the flats to pull out of alignment. This can be prevented with "stop cleats." Stop cleats are placed on the stile of the flat so they will extend ¾" over the edge, thus opposing the direction of stress and preventing the adjoining flat from slipping past. When lashing inside corners, a small stop block made of 1" × 2" can be set ¾" back from the edge of the downstage flat to prevent the upstage flat from slipping past the joint, or stop cleats can be mounted on the face of the upstage flat to accomplish the same thing. After the set is painted, only very close scrutiny can detect these small cleats. (See illustration.)

Bracing Hardware

Most assembled units of scenery require some form of offstage support for stability. A "stage brace" made of wood or aluminum tubing is a traditional support. A stage brace is an adjustable pole which can be attached quickly to the back of a set piece by hooking it into a "brace cleat" mounted on the back of the unit. The bottom of the brace has a bracket that rests on the floor and is secured in place with a "stage screw." The length of the stage brace is adjusted by releasing a thumbscrew which allows the two-piece pole to slide in or out. The top of the brace is fitted with a two-pronged hook that fits into the hole in the cleat by inverting the hook, then rolling the brace right side up so the open side rests on the face of the brace cleat.

A stage screw has a coarse spiral thread tapering to the handle which is rounded and shaped to be turned by hand. Where one is not permitted to put stage screws in the floor, stage braces are available with nonskid floor plates. Threaded steel plugs may also be used. The plug is threaded on the outside to screw into the floor, and the inside is threaded for a bolt threaded stage screw. The plugs can remain in the floor, or be removed and the hole plugged with a dowel. (See illustration.)

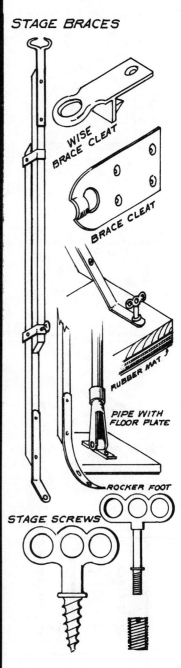

STAGE BRACES

WISE BRACE CLEAT

BRACE CLEAT

RUBBER MAT

PIPE WITH FLOOR PLATE

ROCKER FOOT

STAGE SCREWS

FOOT AND SILL IRONS

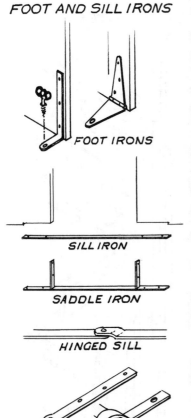

FOOT IRONS

SILL IRON

SADDLE IRON

HINGED SILL

FLAT AND PIPE FOOT IRONS

FLYING HARDWARE

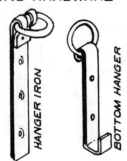

HANGER IRON

BOTTOM HANGER

Foot Irons and Sill Irons

A "foot iron" is a rigid L-shaped bracket attached to the back of a unit of scenery to anchor it to the floor. The bracket is $\frac{1}{4}'' \times 1''$ or $1\frac{1}{8}''$ strap iron with holes in the upright portion for flat head screws or stove bolts. The bracket that rests on the floor has a large hole for a stage screw. For units that must be flown, a "hinged foot iron" has a hinged floor plate that drops down when the unit is raised so it will not snag other scenery in the flies. (See illustration.)

A "sill iron" is a single strap of $\frac{3}{16}'' \times \frac{3}{4}''$ to $1''$ wide strap iron that serves as a bottom rail at the base of a door opening. The sill iron is long enough to extend at least $6''$ along the wood rail on either side of the opening. The rails should be mortised so the metal lies flush with the base of the flat, and screw holes must be countersunk so that screw heads will not mar the floor. Large openings are often made in two sections hinged together. The sill iron must be made in two sections with a center rivet that will allow the iron to pivot correspondingly with the flat. Some technicians prefer that the sill iron extend entirely across the flat, with each end bent at 90° to run $6''$ to $8''$ up the outer edge of the stiles.

A "saddle iron" functions in the same way as a sill iron. The difference is one of design: Two straps are welded or riveted on to the sill iron to align with the inner stiles of the opening. This gives added reinforcement to an otherwise flimsy assembly. (See illustration.)

A "flat foot iron" is a flat strap of $\frac{1}{4}'' \times 1''$ steel designed to mount on the base of a free-standing scenic unit. An enlarged hole on one end for a stage screw makes it possible to secure the unit in a stationary position.

Flying Hardware

When flying hard scenery, that is units with rigid frames covered with canvas or muslin, it is essential that special hardware be used which will not split the wood or pull free from it. Neither screw eyes nor eye bolts can be used safely. Two types of hanger irons may be used: the regular "hanger iron" made of $\frac{3}{16}'' \times 1''$ steel with a D ring at the top and holes for bolt mounting to the rigid framework of the unit; or a "bottom hanger iron" designed to hook beneath the unit, thereby raising the unit by compression, or pushing upward on the load rather than lifting from the top. The latter method is best, but a hook must also be used at the top of the unit for the line to pass through to prevent it from toppling. (See illustration.)

With box style settings, a "ceiling piece" is often used to add to the visual realism, as well as an aid to vocal projection. A ceiling piece is actually a large wooden frame covered with canvas that can be lowered horizontally to rest on top of the set walls. Fly-lines are attached to "ceiling plates" that are bolted across the joints of the ceiling framework. These are $1/8'' \times 2\frac{1}{2}'' \times 7''$ steel plates with a heavy D ring attached for securing lines. (See Figure 4-31, a., p. 196.)

A "passing link trim chain" provides a convenient and safe means of attaching a flown unit, such as a ceiling piece or drop to a pipe batten. Trim chains may be obtained in lengths from 18" to 48". There is a 2" ring on one end and a snap on the opposite end. The snap is passed through the ring of the hanger iron and over the batten then snapped into its own ring.

A "drop holder" is a scissor type clamp designed to fit around a wooden top batten on a painted drop. The eye will accept a rope, cable or chain, and a safety ring locks over the scissor bolt so that the holder cannot open during operation. These are convenient particularly where it is necessary to switch drops during the run of a performance when there is no time to make trim adjustments.

Pulleys and Tackle Blocks

Excluding the sheaves and blocks used in the permanent rigging system, there are several types of loose pulleys used by the stage technician. Some sizes may be available through local hardware sources, but where special service is required, theatrical suppliers are most reliable. In the first place, the reason for using pulleys is to change either the direction of the pull force needed to

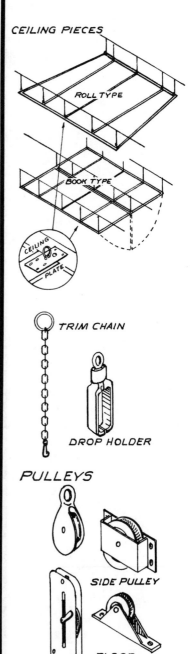

CEILING PIECES

ROLL TYPE

BOOK TYPE

CEILING PLATE

TRIM CHAIN

DROP HOLDER

PULLEYS

SIDE PULLEY

FLOOR PULLEYS

raise or pull a load, or to create a mechanical advantage which will reduce the energy required to move the same load.

Where no mechanical advantage is required, small pulleys made of galvanized malleable iron with sheaves for $\frac{3}{16}''$, $\frac{1}{4}''$ and $\frac{3}{8}''$ rope are often adequate for light blinds and draperies. Pulleys that mount on the wall, or on the back of an opening, can be useful for rigging tableau curtains. These are called "mule blocks" or "side pulleys." The sheaves are 3″ or more in diameter, and are grooved for cotton or manila ropes. (See illustration.)

Pulleys designed for floor mounting are often needed for traveler curtains or spotlines. These may have the sheave mounted in a fixed position, or an adjustable bolt axle to regulate the tension of the handlines.

A "block and tackle" is literally a machine composed of a pair of pulleys, or tackle blocks reeved (threaded with rope) to attain a mechanical advantage over the direct lift of a single pulley. The mechanical advantage can be increased from 1 : 1 to 1 : 5 in this manner, which involves the use of double and triple tackle blocks. This becomes useful when adding heavy sandbags to empty battens and flying operations involving unequal loads. Most technicians prefer tackle blocks with wooden housings because they are lighter weight and more quiet to operate. (See illustration.)

Plates, Brackets, and Hangers

Small L-shaped brackets and corner plates are often used for metal reinforcement of light wood framing. These are available in a variety of sizes at local hardware suppliers, but they are of little value for larger construction. A "mending plate" stamped from $\frac{1}{8}''$ steel, in 6″ × 2″, 12″ × 2½″ and 18″ × 3″ sizes, has many uses besides that of mending wooden flat frames. Open, skeletal framing must appear light, yet it must be strong. Plywood straps not only appear bulky, they lack the strength required. Mending plates, "flat corner plates" and "T-plates" are nearly indispensable for open construction. Such plates could be shop made, but the time and effort required to cut them out of 14 ga. steel makes them quite expensive.

CKLE BLOCKS

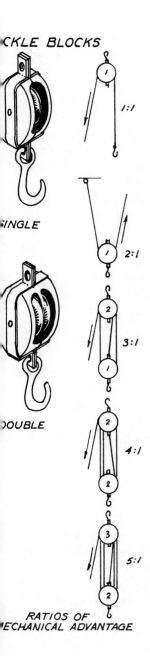

SINGLE

DOUBLE

RATIOS OF
MECHANICAL ADVANTAGE

PLATES
AND BRACKETS

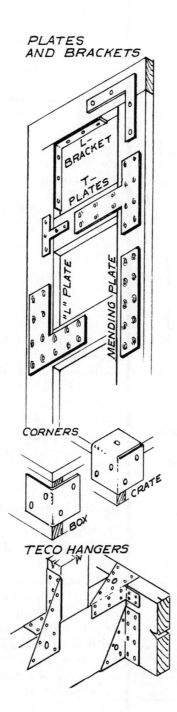

L-BRACKET

T-PLATES

"L" PLATE

MENDING PLATE

1:1

2:1

3:1

4:1

5:1

CORNERS

BOX

CRATE

TECO HANGERS

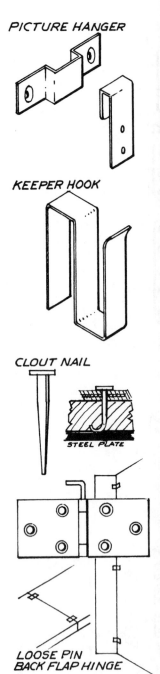

PICTURE HANGER

KEEPER HOOK

CLOUT NAIL

STEEL PLATE

LOOSE PIN
BACK FLAP HINGE

"Box" and "crate corners," as their names imply, are intended for corner reinforcements on shipping crates. They are equally useful to reinforce the corner joints on stage platforms and wagons. Butt joints held only with nails tend to work loose with movement unless a metal binding is added to prevent the joint from opening. In this same category, the metal plates used by the building trade in securing joists are equally effective. These are known as "Teco Trip-L-Grip" framing hangers, and are available at most lumber suppliers. Teco hangers are preformed, zinc coated 18 ga. steel, and are cut to be used with $2'' \times 4''$ to $2'' \times 12''$ fir dimension stock. (See illustration.)

Hanging a false beam or a heavy picture on the set without concern that it will shift askew is simplified with a "picture frame hanger," consisting of two pieces of strap metal, a hook and socket, designed to mount on the back of the frame and the wall. Picture hangers can be used to mount wall panels, sconces, or other heavy objects that must be struck before the setting is shifted. (See illustration.)

Hinged or lashed flat wall units usually require stiffeners in addition to braces to maintain their rigidity. A square S-shaped "keeper hook" hung over the toggle rails of adjoining flats provides a hook for a wooden batten to align the flats. The keeper hook can also be used to support removable cornices, mantle shelves, and valances.

Special Nails and Hinges

Nails used in the construction of scenery must hold securely in the wood and be easy to drive and clinch. The scene builder finds that the "clout nail" offers many advantages over the regular nails described earlier in this chapter. One advantage is that clouts are square and do not turn in the wood; a second is that they are made of softer steel which makes them easy to clinch; and a third, is that they have larger heads than other nails of the same size which makes them easier to drive.

Clout nails are used for nailing the plywood reinforcement plates over the joints of a flat frame. They are started in the plywood and driven through the frame with about a ¼″ extending beyond to be clinched so the nail will not work loose. By placing a 10″ × 10″ × ¼″ piece of steel boiler plate beneath the joint—a "clinch plate"—the nail point will bend over as it strikes the plate, clinching itself. Clout nails are sold in 1 lb boxes or in 25 lb bulk lots in 1″, 1¼″ and 1½″ lengths.

The "loose pin back flap" hinge has more uses in scenic work than any other. The leaves of the back flap are square, which gives them a broad fastening surface. This is a decided advantage when hinging 1″ × 2″ and 1″ × 3″ scenery stock. By removing the hinge pin, the leaves can be separated, thus the back flap may be used to join, as well as hinge, two units together. When assembling hinged flat units, the hinges are located along the joint so the units will fold like a book. Dutchman strips, used to cover the crack between the units, are laid over-top the hinges. A step unit may be joined to a platform with loose pin back flap hinges. To separate the units, the hinge pin is withdrawn. Hinges are in two sizes: 1½″ × 3⁷⁄₁₆″ and 2″ × 4⅜″ with either fast or loose pins.

It should be obvious at the end of this chapter about the materials of the scene that theatre technology recognizes no limits. The lack of creative imagination and ingenuity to use these materials and new ones as they appear is the most serious problem that the technician may encounter. The materials are limitless; the descriptions presented are only the most familiar ones we have to work with today. There will be new ones tomorrow!

While a few notations have been included to suggest how these materials and pieces of hardware may be utilized, this discussion hardly scratches the surface. To grasp fully the extent and use of scenic materials, a person must have an opportunity to work with them. Through this experience, one learns to appreciate the value of this body of technical knowledge, and its relevance to the technology of the theatre. This is the key to the development of technical skills, and to the stimulation necessary to inspire creative utilization of existing materials, as well as the many new ones that will continue to appear.

SUGGESTED READINGS

Burris-Meyer, Harold and Cole, Edward. *Scenery for the Theatre.* Boston: Little, Brown, 1972.

Gillette, A. S. *Stage Scenery: Its Construction and Rigging,* 2nd ed. New York: Harper & Row, 1972.

Clancy, J. R. *Hardware Catalog.* Syracuse: J. R. Clancy, 1975.

Mutual Hardware Corp. *Theatrical Hardware Catalog.* Long Island City: Mutual Hardware Corp., 1973.

Parker, W. Oren and Smith, Harvey K. *Scene Design and Stage Lighting.* New York: Holt, Rinehart & Winston, 1963.

Ramsey, Charles G. and Sleeper, Harold R. *Architectural Graphic Standards,* 5th ed. New York: Wiley, 1956.

Seldon, Samuel and Sellman, Hunton. *Stage Scenery and Lighting.* Englewood Cliffs, N.J.: Prentice-Hall, 1959.

U.S. Forest Products Laboratory. *Wood Handbook.* Washington: Government Printing Office.

BUILDING AND HANDLING SCENERY

Although the scene shop is the hub of technical activity during the preparation of scenery for a play, the physical characteristics which comprise an efficient shop can only be those of the author of any suggestions. The tools that lead to efficiency are a basic concern, for they are essential for all construction activity. Regardless of how expert one may become in the use and manipulation of tools, the tools themselves require care and proper usage in order to produce quality workmanship. No amount of verbalizing will teach a beginning technician how to use tools; this he must acquire through direction and experience.

SHOP TOOLS: SAFETY AND CARE

General Safety Practices

As a prerequisite to starting any production work involving tools and materials of the scene, the following suggestions pertaining to safety must be regarded as fundamental procedures:

1. Report for work in attire suitable for the job. Stage and shop work is dirty work. Heavy work clothes that will withstand hard wear, yet provide freedom of movement, are recommended.
2. Long hair should be tied back securely or confined with a cap or scarf. Loose hair obstructs vision and increases the likelihood of getting it entangled in rotating hand and power equipment.
3. Always wear shoes, preferably with a covering over the toes. Dropping a tool or unit of scenery on one's foot can occur and result in painful injury.
4. Be constantly alert for boards with protruding nails or screws. Be sure that you were not responsible for leaving stock in that condition.
5. Know where the first aid supplies are kept, and report any injury, regardless of how minor, to the person in charge.
6. Request and get instruction about the operation of power equipment before attempting to use it, then exercise caution.

7. Check every hand tool before using it. If repairs or conditioning is necessary, either make them yourself, or seek the assistance of the person in charge. Dull tools are more hazardous than sharp ones.

8. Use tools for the purpose they were designed. In other words, don't pry with a screwdriver or cut wire with tinners snips.

9. Cutting tools should be laid aside so their cutting edges will not rest on the floor or other hard surface. When a tool is no longer needed, return it to the cabinet or toolroom. Tools must not be left scattered about the shop.

10. Always be alert for hazards and materials that might cause a fire. This applies particularly to highly combustible materials and fumes. Rags used to wipe oil and oil base paint must be disposed of in a closed metal container to prevent spontaneous combustion.

11. Clean up after yourself. Scrap materials, even sawdust, can be hazardous, and they add to the clutter of shop activity.

Hand Tools

It is entirely possible to construct scenery with a few basic hand tools. Although most scenic technicians prefer to use power tools because they are quick and accurate, there are many operations that must be done by hand. One should not be too surprised, however, to discover that many small theatres do not have the necessary funding to supply power equipment, so every technician should strive to learn about the tools of the scene shop, and to develop skills in using them.

All tools, regardless of their functional characteristics, require attention from time to time to maintain them in proper working order. Hammer handles must be securely seated in the heads; screwdrivers must be filed or ground occasionally to keep the edges of the blade sharp and the thickness at the tip right for the slots in the heads of the screws; saws require frequent filing and cutting tools, such as planes, chisels, and knives, may need honing every few minutes. Tools are precision instruments and they should be accorded that level of care.

a. HAMMERS

HAMMERS

CLAW HAMMER

BLOCK

RIPPING HAMMER

TACK HAMMER

BALL PEIN HAMMER

Curved Claw Nailing Hammer

Sizes: 10 oz, 13 oz, 16 oz

Characteristics: Head drop-forged steel with bell face and curved claw for removing nails; handles may be steel with neoprene rubber grip, or hickory; head of wood handled hammer secured with wedge

Uses: A nail driving hammer; should not be used when working on anvil or vise; a leverage block should be used when withdrawing nails longer than 8d

Care: Head must be kept tight by adding additional wedges or replacing handle completely; if face becomes chipped or pitted from misuse, hammer should be replaced

Straight Claw or Ripping Hammer

Size: 16 oz.

Characteristics: Same as curved claw hammer except the claw extends nearly 90° to the throat so that it can be driven between boards as a pry to loosen nail joint

Uses: Nail driving and destructing hammer; use only for woodworking; leverage block recommended when withdrawing nails larger then 10d

Care: Same as curved claw hammer

Tack Hammer

Sizes: 5 oz and 7 oz

Characteristics: A very lightweight hammer with long slender head, usually magnetized to hold tack on the face

Uses: For upholstery tacking with upholsterers' tacks

Care: Slender handle easily broken; head must be tight

Ball Pein or Machinists Hammer

Sizes: 12 oz and 16 oz

Characteristics: Cylindrical face with a ball shaped
pein; oval wooden handle; harder steel than
nailing hammer

Uses: For working on metal, bending metal and
riveting

Care: Slender handle tends to break if using too
light hammer for the job; head must be tight on
handle

b. TACKERS

Heavy Duty Staple Tacker

Sizes: For staple sizes ¼″, ⅜″, and ½″

Characteristics: Heavy spring loaded staple gun;
staples ejected by pressing or squeezing heavy
lever; must have sufficient force to imbed ½″
staple in white pine board

Uses: Stapling muslin or canvas on flats, tacking
covering on platforms, steps, and drops to wood
battens

Care: Springs require frequent oiling; attention to
case bolts and rivets; occasional jamming

Hammer Tacker

Size: 11″ to 12″

Characteristics: An extended handle like a hammer with a stapling tacker head; requires ham-
mering action with enough force to imbed staple

Uses: Tacking covering on flats, tacking easy
curve, platform covers, and laying canvas ground
cloth

Care: Avoid beating too hard; attention to bolts
and rivets; occasional oiling of moving parts

c. SAWS

Crosscut Saws

Sizes: Points per inch: 8, 10, 12; length 26″

Characteristics: Teeth filed to 65° angle and triangular tooth cross filed 60° toward the tip end
of the blade from alternate sides, thus each
tooth becomes a cutting blade as it is pushed
through the wood; teeth are bent outward
slightly in alternating directions to open the kerf
for the blade to pass freely (the set of the saw)

STAPLE TACKERS

STAPLE GUN

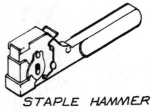

STAPLE HAMMER

SAWS

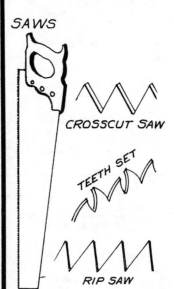

CROSSCUT SAW

TEETH SET

RIP SAW

Uses: For cutting across the grain of wood; a 10 point crosscut saw meets most shop needs; a 12 point will make cleaner cuts in plywood

Care: Avoid sawing into nails or staples; hang the saw when not in use to avoid dulling; sharpen frequently

Rip Saw

Size: 6 points per inch

Characteristics: Slightly wider and heavier steel than crosscut saw; teeth filed at more acute angle so that angle facing end of saw is nearly perpendicular and each tooth is filed straight across, thus each tooth gouges the wood out like a small chisel; teeth are set alternately to widen the kerf

Uses: For ripping or cutting with the grain of the wood

Care: Frequent sharpening

Back Saw and Miter Box

Size: 12 points per inch

Characteristics: Rectangular shaped crosscut saw with a rigid steel cap along the back edge; more accurate because blade does not bend; steel cap fits into guideways on miter box; crosscut filed

Uses: Fitting accurate cabinet and furniture joints; with miter box, for cutting mitered joints 90° to 45°

Care: Same as other saws

Keyhole Saw

Sizes: 10 and 12 points per inch

Characteristics: Long tapered blade, ¼" to 1¼", that fits into pistol grip wood or plastic handle; crosscut filed

Uses: Curvilinear cuts; blade can be started in ⅜" hole

Care: Thin blade easily bent; keep saw sharp and do not force

Coping Saw

Size: 8" × 3⁄16" blade, 16 to 18 teeth per inch

Characteristics: Blade extends across open throat

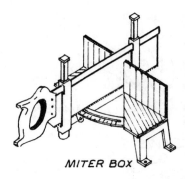

MITER BOX

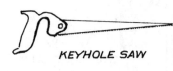

KEYHOLE SAW

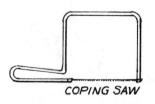

COPING SAW

HACK SAW

of frame; blade can be turned 90° or 180°; blade held in position by spring tension

Uses: Fine scroll cutting in plywood; blade inserted through hole in stock and snapped into frame

Care: Thin blades easily broken; cannot be sharpened; various size blades can be replaced

Hack Saw

Sizes: 8″, 10″ and 12″ blades

Characteristics: Open throat frame adjustable for different size blades; pistol grip handle; blade may be rotated 90° to 180°

Uses: A saw for cutting strap, angle or channel iron; cutting off bolts and rivets; pipe

Care: Cuts only on push stroke; avoid overheating blade by adding oil or kerosene to kerf during saw operation; blade cannot be sharpened, but replaceable

d. CHISELS

CHISELS

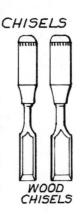

WOOD
CHISELS

Wood Chisels

Sizes: ¼″ to 1¼″ wide blade

Characteristics: A finely sharpened wood cutting tool; steel shank and blade with amber or clear plastic grip and steel capped handle; blade ground to 30° angle

Uses: Mortising, mortise and tenon joints or shaving operations; cut made by pressing or tapping head of chisel with heel of hand or mallet

Care: Should be sharpened before each use by honing on oiled carborundum stone; should be reground occasionally to maintain cutting edge, but avoid burning—turning tip blue—during grinding; burning removes temper from steel so it will not hold a cutting edge

COLD
CHISELS

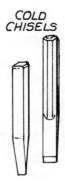

Cold Chisel

Sizes: ¾″ diameter × 7″ long (other sizes are available)

Characteristics: Octagon tool steel, very hard; point forged to flat bevel with short ground cutting tip

PLANES

BLOCK PLANE

SMOOTHING
PLANE

Uses: For shearing mild steel rivets and bolts by
driving cutting edge beneath head or nut with
ball pein hammer; can be used to shear heavy
sheet metal

Care: Frequent grinding to restore cutting edge;
dip frequently in cold water during grinding
operation

e. PLANES

Block Plane

Size: 7″ overall; blade 1⅝″ wide

Characteristics: Small hand plane with blade angle
between 12° and 20°; blade can be adjusted for
shallow and deep cuts

Uses: Planing end grain; plane blade must not move
across edge of wood to avoid splitting

Care: Frequent sharpening, grinding then honing;
same precautions to avoid losing temper of cutting edge; always lay plane on its side

Smoothing Plane

Sizes: 8″ to 14″ long, 2″ wide (9″ bench plane
serves most construction purposes)

Characteristics: Planing with the direction of wood
grain; blade rests at 30° angle; adjustable cutting depth; pistol grip

Uses: Planing face or edge surface of wood; often
required when fitting doors and windows

Care: Frequent honing and occasional grinding to
maintain cutting edge of plane blade; lay on its
side

f. FILES AND RASPS

"Surform" Tools

Sizes: Pocket size, 5½″, flat, 16⅝″, plane, 10″

Characteristics: Patented tools with thin steel
blades perforated with holes that have dis-
tended, sharpened edges

Uses: Like wood plane, but cuts wood away by
grating action; rough forming of chamfers or
rounded edges; may be used on plastics, felt or
leather

Care: Replace blades when dull; lay on side

FILES-RASPS

SURFORM
PLANES

Wood Rasp

Sizes: 10″ and 12″ length; flat, half round

Characteristics: Extremely coarse graterlike file with tine that must be fitted into wooden file handle

Uses: Rough shaping or to remove irregularities on curvilinear shapes not accessible with plane

Care: Occasional brushing with steel brush to remove wood particles; replace when dull

Wood Files

Sizes: 10″ and 12″ length; flat, half and full round

Characteristics: Coarse diagonal ridges or teeth; teeth spiral around round or rat tail file; tine must be fitted into file handle

Uses: Finish filing after rasp; may be used on end grain

Care: Frequent brushing to remove wood particles

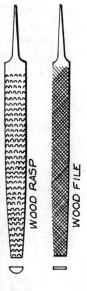

Bastard Cut Metal File

Sizes: 8″ and 10″ length; flat, half and full round

Characteristics: Coarse diagonal cut teeth; very sharp; requires file handle

Uses: Fairly coarse metal filing; bolts, edges of strap, angle, or channel iron

Care: Steel very hard and brittle so do not tap to remove filings; brush with steel brush or file card to remove filings that clog teeth; do not use on wood

Mill File

Sizes: 8″ and 10″ length; flat or tapered

Characteristics: Very fine teeth and thinner than bastard file; file handle required

Uses: Finish filing metal

Care: Frequent cleaning to remove filings; do not use on wood

g. DRILLS AND BITS

Brace and Auger Bits

Sizes: Brace, 10″ sweep; auger bits from 4 to 16 (auger bit size is given in number of sixteenths of an inch: Size 4 = ¼″, etc.)

Characteristics: Brace is a crank with pommel,

DRILLS AND BITS

BRACE

AUGER BIT

HAND DRILL

TWIST DRILL BIT

PUSH DRILL

turning handle and chuck to hold the bit; chuck may have ratchet to permit partial turns; bit has square taper at end of shank which fits in chuck; tapered screw precedes cutting blade and auger raises chips

Uses: Boring holes in wood only; with expansion bit, holes to 2½″ may be bored for poles

Care: Brace ratchet requires occasional light oil; avoid nails, tacks or staples; auger cutter may be sharpened with needle file; avoid dropping

Hand Drill and Twist Drill Bits

Sizes: Drill capacity, $\frac{1}{64}$″ to ¼″ and $\frac{1}{64}$″ to ⅜″, straight shank twist drills sized by fractional diameter of shank

Characteristics: Hand drill often referred to as "eggbeater" drill; geared sprocket with turning handle and chuck to hold bit; bits have straight round shank of drillrod; high speed, high carbon steel

Uses: Predrilling holes for screws in wood, or for bolts and rivets in mild steel

Care: Drill requires frequent oiling of gears and moving parts; do not drop, gears are cast iron and will break; drill bits must be lubricated when drilling in steel; bit points require frequent grinding to maintain sharp cutting edge

"Yankee" or Push Drills

Sizes: Drill capacity, $\frac{1}{64}$″ to $\frac{11}{64}$″

Characteristics: Spring loaded shaft that spins drill points; collet type chuck; drill points only

Uses: Drilling small holes for screws, particularly for starting holes for screws when mounting hardware

Care: Occasional light oil; avoid dropping or bending shaft

h. RULES AND SQUARES

Steel Tapes

Sizes: 8′ and 12′ × ½″ wide

Characteristics: Steel measuring tape encased on self-return or push reel, with or without brake to hold in extended position; calibrated in ⅛'s, inches and feet

Uses: In all measuring operations; reasonably accurate for scenic construction

Care: Spring steel tapes will split if stepped on or twisted; tapes replaceable

Folding Wood Rules

Sizes: 6′ and 8′ × ½″

Characteristics: Folding ruler, usually of wood, very accurate

Uses: All measuring operations

Care: Susceptible to breakage; keep off floor

Yard and Meter Sticks

Sizes: 36″ or 1 meter

Characteristics: Metal or wood; printed wooden sticks only moderately accurate; metal rule very accurate

Uses: All measuring operations; wood sticks not accurate enough for construction measuring

Care: Avoid scratching or dents along edges

Tri-Square

Size: 7″ blade with 5″ handle

Characteristics: Small hand square with steel blade and steel, wood or composition handle; blade calibrated ¹⁄₁₆″, ⅛″, ¼″ and inch segments

Uses: Marking for square cut across narrow stock; too short for squaring flat frame corners; convenient for marking out dado and half-lap joints

Care: An accurate tool; avoid damage to blade and handle

Combination Square

Size: 12″ blade; 90° and 45° handle

Characteristics: An accurately calibrated scale ¹⁄₃₂″ to 1″; each face shows two scales, each segmented differently; rule may be removed from handle or set at any depth; 45° angle on one face of handle convenient for laying out miter joints; some models have spirit level and steel scriber point in the handle; protractor and "V" center finder attachments available

RULES AND SQUARES

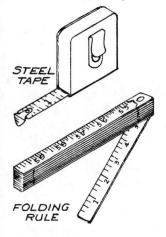

STEEL
TAPE

FOLDING
RULE

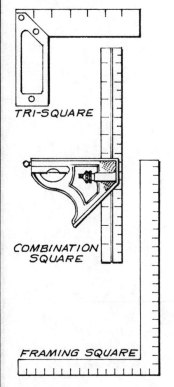

TRI-SQUARE

COMBINATION
SQUARE

FRAMING SQUARE

Uses: An accurate squaring tool for small operations and measurements; particularly useful in
metal working operations

Care: Avoid dropping or uses that might nick or
damage the edges of the rule

Steel Framing or Carpenters Square

Size: Tongue measures 18″ along outside edge,
16″ along inside edge; blade measures 24″ on
outside, 22½″ on the inside edge

Characteristics: Steel or aluminum square with
$\frac{1}{16}$″ and $\frac{1}{8}$″ graduations on one face, $\frac{1}{12}$″ and
$\frac{1}{16}$″ graduations on the opposite; one side of
tongue is laid out in $\frac{1}{12}$″ and $\frac{1}{10}$″ graduations;
rafter scales, brace measure, octagon scale,
board measure, and a 100th scale are imprinted
on surface of some models

Uses: Squaring, framing operations, and accurate
measuring instrument; essential for layout of
stair carriages, flat construction, and platform
construction

Care: Avoid dropping or uses that might nick or
damage edges

i. SCREW DRIVERS

Hand Screw Drivers

Sizes: Blade length from 2″ pocket size to 8″;
blade width varies from $\frac{1}{8}$″ to $\frac{3}{8}$″

Characteristics: High carbon steel shaft flattened
at tip to fit slot cut in screw head; fitted with
handle of hard wood or plastic composition;
length designates length of shaft extending from
handle to tip

Uses: Turning screws

Care: Occasional filing or grinding of tip to maintain square face; do not use screw driver as a
pry or chisel

Phillips Screw Driver

Sizes: Point sizes, 0, 1, 2 and 3; shaft lengths from
2¾″ to 5¾″

Characteristics: Tip pressed into blunt point with

four tapered flanges to fit Phillips screw head; handle plastic composition

Uses: Turning Phillips screw only

Care: Avoid abuse; discard when flanges no longer seat firmly in screw head

Spiral Ratchet Screw Driver (Yankee)

Sizes: Standard and heavy duty

Characteristics: The shaft is a spiral ratchet with a spring chuck to hold two or more sizes of screw driver bits; upper shaft and handle may contain spring to return shaft, or may be ordered without quick return; three position adjustment sets forward, reverse or lock position of shaft; downward pressure spins ratchet

Uses: For setting or removing screws quickly; because of long shaft, must be used only where direct body pressure is possible; avoid reaching over head

Care: Particular care required to avoid bending ratchet; ratchet requires frequent oiling; bits must be kept sharp

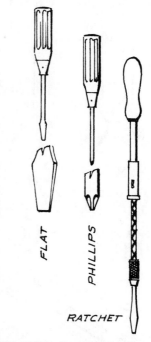

SCREW DRIVERS

FLAT   PHILLIPS

RATCHET

j. PLIERS AND WRENCHES

Combination Pliers

Sizes: 6″ and 8″

Characteristics: Common pliers with two position slip joint to permit enlargement of jaw opening

Uses: General purpose for bending wire, holding nut while tightening stove bolts, or grasping operations

Care: Frequent attention to bolt and nut which forms axis for jaws; proper tension necessary for efficient operation

Vise Grip Pliers

Sizes: 7″ and 10″ over-all

Characteristics: Combines characteristics of common pliers with adjustable wrench; adjustment bolt in end of one grip handle and lock spring creates vise action with great pressure

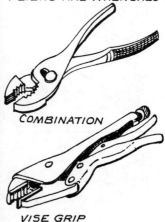

PLIERS AND WRENCHES

COMBINATION

VISE GRIP

ARC-JOINT PLIERS

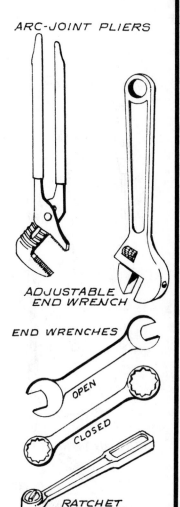

ADJUSTABLE
END WRENCH

END WRENCHES

OPEN

CLOSED

RATCHET

SOCKETS

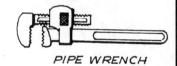

PIPE WRENCH

Uses: General purpose wrench for tightening nuts and gripping small pipe

Care: Occasional oil on screw threads

Arc-Joint or Tongue and Groove Pliers

Sizes: 10", open to 1½"; 16", open to 2½"

Characteristics: Arced grooves in jaws shifts pivot pressure away from bolt; sharp teeth inside each jaw give good grip on cylindrical forms; long handles give strong leverage

Uses: A wrench to grip pipe

Care: Occasional grease in grooves of jaw

Adjustable End Wrench

Sizes: 8" and 10"

Characteristics: An end wrench with knurled adjustment set into larger jaw and heavy steel handle; smooth jaws

Uses: Tightening bolts; an excellent general wrench

Care: Occasional light oil

Socket Wrenches and Ratchet

Sizes: ¼", ⁵⁄₁₆", ⅜", ½" hexagon

Characteristics: Ratchet tool with interchangeable wrenches to fit nuts of more common bolt sizes

Uses: Tightening or loosening nuts quickly

Care: Occasional light oil on ratchet mechanism

Pipe Wrench

Size: 10" for up to 1¾" pipe

Characteristics: A wrench for pipe work; hook jaw moves against flat spring to permit ratchetlike action when tightening or loosening pipe; knurled opening adjustment, sharp pipe grip jaws

Uses: For holding pipe or pipe fittings; two wrenches are often needed

Care: Occasional light oil on threads

k. SHARPENING STONES AND ABRASIVES

Carborundum Stone

Size: ¾" × 2½" × 6"

Characteristics: A trade name for sharpening stone made of silicon carbide or other abrasive compounds; different grades of coarseness, or one side fine, the other coarse; stone coated with lubricating oil to free metal particles deposited by grinding action

Uses: To sharpen chisels, plane irons, knives

Care: Add few drops of oil with each use; do not drop

Sandpaper

Size: Sheets, 9″ × 12″, grades fine, medium, coarse, or No. 000, No. 0 and No. ½

Characteristics: Finely graded silicon sand adhered to heavy paper, available in both regular and waterproof

Uses: Fine abrasive effective on wood, plastics, and plaster

SHARPENING STONES AND ABRASIVES

CARBORUNDUM STONE

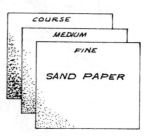

COURSE

MEDIUM

FINE

SAND PAPER

1. SHEARS, SNIPS AND KNIVES

Shears and Scissors

Sizes: 6″ and 8″ blades

Characteristics: Heavy duty scissors; high carbon steel

Uses: For cutting paper, canvas, and muslin

Care: High carbon steel very brittle, so avoid dropping; for use on soft goods only; frequent sharpening to maintain cutting edge

Tinners Snips

Sizes: 7″, 10″ and 12″ lengths

Characteristics: Drop forged steel shears with straight bill, duck bill, or curved bill patterns, or aviation type which have compound leverage to reduce cutting pressure

Uses: For cutting sheet metals up to 18 ga. thickness

Care: Avoid cutting nails, wire, or other round objects; occasional sharpening

Utility Knife

Size: 6″ long with 2½″ double end blade

Characteristics: Compact heavy handle with short blade that can be turned end for end; cast aluminum

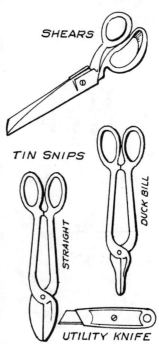

SHEARS-SNIPS-KNIVES

SHEARS

TIN SNIPS

STRAIGHT

DUCK BILL

UTILITY KNIFE

Uses: Trimming away excess material on flat covering; general cutting on corrugated paper, Upson board, or other paper stock; carving

Care: Frequent honing; blade replacements; avoid dropping

m. CLAMPS AND VICES

"C" Clamps

Sizes: Throat opening 2″ to 8″; throat depth 2½″ to 3¼″

Characteristics: A C-shaped clamp with screw and handle; malleable iron with free turning pressure foot

Uses: To clamp glued surfaces; clamp joining light framed scenery; holding work securely for other tool operations

Care: Malleable frame can be sprung out of shape if too great pressure exerted

Bar or Pipe Clamps

Sizes: Bar clamps available in lengths from 2′ to 6′; pipe clamp sets threaded for ½″ and ⅝″ pipe

Characteristics: Bar clamp has ¼″ × 1¼″ flat bar with sliding pressure plate which catches in spaced notches in top of bar; opposite end has threaded shaft with surface plate and hand crank for adjusting clamp pressure; pipe set has similar hardware which is fitted to pipe provided by shop

Uses: For clamping edge to edge glue joints; all other clamping operations; different length pipes can be substituted

Care: Occasional oil on pressure screw

Carpenters Bench Vise

Size: Vise faces 4½″ × 6″, opens to 10″

Characteristics: Face plates kept in alignment by two guide bars and heavy screw that opens and closes the vise; mounted on edge of work table, flush with the counter top; face plates covered with ¾″ pine to protect clamped material

Uses: To clamp wood for planing, sawing, or drilling

Care: Wood facings must be replaced occasionally

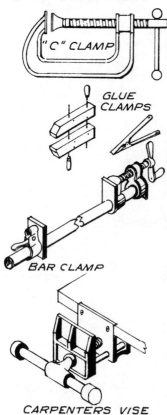

CLAMPS AND VISES

"C" CLAMP

GLUE CLAMPS

BAR CLAMP

CARPENTERS VISE

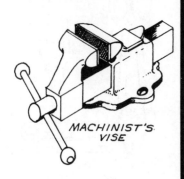

MACHINIST'S VISE

Machinist's Vise

> Size: Several sizes from jeweler's vise to one that
> opens 8"; common shop size, 4" wide × 6"
> throat opening
>
> Characteristics: Metal working vise, with small
> anvil surface and swivel base; bench top mount;
> pipe jaws
>
> Uses: To hold metal while sawing, bending strap
> iron, and general metal working operations
>
> Care: Frequent cleaning and oiling

n. PINCH OR CROW BAR

Pinch Bar

> Sizes: 12", 18" and 24"
>
> Characteristics: Octagon tool steel flattened and
> bent slightly to acquire leverage fulcrum for
> prying heavy boards; opposite end flattened with
> claw cut and formed in half circle for pulling
> heavy nails
>
> Uses: For forcing apart nailed boards and remov-
> ing long nails; indispensable for dismantling
> platforms

Power Tools

Discretion must be exercised in determining what machines shall be used in a scene shop. One assumes it
would be ideal to have every conceivable wood and
metal working machine, except that every production
has unique scenic requirements, some very simple,
others technically complicated. The chances are that
many of the more specialized pieces of power equipment would stand idle much of the time. It is often more
important to have large open floor areas than to have
valuable floor space taken up with equipment which is
not being used.

Skilled operators who are knowledgeable in the uses
and maintenance of power tools must also be considered when one selects essential equipment. Skilled technicians can be trained, but this presents a crucial
problem for community and college theatres where there
is frequent turnover of qualified technicians, and sometimes no one qualified at all. Thus, there are many argu-

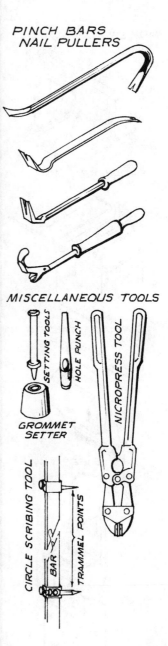

PINCH BARS
NAIL PULLERS

MISCELLANEOUS TOOLS

SETTING TOOLS

HOLE PUNCH

NICROPRESS TOOL

GROMMET SETTER

CIRCLE SCRIBING TOOL

BAR

TRAMMEL POINTS

POWER SAWS

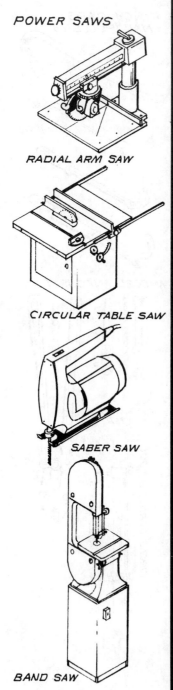

RADIAL ARM SAW

CIRCULAR TABLE SAW

SABER SAW

BAND SAW

ments that favor minimal numbers of power tools, and where such equipment is essential for technical efficiency, stationary machines should be mounted along the walls of the shop so the floor area is left open, or machines should be portable so they can be moved easily.

This is not to imply that power tools should be eliminated; there are many that should appear on the list of essential equipment, and these are described because their frequency of use is high and a few minutes of instruction will teach individuals the basics of safe operation.

POWER SAWS

Radial Arm Saw

Description: Saw and motor suspended from an arm above the work to be cut; saw moves back and forth in a track mechanism on the arm; operating handle permits operator to pull the saw through the stock and push it back where it can be locked in safety position; radial arm can be raised and lowered, or pivoted 45° either direction; motor can be tilted 45° for compound miter cuts, or turned 90° laterally for ripping stock; table mounting variable

Uses: Cross cuts in stock to 12″ wide; rip cuts to 10″ wide; angular cuts from 0 to 90°

Advantages: Saw can be set against a wall; reasonably safe to use because operator pulls saw across the wood rather than pushes wood across saw blade, and when cut is complete, saw is pushed completely back of the stock

Disadvantages: Tends to be less accurate on ripping cuts; blade guard causes some difficulty with deep compound miter cuts

Circular Table Saw

Description: Saw and motor mounted below saw table with blade extending through slot in table; blade can be raised, lowered, or tilted to adjust depth and angle of cut; adjustable rip fence used to determine width of rip cut; crosscut fence moves in channel ways in top of table for guid-

ing cross grain cuts; crosscut fence has protractor adjustment for miter cuts; blades for crosscut, ripping, and combinations

Uses: For cross grain and ripping cuts; very accurate for mitering and dado cuts

Advantages: Considered more accurate for cabi-
netry; extension accessories to enlarge table and
guide fence limits makes it possible to handle
wider stock than on a radial saw

Disadvantages: Saw table must be secured to floor
with minimum of 14' in the clear in all directions;
even with blade safety guard, there are greater
hazards because the hands must often move past
the blade

Saber Saw

Description: A small hand-held jig saw which uses
rigid saber blades; blades in a variety of tooth
sizes for pine, plywood, and masonite

Uses: For curvilinear cuts, piercing, as well as
straight cuts

Advantages: Excellent power tool for cutting plywood and Upson where free form curves are required; lightweight and portable

Disadvantages: Vibration of blade makes it difficult
to guide saw with accuracy; blades overheat
quickly in ¾" stock causing them to lose temper
and drift

Band Saw

Description: Narrow, continuous blade passing over
two rubber tired drive wheels and through center
of cutting table; table may be tilted to 45° angle
cuts; blades for wood ¼", ⅜", and ½" widths

Uses: Curvilinear cutting; excellent for plywood,
pine, and composition boards; ¼" blades for
smaller curves, ⅜" and ½" for larger sweeps

Advantages: Simple and safe to operate with mod-
est maintenance; preliminary instruction simple,
but must include changing blades, alignment, and
tension adjustment

Disadvantages: Broken blades can be hazardous;
constant attention necessary to proper tracking

CIRCULAR PORTABLE SAW

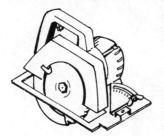

CUT-AWL

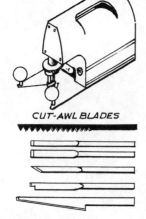

CUT-AWL BLADES

POWER DRILLS

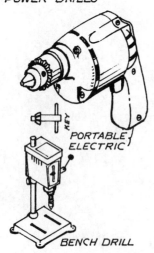

KEY

PORTABLE ELECTRIC

BENCH DRILL

and tension of blade; not an effective tool for small detail cutting

Circular Portable Saw

Description: Hand-held circular saw, with 7″ to 8″ diameter saw blade; small adjustable plate sets depth and angle of cut; crescent safety guard covers blade completely when removed from stock

Uses: Light portable power tool for cutoff and rip cuts; a time saver when constructing platforms, cutting large sheets of plywood and heavy framing

Advantages: Avoids tying up other saws and much faster than hand sawing; can be used at site of construction

Disadvantages: Hand guiding results in blade binding or jamming, causing the saw to buck; cannot be used to trim off short pieces of stock; only moderately accurate; a hazardous tool in the hands of a novice

Cut-Awl

Description: Combines cutting characteristics of band saw and saber saw; swiveling blade mounting and vertical jig action permits cutting extremely intricate patterns; small saber saw blades for cutting wood, and a wide variety of chisels for cutting Upson board, masonite, and cloth; adjustments for depth and length of stroke

Uses: Cutting plywood and ¾″ pine; Upson board, fiber board, and canvas; pierced cut out on soft goods

Advantages: Simple and safe to operate; only power tool for small curvilinear details

Disadvantages: Blades easily overheated and broken; requires frequent attention to lubrication and mechanical adjustment

POWER DRILLS

Portable Electric Drills

Description: Compact electric drill with keyed chuck, pistol grip, and trigger switch; may be single or dual speed; drill size capacity, ¼″, ⅜″; housing cast aluminum; accessory: sanding disc

Uses: Portable drill for predrilling holes for screws
and bolts; light disc sanding

Advantages: Portable, very fast, and simple to
operate

Disadvantages: Aluminum case easily broken if
dropped

Bench Drill

Description: A stationary drill and motor mounted
on bench or stand; keyed chuck and variable
speed pulleys; manual lever to lower drill into
work; base drilled for drill vise; ¼" and ⅜" drill
capacity

Uses: For accurate drilling, particularly in metal
and pipe

Advantages: A stationary drill with variable speed

Disadvantages: Takes up necessary floor or bench
space; degree of accuracy this machine offers is
seldom called for in scene shop

SOLDERING AND WELDING EQUIPMENT

Electric Soldering Iron

Description: A straight soldering tool with heating
element and interchangeable copper soldering
tips

Uses: General soldering of galvanized sheet steel or
heavier gauge copper; requires acid core solder,
or bar solder and acid flux

Soldering Pencil

Description: A small soldering instrument with replaceable soldering tips

Uses: Ideal for electrical soldering in confined areas

Pistol Grip Soldering Gun

Description: A pistol shaped composition plastic
case and trigger heat control switch; thin copper
tip

Uses: Soldering thin metals, electrical connections,
and light copper or tin properties

Propane Torch

Description: A burner or jet fitted atop a steel bottle
containing propane or similar gas under pressure;

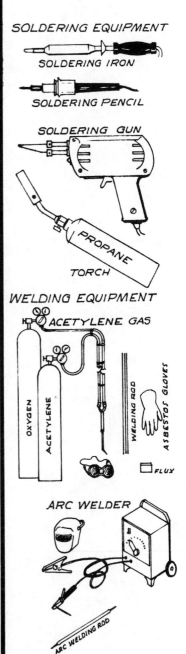

SOLDERING EQUIPMENT

SOLDERING IRON

SOLDERING PENCIL

SOLDERING GUN

PROPANE TORCH

WELDING EQUIPMENT

ACETYLENE GAS

OXYGEN

ACETYLENE

WELDING ROD

ASBESTOS GLOVES

FLUX

ARC WELDER

ARC WELDING ROD

intensity of flame regulated by thumb screw controlling gas flow

Uses: General soldering on heavier metal where more heat is necessary; sufficient heat for hard soldering with silver solder

Gas Welding

Description: By combining oxygen and acetylene under pressure through a nozzle where the proper mixture can be controlled and ignited, an extremely high temperature flame can be produced to fuse two pieces of metal together; an alloy metal which melts at a lower temperature is required for the fusion; special torches available for cutting steel and brazing

Uses: For welding steel for scaffolding, platforms, and metal set pieces, including heavier sheet steel

Advantages: Eliminates need for bolts or rivets when working with heavy steel

Disadvantages: Hazard of fire from flying sparks; workers must wear goggles and heavy gloves; infrequent use of equipment seldom warrants investment and storage (renting or borrowing may be best solution)

Arc Welder

Description: Uses an electrical arc as heat source; amperage from 35 to 230; electrode welding rod strikes the arc when brought in contact with grounded metal surface

Uses: For all types of welding on ferrous and non-ferrous metals; spot welding, cutting, brazing, and bending

Advantages: Cleaner, less fire hazard, and less equipment to handle

Disadvantages: Considered more difficult to master; arc gives off ultraviolet rays injurious to eye and skin tissue unless proper safeguards are used: helmet with ray-absorbing glass, apron, gloves, and other covering over all exposed skin areas of operator, as well as of other people in immediate area

MISCELLANEOUS POWER TOOLS

Bench Grinder

　Description: Grinding wheels mounted on one or both ends of motor axle; ¾ of wheel enclosed with guard, safety glass shield, and adjustable tool rest; bench or stand mount; wire brush, buffing, and sandwheels available accessories

　Uses: For general grinding, buffing, sanding, and sharpening plane blades, chisels, and drill bits

Electric Impact Wrench (also compressed air)

　Description: Torque action wrench that can tighten or loosen nut by impact; socket wrench heads for square or hexagon nuts

　Uses: Timesaving and fast when assembling or dismantling bolted scaffolds, platforms, and scenery

Router

　Description: Hand held electric shaping tool with wide range of decorative cutting heads for edging or routing operations

　Uses: For cutting moulded edges, dado joints, and incised designs in wood

Wood Turning Lathe

　Description: Wood turning tool with a variety of hand held chisels and gouges for shaping wood

　Uses: For turning spindles, furniture parts, and ornamental pieces

SCENERY CONSTRUCTION

Construction Drawings

Building scenery, like any other operation involving technical skills, must proceed according to plan, rather than intuition, if the outcome is to be successful. Hopefully, a scene designer will have worked out the details of construction before the plans are handed to the building carpenter. While one may expect some eccentricities in the style and form in which a designer prepares his drawings, there are standards of mechanical drafting

MISCELLANEOUS POWER TOOLS

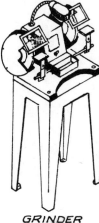

GRINDER

IMPACT WRENCH

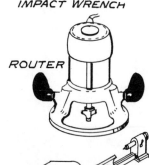

ROUTER

WOOD LATHE

which every technician should be able to read and understand.

In the first place, plans for a production should include scale drawings of the stage with the floor plan of the set clearly indicated. Doorways, steps, windows, platforms, or ramps should be noted. Groundrows, fences, rocks, and trees should be marked in their exact position. Flown units should be indicated with solid lines, or with broken lines if they do not contact the floor.

Second, a set of plans should include elevation drawings in scale for every unit shown on the floor plan. An elevation drawing is a flat view showing one or more sides with outside dimensions. Surface detail is shown, as well as notations on painting detail, the location of properties attached to the surface, draperies, and bric-a-brac. Some designers also include notations on assembling the scenery; others prepare a rear elevation showing the structural framing, placement of hardware, and lashing detail.

Third, detailed working drawings for every unit of scenery to be constructed must be provided for the carpenters. These must be scaled drawings with all dimensions, notations pertaining to stock, and sufficient views of each piece to explain construction procedures. Occasionally the set designer may provide only a rough sketch for the carpenters to follow, but this is a risky practice unless the head carpenter is able to make shop drawings for the crew to follow. This practice is usually the result of some last minute set change. Freehand drafting would be acceptable in this case.

Plan drawings utilize symbols to communicate, and since lines are the primary elements, beginning technicians should familiarize themselves with the symbols if they are to understand the language.

Drafting Conventions

Looking first at the set floor plan—often called a ground plan—one sees the structural walls of the staging area shown in two heavy lines spaced apart the scale thickness of the actual walls. The space between the lines is

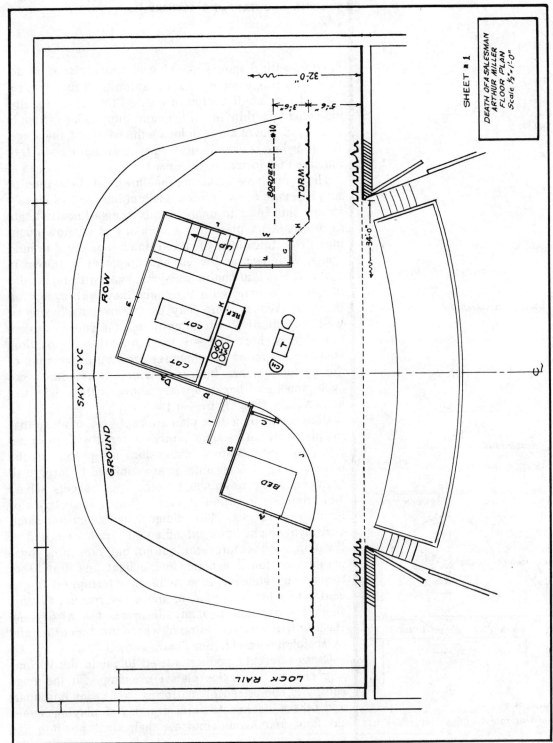

Figure 4–1. *Floor plan.*

filled in with diagonal hatching to connote solid structure. Stage extensions, like an apron or thrust, are indicated by a continuation of a single line. A center line indicated by a thin line of long and short dashes extends from up to down stage to locate the center of the stage. A center line is usually marked with an italicized *CL* to indicate the purpose of the line.

The main lines indicating the outline of the setting or set pieces are drawn with a medium line, or two closely spaced thin lines to denote walls. Single lines indicate furniture, steps, platforms, and door and window openings. The thickness of the framed openings around doors, windows, archways, and fireplaces is shown in scale. Tables and chairs are symbolized with rectangles or circles in scale with the space they will occupy on the floor. Where there may be overhanging beams or wall projections which do not touch the floor, a broken line of very short dashes is used to mark their location. Hanging draperies, whether set dressing or sections of the cyclorama, are indicated with a wavy line. Sky cycloramas and backdrops are shown with single, unbroken lines. (See Figure 4–1.)

Dimensions on a floor plan are kept very small so that the plan will not become overly cluttered with information. For the most part, dimensions are placed on the offstage side of each unit, or are confined to large wall segments with reference to other plan sheets where more detailed information can be found. Two types of lines are used to relate dimensions: *extension lines,* very lightweight lines extending 90° from each end of the points of measurement, but not quite touching these points; and the *dimension line,* a light line drawn between the extension lines with an interruption in the center to allow insertion of the measurement. A tiny, slender arrow point—many designers use a diagonal slash or half arrow—is drawn where the dimension and extension lines meet. (See Figure 4–2.)

Cross reference coding is used to relate the various segments of the design plan. For example, if the stage setting is comprised of platforms, some standing apart and others stacked to form a series of playing levels, the floor plan would indicate their stage position and

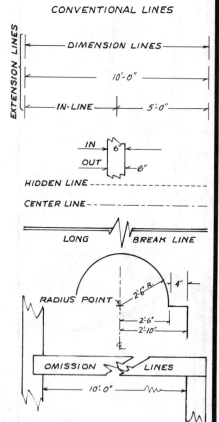

Figure 4–2.
Conventional drafting lines.

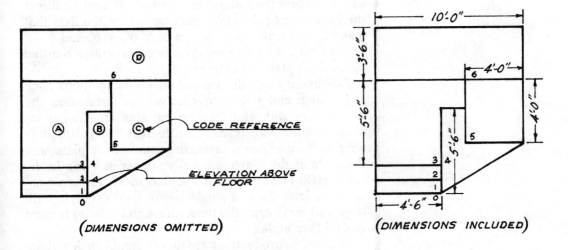

(DIMENSIONS OMITTED)

(DIMENSIONS INCLUDED)

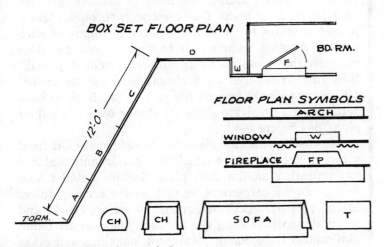

Figure 4–3. *Floor plan symbols.*

their projected shape as performance areas. To include all the hidden lines that would indicate boxes piled on top of boxes would clutter the floor plan. An alphabetical cross coding mark on each level enables the technician to refer to elevation drawings and construction details on other plan sheets. The same system is found on floor plans of a box type setting. Where the right stage wall may have a dimension indicating its length as 12', code letters along the wall, A, B, and C, direct the carpenter to the elevation plan where the flats that make up the wall are shown to be 3' 0", 4' 0" and 5' 0", respectively, thus detailed dimensions are often omitted on the floor plan. (See Figure 4–3.)

Explanatory notations to identify offstage units such as backings and groundrows, as well as tormentors, the proscenium wall and traveler curtains are always included on the floor plan. The title of the play, the playwright, the designer's name, the name of the plate, and the scale of the drawing usually appear in a box in the lower right-hand corner of the plan sheet. The most acceptable lettering is a single stroke, vertical style with large and small capital letters, although legibility is more critical than style.

Multiscene productions are more complicated, and designers employ different methods of indicating scene changes on floor plans. One method is to render transparent overlays to show the relative positions of each setting. Another technique is to superimpose one floor plan on the other by using different colored pencils. Still another reduces the scale of the drawings so that all plans can be shown on the same page. Back to back settings on a revolving stage are shown on a single floor plan. (See Figure 4–4.)

As noted earlier, the elevation drawings are flat front views of the set pieces which add height and contours not indicated on the floor plan. Surface detail which will guide the carpenters, as well as the scene painters in applying trim, is drawn on the elevation. Height and width dimensions are given for each piece, as are detail dimensions for openings, wainscot, paneling, and other forms of surface trim. Dimension lines are always enclosed between extension lines. Where possible, horizontal dimensions are indicated at the base of the drawings, while vertical dimensions may be at either right or left, but the figures always read from the right side of the plan. The exception is on the diagonal: Those slanting to the right should read from the right to horizontal; those on the left should read from the horizontal base. (See Figure 4–5.)

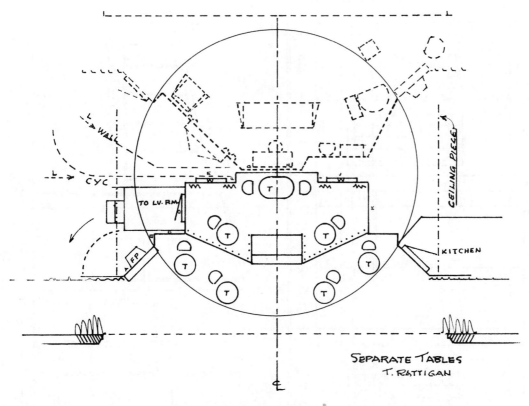

Figure 4–4. *Floor plans, back-to-back sets on revolving stage.*

The scale of elevation drawings is usually enlarged so that details can be brought out more clearly. A floor plan may be done in a scale of ¼″ or ⅜″ to the foot, and the elevations may be in ½″ or ¾″ scale. This creates no problem until a large unit exceeds the limits of the drawing page. If the dimensions of the unit are uniform, the drawing can be shortened by interrupting it with an omission line which signals that a portion of the drawing has been omitted. The dimension is noted in full, but the dimension line also contains a zigzag to indicate the omission. Explanatory notes can be inserted on the drawing wherever they are required. They are underscored with a line which extends to the object of notation, ending with an arrow point.

On large two-dimensional units, like a false proscenium, the designer may draw only half an elevation,

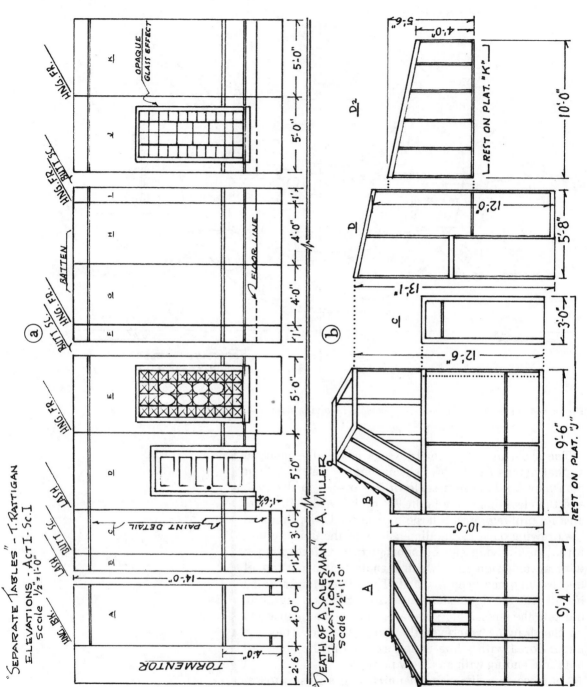

Figure 4–5. Elevation drawings. (See Figure 4–1 and Figure 4–4.)

with the other half shown with the covering removed to show the details of construction. There should be a notation, but be certain that assembly of the unit is reversed if there is any variation in the two halves. (See Figure 4–6.)

Three-dimensional units often require two or three elevation views. If so, these will usually be arranged in a line, and dimensions that are common to all views will only be noted once. The designer may also switch to a

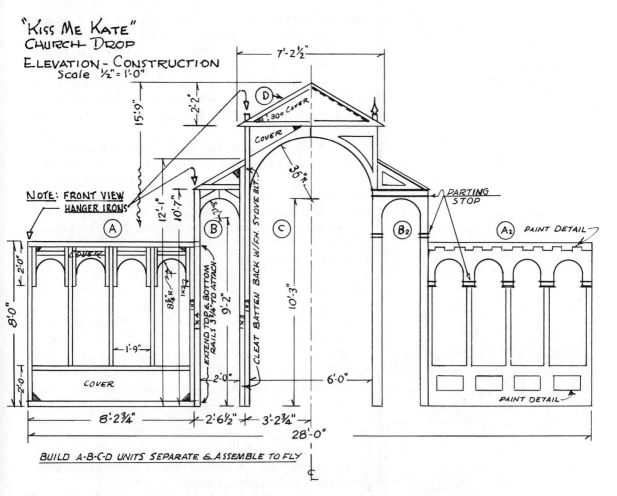

Figure 4–6. *Elevation-construction detail.*

form of drawing which places the scenic unit in a position so that three views may be observed simultaneously. This is called an isometric drawing and is often used to show the elevations of rectangular objects. All dimensions are exact, although the absence of perspective foreshortening distorts the visual appearance of the object somewhat. (See Figure 4–7.)

A rear elevation drawing is used primarily as a guide for the assembly of flats for a box or unit set. The structural characteristics, as well as lashing detail, the location of stiffeners, and special toggles and rails are shown. Many designers omit the rear elevation because it is a miniature construction layout, but too small to actually be used as a building plan. If the designer is satisfied with the front elevations, and he is confident that his technicians know how to assemble the set, he will make notations along the tops of his elevations to indicate the assembly of each unit with the next. (See Figure 4–5.)

Construction details are labeled and cross-coded to refer to the floor plans and elevations. Since some construction problems are more complicated than others, each unit is drawn in the scale suitable for showing the detail effectively and the scale is noted with each drawing. Where two or more units that are the same size are needed, a single construction detail is shown with the notation that a certain number are to be built. Where two units are alike but opposite one another, the notation, "build two, one opposite hand," may be used. Each segment of a construction detail sheet is usually set apart with double lines broken with a squiggle. (See Figure 4–8.)

Arch and sweep details must include the exact location of radius points and the dimensions. Free form sweeps are laid out on a gridwork of squares with each square of the grid equivalent to a given number of inches in scale with the actual dimensions. This makes it simple to enlarge the drawing to full scale by enlarging the squares to full scale on the surface of the construction material. This technique is used·for details of painted drops and groundrows.

Two-dimensional construction drawings require a

Figure 4–7.
Isometric elevation detail.

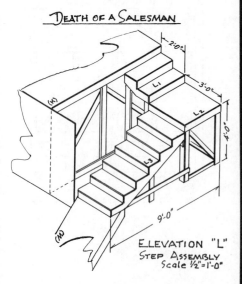

DEATH OF A SALESMAN

ELEVATION "L"
STEP ASSEMBLY
Scale ½"=1'-0"

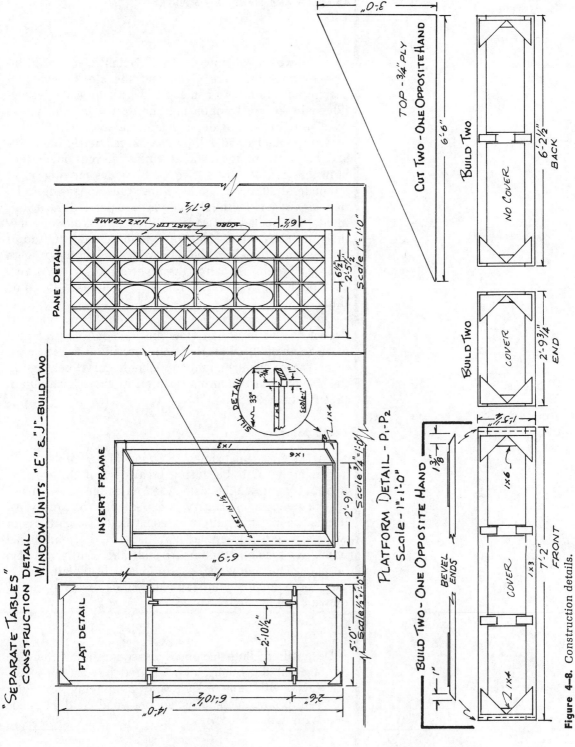

Figure 4-8. Construction details.

single view shown from the back. Height, width, and internal dimensions are given and the stock, including bracing and reinforcements, are drawn to scale. Three-dimensional construction may be drawn in plan views consisting of front, side, and top rendered individually, or with isometric or oblique views. Isometric drawings show a platform, for instance, turned so that one corner is in the front, with the two visible sides moving off at an angle of 30° from the base line, thus appearing to be below eye level so that the top is revealed. All measurements are scaled accurately. Since this kind of view does not show back side construction detail, the top of the platform may be tilted upward 45° as though it were hinged, thereby revealing the inner structure, or drawn as though the top were lifted to accomplish the same thing.

Oblique drawings differ in that the front view is drawn flat, as in a plan view, but one side is projected at an angle of 30°. This drafting convention is used most often where construction may include curvilinear vaulting. Scenic draftsmen may use all of these techniques. (See Figure 4–9.)

Basic Joinery

Most scenery constructed of wood is assembled with very simple joints because a great deal of the work is temporary and will be dismantled when the show closes. At the same time, scenery is expected to be sturdy, so it must be exceptionally well constructed. Regardless of what strength the lumber may have, if the joints used in making the construction are poor, the results will also be poor. The following descriptions will explain briefly the most common joints and the kinds of construction on which they might be used.

BUTT JOINT

> Description: Both members cut square and fitted one against the other; joint secured by fastening surfaces with nails or screws, or overlaying joint with reinforcing plate of steel or wood held in place with nails or screws

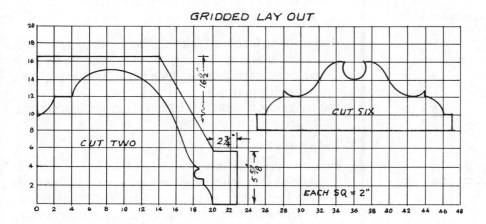

GRIDDED LAY OUT

CUT TWO

16½"

2¾"

5⅝"

CUT SIX

EACH SQ = 2"

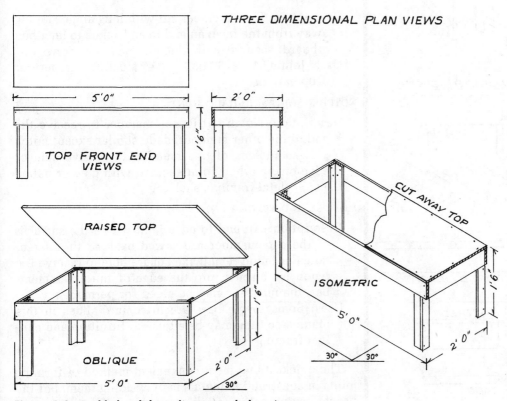

THREE DIMENSIONAL PLAN VIEWS

5'0"

2'0"

1'6"

TOP FRONT END
VIEWS

RAISED TOP

CUT AWAY TOP

ISOMETRIC

1'6"

5'0"

2'0"

30°   30°

OBLIQUE

1'6"

2'0"

5'0"

30°

Figure 4-9. Gridded and three-dimensional plan views.

JOINTS USED IN SCENERY CONSTRUCTION

BUTT JOINTS

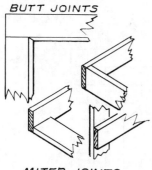

MITER JOINTS

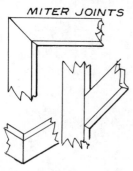

HALF-LAP JOINTS

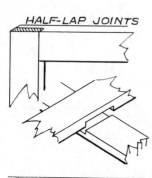

SCARFED JOINT

NOTCHED

DADO

Uses: Flat construction, platforms, and scaffolding; simplest and most commonly used joint

MITER JOINT

Description: One or both members cut to 45° angle to form brace or 90° corner; joint secured by nailing, using corrugated fasteners, or overlaying with reinforcing plates

Uses: Framing, molding corners, corner braces, stationary jacks

HALF-LAP JOINT

Description: Half the thickness of each member cut away so that when they are joined, each laps over the other; joint secured with glue, nails, or screws

Uses: Open frames, screens, continuous long battens

SCARFED JOINT

Description: Each member cut with long angle sloping away from the face; an end to end splice to lengthen a board; secured with glue and nails or screws

Uses: Joining $1'' \times 3''$ or $1'' \times 4''$ stock for drapery or drop battens

NOTCHED JOINT AND DADO JOINT

Description: Notch cut in one member to receive the end of the other member; dado similar except notch plowed in face of one member to receive side or edge of the other; joint secured with glue or nailed

Uses: Skeletal framing, shelving

MORTISE AND TENON JOINT

Description: An end to edge joint where the surfaces of the end member are sawed back so that a rectangular tenon remains; a square hole to receive the tenon is chiseled into the edge of the other member, the mortise; may be glued for permanency

Uses: Some toggle bars are fitted into shoes in this manner so they may be adjusted; furniture and cabinet framing

The quickest and most convenient method of forming joints in construction metals is by welding them, but the proper equipment is not always at hand. The illustration shows some of the methods of making joints with metals. (See illustration.)

Two-Dimensional Hard Scenery

Constructed scenery falls into three general categories: two-dimensional hard scenery, two-dimensional soft scenery, and three-dimensional scenery. Hard scenery is constructed to stand on the floor and is therefore framed and rigid. Soft scenery refers to hanging drapery or drops and borders which are not self-supporting. Three-dimensional scenery refers to units of scenery which have sufficient mass to stand by themselves.

Flats are light frames over which canvas or muslin has been stretched. To maintain light, portable units that are strong enough to be self-supporting, it is more practical to construct several small flat units which can be joined than to build a single large unit that would be so cumbersome and flimsy as to be unmanageable. Because flats must be strong and must fit together, the lumber selected for the framing must be strong and light, but above all, straight.

The outer frame of a flat is made up of four pieces of lumber: A *top* and *bottom rail,* and two uprights called *stiles.* Where the height of flats will not exceed 14', 1" × 3", B or Better, or C Select pine that is clear of imperfections, is sufficiently strong for flat construction. A flat can be built any desired size, but most theatres that have space for storage use flats over and over so a uniform height is usually established. The narrowest flat is 12" wide and is usually referred to as a *jog.* The width of other flats start at 1' 6", and may run as wide as 5' 6" or 6' 0". By constructing flats that vary in width in 6" modules, there is usually sufficient variation without having a stock of units with odd dimensions. In many references, 5' 9" is given as the maximum flat width. This stems from the myth that flats wider than that would not pass through the door of a baggage car. A more logical reason is that for many years the widest fabric available was 72" which, after it was flame-proofed, shrank to 69".

The corners of flats are assembled with butt joints

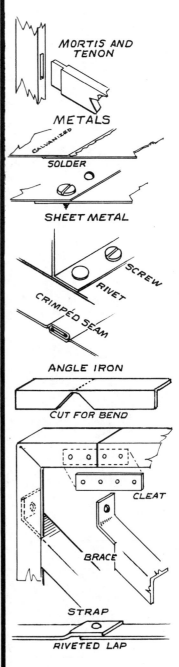

MORTIS AND TENON

METALS

GALVANIZED

SOLDER

SHEET METAL

SCREW

RIVET

CRIMPED SEAM

ANGLE IRON

CUT FOR BEND

CLEAT

BRACE

STRAP

RIVETED LAP

with the ends of the stiles butting into the edges of the top and bottom rails. They are assembled in this manner because when shifting flat scenery, the flat is held upright so the rail serves as a skid. If the stile were extended to the floor, the edges of the frame would soon split from the skidding action. Thus, the top and bottom rails are cut the exact width of the flat, with the stiles fitted in between and shorter than the height of the finished flat by the sum of the widths of the top and bottom rails. For example, if the flat is 5' 0" wide by 14' 0" high, the rails would be 5' 0" long, and if the 1" × 3" stock was 2¾" wide, the stiles would be cut 13' 6½" long.

One or more additional rails are required to keep the stiles parallel. These spreaders are called *toggle rails*. If a single toggle is used, it should be placed midway between the top and bottom rails. If the stiles are bowed slightly, two toggles are often used. Toggle rails are cut to length, accounting for the widths of the stiles; do not measure the distance across the center and cut the toggle to fit because this only builds in any irregularity in the width of the finished flat.

In laying out stock in preparation for cutting the rails, stiles and toggles, the following procedures mark a good scenic technician:

1. Select clear straight stock.
2. Check the ends of the stock for small splits and for square: If the board is not square on the end, or hair splits are apparent, mark the board, using a tri-square, back from the end far enough to eliminate both conditions and cut off the bad end with a cross-cut saw, staying on the waste side of the mark. Re-check the square after cutting.
3. Measure off the length of piece and mark with square: cut off on waste side of mark and recheck for square.
4. Repeat procedure for all required pieces of lumber.

Supplementary bracing is often used to reinforce the flat frame, particularly where a single toggle bar is used, and on flats wider than 3' 0". This is a diagonal *corner*

brace of 1″ × 2″ running from the center of the rail 45°
to one of the stiles.

The precut parts can be laid out for assembly, but
first four plywood corner blocks, keystones or wide
straps for toggles, a carpenter's framing square and claw
hammer, a clinch plate, and clout nails will be required.
Corner blocks are ¼″ plywood made by cutting 8″ or
10″ squares diagonally. Straps are also plywood cut 2″ ×
7″ with the grain running the long way of the strap;
narrow 1½″ straps will be needed for corner braces.

Using the framing square around the outside, one stile
and rail are abutted and a corner block, laid with the
plywood grain running parallel to the stile, is placed
over the joint, but ¾″ back from the edges of both stile
and rail. While holding this assembly securely in place
and firmly against the tongue and blade of the square,
start a clout nail in each of the corners of the corner
block, but drive it no more than halfway. Next, start
two nails ⅜″ back from the joint on the stile, then two
on the rail side, but stagger these slightly so that the
nails do not enter the same grain line of the rail. Now
the joint is tacked in position so that the 10″ square
clinch plate can be slipped beneath the joint assembly
and the nails driven down. The reason for tacking the
corner block securely before driving any nails down
against the clinch plate is that when the nails strike the
plate, the wood tends to shift, throwing the joint out
of square. Additional nails can now be driven. (See
Figure 4–10.)

After the four corners of the flat have been nailed,
toggles and corner braces are laid in position. The straps
or keystones are also set back from the edge ¾″. Three
nails on either side of each joint will be sufficient. There
is an advantage in having the toggle bar attached so that
height adjustment can be made. This may be done by
fitting the ends of the toggle into shoes held in place
with two screws on each stile, or by using ¾″ wood
screws to hold the straps to the stile, instead of clout
nails.

The basic procedure just described is followed in constructing all two-dimensional hard scenery where the
basic wood framework will be covered with some other

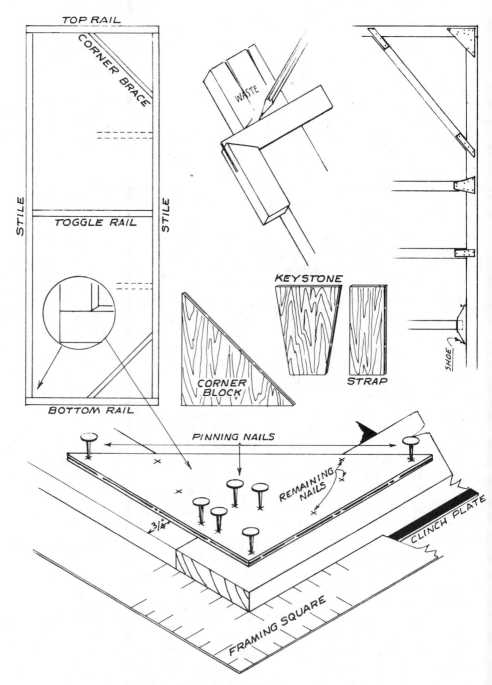

Figure 4–10. *Flat nomenclature.*

material. Flats with door openings differ only in the placement of the toggle bar so that it forms the top of the door opening, and the bottom rail is made in two sections with vertical door stiles rising to the toggle to form the door frame. A sill iron joins the two bottom rail sections. Short toggles or spreaders, located between the door stile and the stiles of the outer frame, should be placed midway between the bottom and main toggle rails. (See Figure 4–11, a.)

For the sake of appearance, openings for doorways usually conform to those of standard door sizes. Door widths range from 2' 6", 2' 8", and 3' 0". Standard heights are 6' 6", 6' 8", and 7' 0". However, the manner in which the door is to be hung will affect the size of the opening built into the flat. To create the illusion that the flat walls have more substance than their actual ¾" thickness, "thicknesses" are added around door and window openings. These thicknesses may be 1" × 6" stock, or wider material, and if the thickness of a castle wall is needed, the thickness may be made of covered frames like flats. A thickness can be attached directly to the back of the opening with screws, or it is sometimes more convenient to construct an insert framework that has the door attached which will slip through the opening in the flat. Where insert thickness units are used, the opening must be 2½" wider and higher than the outside measurement of the thickness unit. If the thickness is attached directly to the flat, the opening for a door that will swing onstage should be ⅜" wider and ½" higher than the actual door. A door that will swing offstage may be hung on the back of the thickness frame with bent strap hinges: The opening can be standard and the door can be constructed to fit the thickness surrounding the opening. (See Figure 4–11, e.)

The door facing trim on a unit where the thickness is built into the flat opening is attached to the flat frame around the opening. On an insert unit, the facing is attached to the thickness frame so that it extends out to cover the crack around the opening. The insert unit can be secured in place by setting screws from the back into the facing, or by using a 6" strap hinge attached to the offstage face of the thickness. (See Figure 4–11, f.)

DOORWAY AND THICKNESS DETAIL

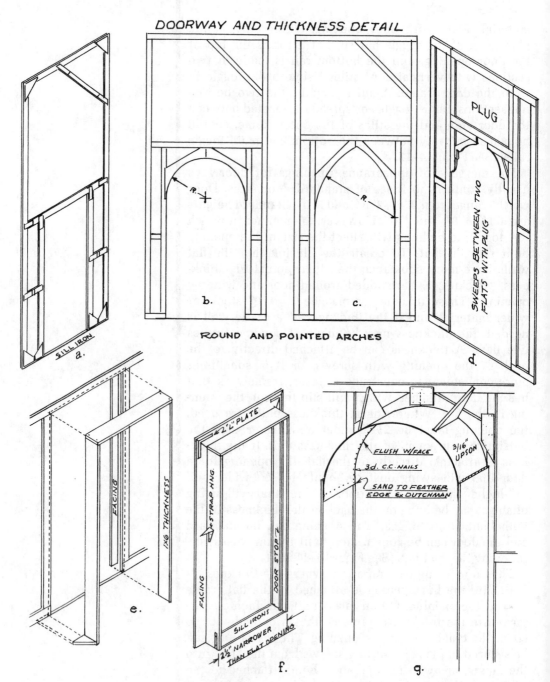

ROUND AND POINTED ARCHES

Figure 4–11. *Door, archway, and thickness detail.*

Door shutters, the actual doors, may be purchased at any lumber supplier, or they can be constructed at considerably less cost. Doors that are to be hung on the back of the thickness so they will swing offstage may be built like small flats. There must be adequate wood to hang the latch or knob and surface plate. The conventional height for a door knob is 36″, although this will vary in some European countries. By fitting the frame with a 1″ × 6″ toggle, instead of 1″ × 3″ centered 36″ off the floor, ample mounting area for the knob and plate is assured. Whereas this type of door would be covered with canvas and painted to represent wood, a paneled door can be made with the framing on the face side with ¾″ pine. This can be done with 1″ × 6″ stock ripped down to 5″. Framing joints may be either miter or butt, but they must fit precisely. The paneling may be ¼″ fir or other plywood, attached to the back of the face frame with ¾″ wood screws, or if the door must be double-faced to swing onstage, paneling may be inserted between the front and back facing. (See Figure 4–12, b.) The addition of narrow molding, such as half-round, cove or quarter-round, will soften the heavy appearance of the door.

Window openings in flats require two toggle rails placed to form the top and bottom of the openings. Side stiles are then fitted between the toggles. The size of window openings is more critical to the general appearance of the setting than doors because the wall mass tends to make window openings appear out of scale, that is, a standard window placed in a flat at the normal distance above the floor will seem too small due to the great mass of wall above it. Most designers plan window openings that appear right, rather than adhere to uniform rules. Window thicknesses can be attached directly or made as insert units which can be slipped into place. (See Figure 4–8.)

The pane dividers—muntins—can be constructed in a variety of ways. If the details of the window will be obscured with glass curtains and draperies, it can be a waste of time to spend hours cutting and fitting wooden muntins that will only be seen as silhouettes. Such shortcuts as stretching ½″ cotton twill tape across the

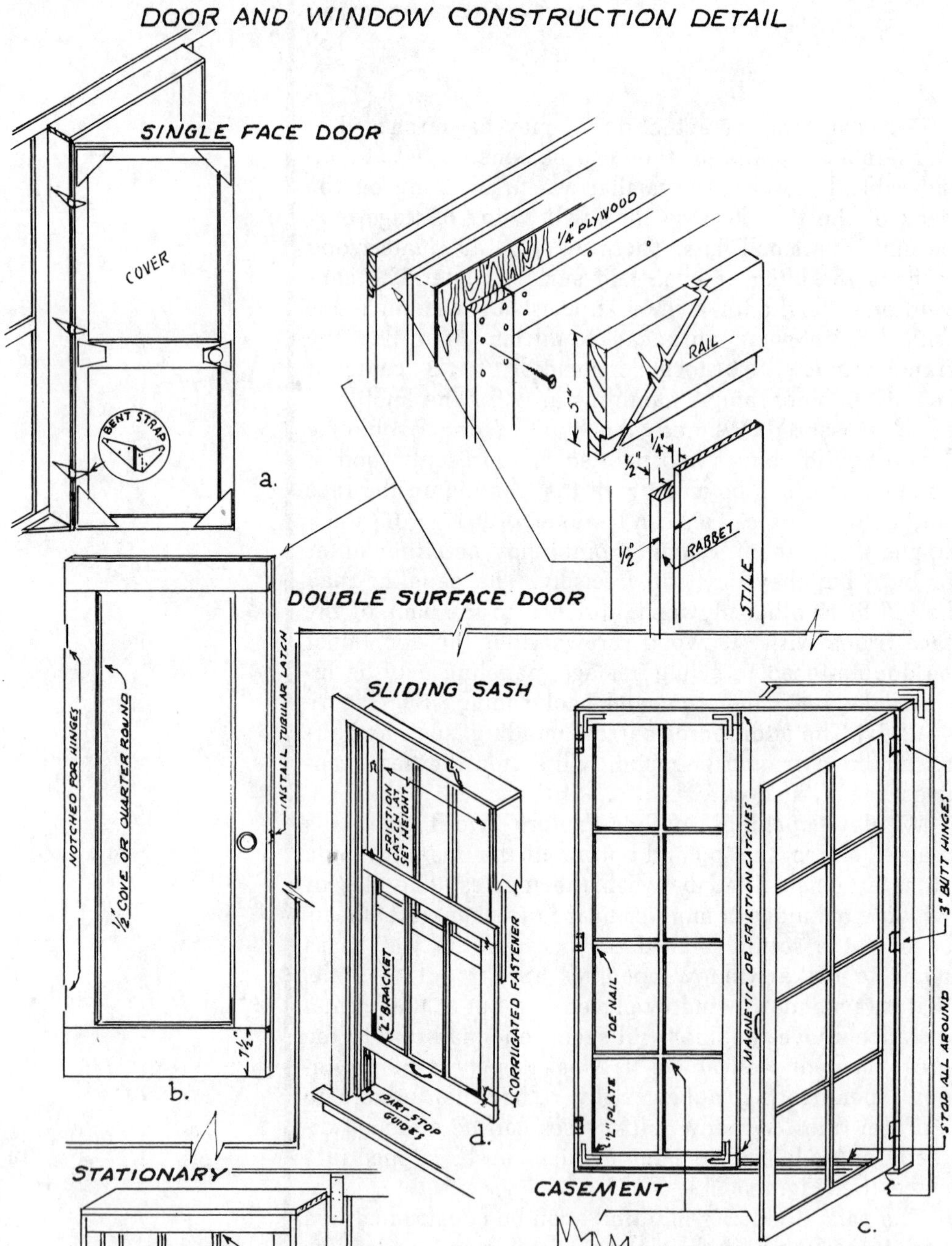

DOOR AND WINDOW CONSTRUCTION DETAIL

SINGLE FACE DOOR

COVER

BENT STRAP

a.

¼" PLYWOOD

RAIL

5"

¼"

½"

RABBET

STILE

DOUBLE SURFACE DOOR

NOTCHED FOR HINGES

½ COVE OR QUARTER ROUND

INSTALL TUBULAR LATCH

1½"

b.

SLIDING SASH

FRICTION CATCH AT SET HEIGHT

L BRACKET

PART-STOP GUIDES

CORRUGATED FASTENER

d.

CASEMENT

TOE NAIL

MAGNETIC OR FRICTION CATCHES

3" BUTT HINGES

STOP ALL AROUND

½"PLATE

c.

STATIONARY

NAIL-BACK OF FRAME

NAIL

TOE NAIL

1 X 2

THICKNESS

e.

Figure 4–12. Door and window construction detail.

back of the thickness frame to give the effect of muntins, or using No. 6 cotton rope dyed black stretched across the frame in diamond patterns to simulate leaded glass, can be effective under these conditions. Wooden muntins made with parting stop, with notched joints where the horizontal and vertical members cross, require time and patience, but their appearance is well worth the effort. (See Figure 4–12, c., d., and e.)

Flats which contain arched or contoured openings are constructed in the same manner as a door or window unit. Laying out the stock and marking the sweep are usually the most complicated problems. Most carpenters lay out and assemble the basic flat frame that will hold the arch first. If it is an arched doorway, the framing is like that of a standard door except the toggle rail is set 3″ higher than the highest point of the arch. Since the sweep of the arch will be tangent to the side stiles of the opening, it is often helpful in laying out the arc to fit a temporary toggle between the inner stiles with the top edge even with the tangent points. It is seldom possible to cut the sweep from a single piece of stock, and it is not economically feasible to use ¾″ plywood for this purpose. A sweep with a 2′ radius can be cut from 1″ × 12″ stock; anything wider will require four sections or more. The width of the remaining stock at the narrowest part of the sweep should never be less than 2″. (See Figure 4–6.)

Free form sweeps are fitted into, or added to the supporting frame in the same way that the arch was assembled. The stock from which the sweep is to be cut can be gridded to correspond to the working drawing, but the simplest method is to enlarge the drawing on wide kraft paper which is easier to grid accurately. If the drawing is laid out in charcoal, corrections are easy to make. After the cartoon is complete, the drawing is laid over a sheet of Celotex and perforated with a tracing wheel, then turned over and sanded lightly to open all of the holes. The pattern is then laid over the stock and the design pounced on with a small pounce bag filled with blue chalk dust. It is a good practice to draw over the pounced outlines with a soft pencil because the vibration occurring during the cutting process often obliterates the chalk detail. (See Figure 4–9.)

Many interior settings call for fireplaces, if not for practical reasons, then because they are decorative. If the stage dressing is to include a pair of andirons or coal grate, the depth of a fireplace unit merely set against the wall of the set will not accommodate these properties. Where realism is essential, a special fireplace flat may be constructed which has an opening that will allow these instruments to extend through the set wall. The construction is similar to a door flat, with the toggle adjusted to the height of the opening, and a second toggle higher up which can be adjusted to provide a hanging batten for pictures, mirrors or sconces. (See Figure 4–13, a.) A three-fold backing screen will be required behind the opening which can be painted to represent blackened bricks or stone.

It is not always practical to construct flats which have unusually wide openings, or wide spans above alcoves or window bays. In these instances, plugs or small flats are used to bridge the opening. These are attached to the adjoining units with hinges or with wooden battens screwed to the backs of the units. Plugs are built like the flats, often of $1'' \times 2''$ stock, and the bottom rail may be arched or straight to conform with other set openings. Plugs should be considered temporary and be constructed with $\frac{3}{4}''$ screws, rather than clout nails. (See Figure 4–11, d.)

Two dimensional groundrows may be constructed of several materials, depending on the size and the structural durability. Groundrows are generally free standing units, therefore the materials must be rigid enough to be self-supporting with a minimum of back framing.

The most durable stock for groundrows is $\frac{1}{4}''$ plywood, but it is also the most expensive, and unless the proper tools are available, delicate cut-out work can be quite difficult. The easiest material to cut is corrugated paper, but it is also very fragile and requires rigid framing for support. Easy Curve ($\frac{1}{8}''$ Upson) or $\frac{1}{4}''$ Upson board is more rigid than corrugated stock, but the density of the laminated paper is difficult to cut with a knife. Nevertheless, Upson board is strong enough for intricate cuts and accepts paint better than either plywood or corrugated paper.

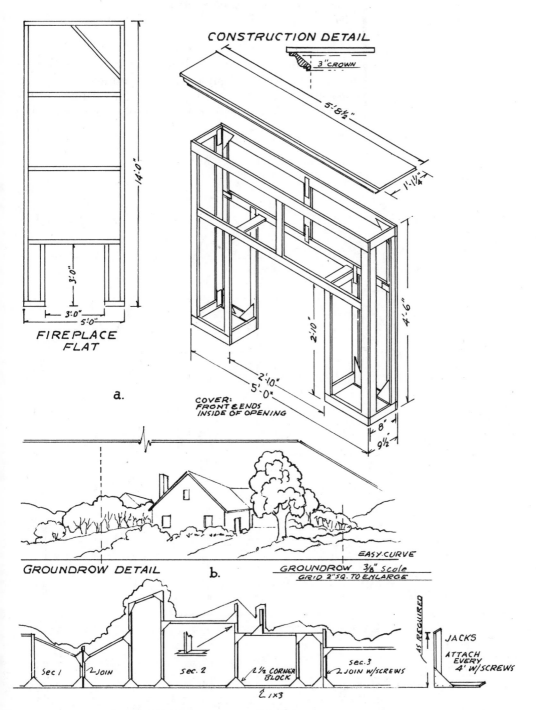

CONSTRUCTION DETAIL

3" CROWN

5'-8½"

1'-1¼"

4'-6"

2'-0"

2'-0"
5'-0"

COVER:
FRONT & ENDS
INSIDE OF OPENING

8"

9½"

a.

FIREPLACE
FLAT

14'-0"

3'-0"

3'-0"

5'-0"

GROUNDROW DETAIL   b.   GROUNDROW ⅜" scale
GRID 2" SQ. TO ENLARGE

EASY CURVE

Sec 1   JOIN   Sec. 2   2½ CORNER
BLOCK   Sec.3
JOIN W/SCREWS

1x3

AS REQUIRED

JACKS

ATTACH
EVERY
4' W/SCREWS

Figure 4–13. *Fireplace and groundrow construction.*

The contour of a groundrow may be cut out either
before or after the design has been painted in, depending somewhat on the cutting tool and the intricacy of the
design. Gentle curves can be cut with a band saw, but

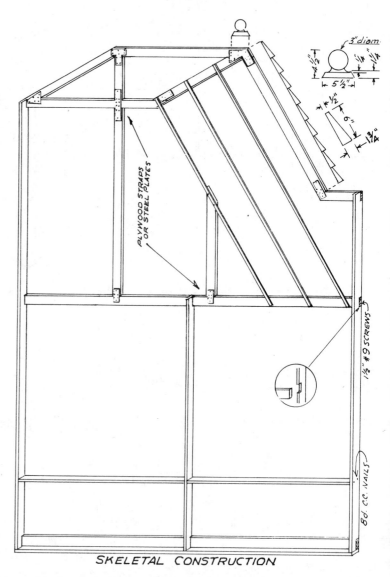

SKELETAL CONSTRUCTION

Figure 4–14. *Skeletal construction.*

where the curves bend in and out, a saber saw can be used effectively if the blades are fine toothed and sharp so the edges will not be splintery or frayed. The most versatile tool for fine cut-out work is the Cut-Awl, because the blade will swivel in any direction with the slightest pressure on the guide knobs.

The backing framework for a groundrow can be similar to flat framing, or framing with the stock assembled on edge. The latter method will give the frame greater rigidity and simplify joining where there are several sections involved. (See Figure 4–13, b.)

Skeletal construction implies open structure that will not be covered, thus the use of corner blocks to reinforce the joints may be visually objectionable. Where a great deal of a skeletal setting may be two-dimensional, it is not unusual to find that the flimsy appearing framework is actually supported by invisible wires from above. By combining edge to face joints with the principles of truss framing and notched and overlapping joints, it is possible to attain an amazing amount of rigidity with very light stock. It is easy to break these fragile structures when raising them off the floor, but with many hands and an assist from flown lines, they can be walked up safely.

Flat joints can be held with plywood straps or with metal corner plates. Corner blocks can be used also if the open portion of the triangle is cut away and the edges tapered back with a wood file. Cement coated nails and wood screws are generally more secure fasteners than ordinary nails for skeletal construction. (See Figure 4–14.)

Two-Dimensional Soft Scenery

When constructing drops and borders, one must consider the characteristics of the effect first. If the unit is to be flat with no draping or fullness, the width must be adequate to extend only far enough into the wings to obscure the ends. If the unit is to hang full with heavy soft folds, additional fabric will be required. When considering a drop that will be made of muslin to be painted, the fabric must be made from several widths sewn together with the seams running horizontally. A drop made of velour must be made with the panels of fabric sewn with the seams running vertically. Thus, the first step is to sew the fabric. Fabric that is to be pleated must have a minimum of 75 percent added to the width, or if fullness is to be formed by gathering the material, a similar allowance should be made. At least 10 percent should be added to the width and height of the material for a painted drop to allow for shrinkage.

Sewing up a large drop is difficult unless there are at least two assistants at hand to manage the material before and after it leaves the machine. Basting the pieces of fabric along the selvedge with small wire staples before sewing saves time and keeps the two pieces of material in line. The stitching should be rather long and at least ½″ from the edge: straight seams will avoid puckers in the finished work. Needless to say, the work area must be spotless.

The top and bottom edges of painted drops may be sandwiched between wooden battens that are made long enough by making lap joints or scarf joints. The bottom batten is laid along a chalk line snapped on the working floor; the fabric is laid along the batten and stapled at six inch intervals, then the second batten is placed on the fabric and fastened with 1½″ wood screws. The same procedure is repeated along the opposite edge. A second method uses a 3″ jute webbing sewn into a hem along the top edge of the drop. Three-eighths inch (#2) grommets are inserted through the webbing at 12″ intervals. The drop is then attached to a batten with No. 6 cotton cords. To weight the bottom, a four-inch hem is sewn into the bottom of the drop so that a pipe or chain may be inserted. (See Figure 4–15.)

Foliage or other forms of contoured border curtains are constructed with battens or webbing and grommets at the top. Bottom hems and weights are usually not required, but large cut-out areas must be backed with a transparent netting cemented over the back of the opening to prevent the fabric from curling or sagging.

As a general rule, seamless scrim drops which are the full width of the stage can be ordered made up ready to hang. These fabrics are so stretchy that it is very difficult to make them so they will hang without wrinkles.

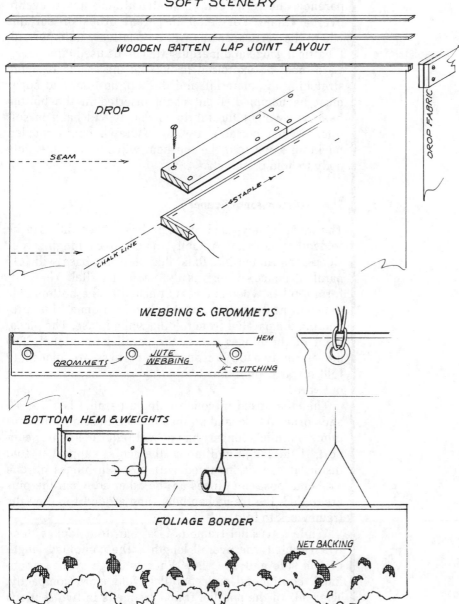

SOFT SCENERY

WOODEN BATTEN LAP JOINT LAYOUT

DROP

DROP FABRIC

SEAM

STAPLE

CHALK LINE

WEBBING & GROMMETS

HEM

GROMMETS

JUTE WEBBING

STITCHING

BOTTOM HEM & WEIGHTS

FOLIAGE BORDER

NET BACKING

Figure 4–15. *Soft scenery construction.*

Bobbinet and sharkstooth scrim fabrics are available, and where only a portion of the setting requires transparency, the scrim can be stretched and tacked evenly over a frame. For semitransparent drops or curtains where the vertical seams will be relatively unimportant, theatrical gauze and marquisette can be used effectively. Care must be exercised in making the seams to avoid stretching the material, and the top, bottom, and edges must be hemmed. Light chain inserted in the bottom hem will weight the fabric so that it will hang in soft folds. When curtains are to be drawn on a traveler, buckram sewn into the top hem will provide adequate body to hold grommets.

Three-Dimensional Scenery

The most widely used platform has a base that can be folded for storage. Actually made up by hinging four sides constructed like flats, this platform base will fold parallel, hence, it derives the name, parallel. The platform top has wooden cleats attached to the bottom side that will fit inside the frame when it is open, thus preventing the parallel from folding while in use. The placement of the hinges makes the parallel functional: The hinges on two of the opposing corners are placed to fold inward; the other two corners are hinged to swing outward.

The stock used in constructing a parallel is $1'' \times 4''$, and corner blocks and straps are used to secure the butt joints. Parallels longer than 3' will require a center support. If the length will allow the center support to fold inside, it can be mounted with fast pin hinges on one side and loose pin hinges on the other so when the pins are pulled, the frame can be swung around to allow the framework to fold.

While a parallel frame is less than four inches thick when folded, the overall length is the combined length of one side and one end. Where storage space is confined, continental style parallels fold more compactly. The ends of the parallel frame are made in two sections and hinged in the center as well as the corners, so they jackknife inside. Separate center support units can be

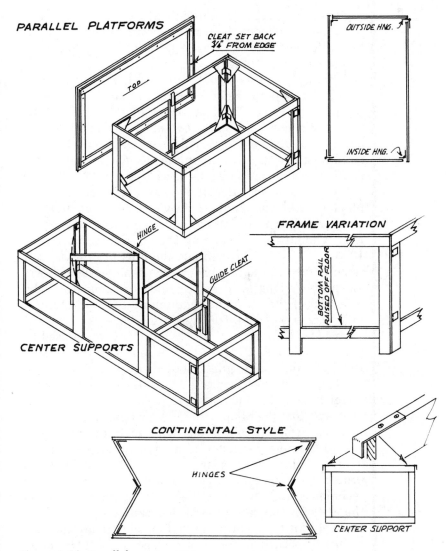

PARALLEL PLATFORMS

CLEAT SET BACK ¾" FROM EDGE

TOP

OUTSIDE HNG.

INSIDE HNG.

HINGE

GUIDE CLEAT

CENTER SUPPORTS

FRAME VARIATION

BOTTOM RAIL RAISED OFF FLOOR

CONTINENTAL STYLE

HINGES

CENTER SUPPORT

Figure 4–16. *Parallel construction.*

set in place by using strap iron hooks that fasten over the sides. (See Figure 4–16.)

It is seldom practical to construct parallel platforms that are less than 12″ high, or higher than four feet, but the shape is not restricted wholly to rectangles: By pulling the pins on one or more joints, most any shape can be collapsed effectively. The major advantage of parallel platforms is that they are lightweight, easy to set up, and remarkably strong.

Greater flexibility can be obtained by constructing simple boxes with sides of 1″ × 6″ stock and either plywood or 1″ × 12″ tops. Boxes of this kind can be used for single step platforms, stacked on top of one another, or raised with wood or metal legs to any desired height. It is a simple matter to mount casters beneath boxes to make wagons. (See Figure 4–17, a.)

Ramps give an interesting transition between one playing level and another provided they are not too steep. A ramp on which an actor can perform comfortably without fear of slipping should rise no more than 18″ to 20″ in 12′ of run. Since the pressure thrust on a ramp is toward the low end, rather than straight down, adequate bracing must be provided to compensate the direction of thrust. If the function of a ramp is to provide access only, the framing of the base can be made from 1″ × 3″ or 1″ × 4″ stock, but if it is to be used as a dance platform, 2″ × 4″ uprights and top rails will be required, and major joints should be bolted with $\frac{5}{16}$″ carriage bolts. (See Figure 4–17, b.) If the ramp is to be wider than 2′, it is advisable to construct a center support, and floor the ramp with ¾″ plywood.

In constructing platforms with pipe or preformed steel, the primary concern is to make joints secure and stable. Welded frames are the best, but without the proper equipment and a skilled welder, other assembly techniques must be used. Black 1½″ pipe threaded on the ends for standard pipe fittings can be assembled effectively for open platforming. Pipe flanges are the best means of securing pipe to the stage or platform floor. These are threaded and the base is predrilled for screws or lag bolts, making attachment to a base or platform top a simple matter. Platform tops should be ¾″ plywood or particle board which has been rimmed with 1″ angle iron to eliminate any springiness. Diagonal bracing may be required to stabilize the structure. Angle iron or ¼″ × 1″ strap iron bracing fastened with ¼″ machine bolts may be used. (See illustration.) If the top

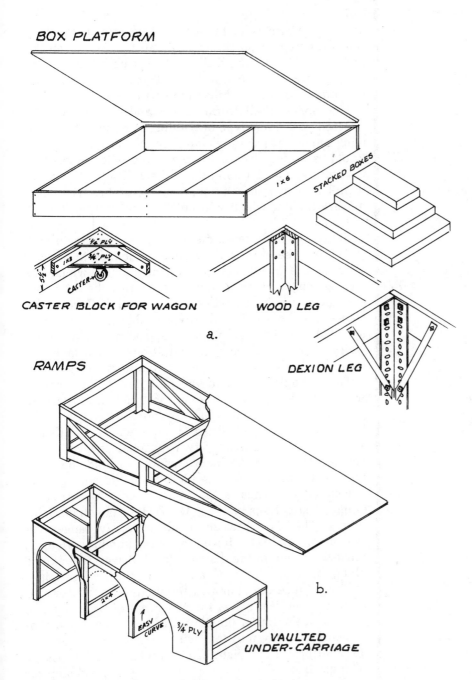

BOX PLATFORM

1 x 6

STACKED BOXES

CASTER BLOCK FOR WAGON

¼" PLY
1 x 8
¾" PLY
5¼
CASTER

WOOD LEG

DEXION LEG

a.

RAMPS

b.

2 x 4

EASY
CURVE

¾" PLY

VAULTED
UNDER-CARRIAGE

Figure 4–17. Box platform and ramp construction.

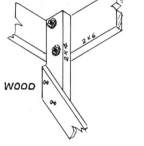

PIPE & FITTINGS

90° ELBOW
NIPPLE
TEE

ANGLE IRON

PARTICLE BRD.
OR
3/4 PLY TOP
CARRIAGE BOLT
MACH. BOLTS

TELSPAR

WOOD

2×4
2×6

Figure 4–18.
Platform legs.

of the platform is to to rest on pipe around the four sides, the angle iron rim can be omitted. To fasten the top in place, holes are drilled through both the top and the pipe for $\frac{5}{16}''$ carriage bolts. This method will hold the top, as well as stabilize the entire unit.

The tops of all platforms, steps, and wagons must be covered with some type of padding to reduce the drumming effect caused by walking on the surface. A layer of old carpeting or carpet pad covered with canvas that is securely tacked around the edges will solve this problem. The canvas can be painted, preferably with latex or casein paint which will not flake off during the run of the show.

Stairways and step units are relatively easy to construct, but there are some simple guidelines to be considered: The tread—that part of the stair on which one steps—must be wide enough for the foot to be set down; and the riser—that portion of the stair between each step—must be a height that will enable the actor to go up or down the stair without appearing awkward. A stairway unit must be solid and strong, but it must not be so heavy that it will be impossible to move.

The strength of a stairway unit lies in the carriage which is the support to which the treads are attached. An onstage stair unit is usually notched out with the tread and riser boards fitted to the notches. An offstage stair unit may be merely two diagonal stringers with cleats attached to the inner surfaces to hold the tread boards. In either case, the plotting of the spacing and placement of treads is the same. Except in extremely cramped situations, a $1'' \times 12''$ ($11\frac{1}{2}''$) is standard for treads. The rise between treads normally ranges between $5\frac{1}{2}''$ and $7''$. With these figures in mind, attention must be turned to the distance the stairway will extend along the floor—*the run*—and the height it will attain—*the rise*. Since the stair will terminate at a platform, it may end one riser below the platform top, or it may end flush with the top of the platform. For example, to construct a stairway unit that will carry us to the top of a $36''$ platform, this height can be divided into six risers, $6''$ high. If we elect to use $1'' \times 12''$ treads, and stop the stair one step below the platform level, there would be five treads at 11½″ wide, so the stair would run 57½″ along the floor. (See Figure 4–19.)

To lay out the carriage board, stock should be selected which will leave a minimum of three inches of space between the deepest part of the notch and the bottom edge of the carriage. Since this is a short run of steps, a 1″ × 10″ will meet this minimum, but if the stair is longer, it would be wiser to use 1″ × 12″ stock. A framing square is used to mark out the carriage for cutting: From the outside corner of the square, measure along the tongue, the height of the riser (a), and along the blade, measure the width of the tread (b); laying the square on the face of the carriage stock so that these two points are exactly even with the edge, mark around the square; move the square over so that the point (b) in the new position meets (a) of the first marking and mark around the outside of the square; repeat until all notches have been marked. (See Figure 4–19, b.) The final step is to shift the square to mark the angles of the carriage that will rest on the floor and the platform, but with these alterations: (1) The height of the bottom riser must be cut ¾″ lower than the others, and (2) the top tread cut must be ¾″ narrower than the other. The reason for this variance is to compensate for stock thickness.

If the width of the stairway unit is to be more than 30″ wide, three identical carriage boards will be required. On narrow units, two carriages will be sufficient. Time will be saved if the two carriages can be cut simultaneously. The boards can be nailed together temporarily during the cutting operation.

The tread boards can now be cut, and the risers will all be 6″ wide except the bottom one, if we use the example cited above. The risers are attached first using 8d box nails. The treads are then laid in place, but treads should be set with 1½″ flat head wood screws rather than nails (nails work up in treads causing the stair to squeak). The carriage should now be turned over and two screws set through the back of each riser into the edge of the treads. Finally, a 1″ × 6″ board should be fitted between the carriage boards to support the top tread. Further details showing method of supporting

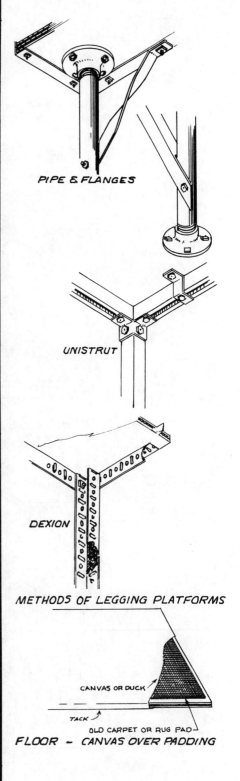

PIPE & FLANGES

UNISTRUT

DEXION

METHODS OF LEGGING PLATFORMS

CANVAS OR DUCK

TACK

OLD CARPET OR RUG PAD

FLOOR – CANVAS OVER PADDING

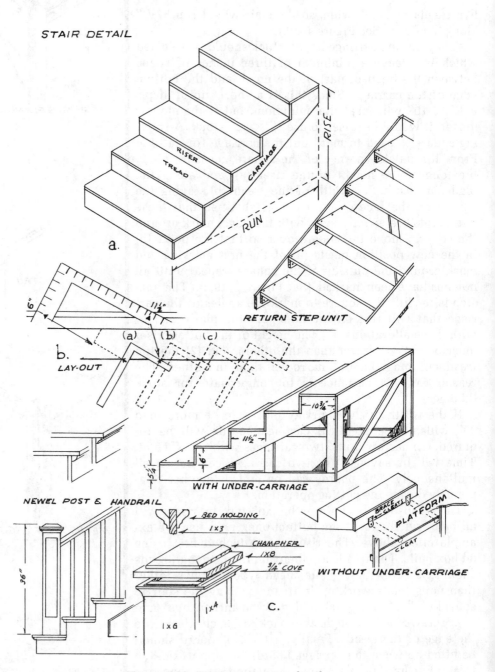

STAIR DETAIL

RISE

RISER

TREAD

CARRIAGE

RUN

a.

6"

11½"

(a) (b) (c)

b.

LAY-OUT

RETURN STEP UNIT

10¾"

11½"

6"

5¼"

WITH UNDER-CARRIAGE

NEWEL POST & HANDRAIL

BED MOLDING

1x3

CHAMPHER

1x8

¾" COVE

36"

1x4

1x6

c.

BRACE CLEATS

PLATFORM

CLEAT

WITHOUT UNDER-CARRIAGE

Figure 4–19. *Stair construction detail.*

and attaching stairs to platform are indicated in the illustrations.

The construction described will produce a step unit where the edges of the treads and risers are flush on the front. If a step with a lip overhanging the riser is needed, the length of the cut for the tread is reduced by ¾″ to 1″. Narrow molding can be added beneath the overhang if desired.

Newel posts, hand railings, and spindles can be constructed which will be practical, as well as authentic in appearance. Fitting spindles so they are evenly spaced and vertical proves to be the most tedious task. Hand rails may be round stock found at the lumber yard, but more interesting shapes can be constructed. (See Figure 4–19, c.) Pipe railings will usually involve bending, which may require a trip to a steam fitter's or plumbing shop where the proper equipment for bending heavy pipe may be obtained.

Stage wagons are basically low platforms mounted on casters. The size and weight which a wagon must carry will affect the construction method and the selection of materials for building. If the wagon is no longer than 8′ × 8′, and the load will consist of only a few units of scenery and a few properties, it may be constructed like the box platforms described earlier. Blocks to hold the casters can be bolted to the underside so that when the wagon is resting on its casters, the bottom edges will clear the floor at least ½″. Casters should be located no further apart than 48″, otherwise the platform will sag under the weight and the floor will tend to spring when walked on. (See Figure 4–17, a.)

Heavier wagons are often required which must be constructed with 2″ × 4″ or 2″ × 6″ understructure. There is, of course, a limit to the size of heavy wagons and the amount of weight that can be moved manually. These factors can be overcome somewhat by using 6″ casters and making up several wagons that will fit together, but which can be moved individually. (See Figure 4–20, a.)

Pariaktoi and jackknife wagons are mounted with a fixed pivot so that they move in a prescribed arc. The shape of the wagon may be round, rectangular, triangu-

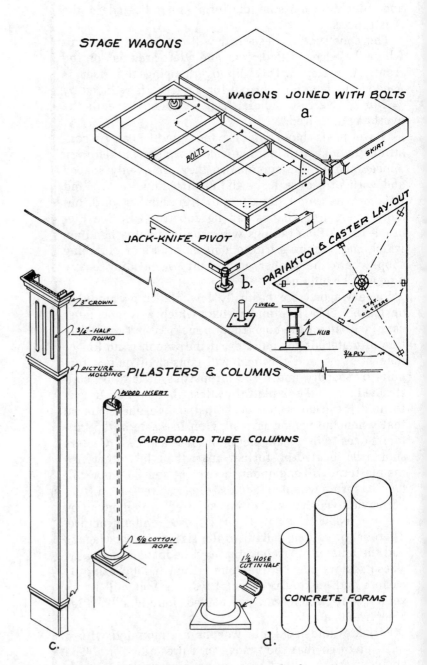

STAGE WAGONS

WAGONS JOINED WITH BOLTS

a.

BOLTS

SKIRT

JACK-KNIFE PIVOT

b.

PARIAKTOI & CASTER LAY-OUT

WELD

STAT. CASTERS

HUB

3/4 PLY

3" CROWN

3/4"-HALF ROUND

PICTURE MOLDING PILASTERS & COLUMNS

WOOD INSERT

CARDBOARD TUBE COLUMNS

5/8 COTTON ROPE

1½ HOSE CUT IN HALF

CONCRETE FORMS

c.

d.

Figure 4–20. *Stage wagons, pilasters, and columns.*

lar, or trapezoidal, but the method of pivoting and the placement of casters is basically the same. The pivot consists of an axle made by using a short length of 1½" pipe mounted in a flange bolted to the floor of the stage. The hub may be a short pipe that will fit over the axle that has been welded to a mounting plate, or if the hub is located on a corner of the wagon, a piece of strap iron ¼" × 1" can be shaped to fit around the axle and bolted to the sides of the wagon. (See Figure 4–20, b.)

The casters used on these types of wagons must be the stationary type, and must be mounted so that the axle of each caster is aligned with the radius point of the wagon's movement. If the wagon is to be rotated several times during the performance, a ¼" plywood track or overlay on which the casters can roll will prevent a depression in the floor of the stage.

Other three-dimensional forms of scenery require special attention. Pilasters, for example, may be constructed of solid wood with a 1" × 8", 1" × 10", or 1" × 12" face and a 1" × 3" or 1" × 4" butted to the edges to set them out from the wall. Various style moldings can be added to the surfaces to give them the proper classical elegance. They may also be constructed like jogs with additional toggles to support the moldings. (See Figure 4–20, c.)

It is seldom practical to attempt to construct round columns that are less than 12" in diameter. Heavy cardboard tubing in sizes up to 4" in diameter can often be obtained from carpeting merchants. By trimming the width of a stock board to slip into the tubing for stability, and covering the outer surface with muslin to obscure the paper wrappings, these make excellent small columns. Where larger sizes may be needed, 6", 8", 10" and 12" heavy cardboard tubing can be ordered from the lumber suppliers. These tubes are also available in diameters up to 36", and in lengths up to 16' long. They are used commercially for concrete forms so the outer surface is waxy and must be covered with muslin before they are painted. (See Figure 4–20, d.)

Tree forms are made by cutting a series of contoured shapes either in full-round or slightly more than half-round. These should be spaced approximately 18" apart

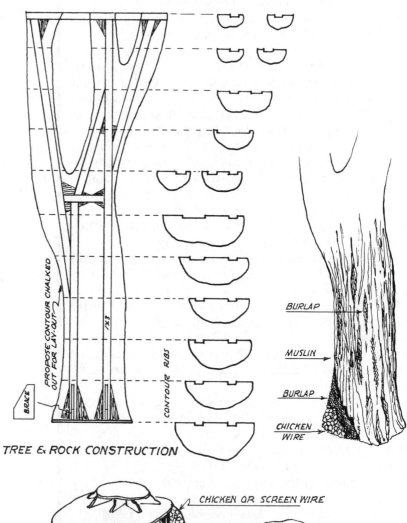

TREE & ROCK CONSTRUCTION

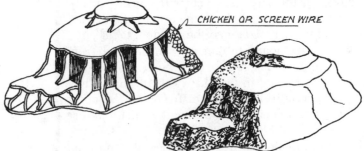

COVER: PAPIER MACHÉ - MUSLIN - CELASTIC OR FIBER GLASS

Figure 4–21. Three-dimensional construction.

and held in position with a rigid inner structure of 1″ × 3″ stock. Chicken or screen wire is then formed over the contour and the outer layer covered with muslin or burlap dipped in scene glue. (See Figure 4–21.)

Rock forms are formed by first building up the basic contours. If the form is to support the weight of actors, a portion of the rock must be like an irregularly shaped platform. The form is filled in with chicken wire then covered with muslin that has been dipped in hot glue, Celastic, or fiber glass, depending on the degree of permanence desired. Where surface hardness is not required, the form may be covered with burlap then covered with a layer of Poly-foam. Poly-foam is obtainable in kits consisting of two parts that must be mixed together. A two quart mixture will expand to approximately 3 cubic feet and may be sprayed or troweled over the surface.

Styrofoam is often used for small architectural details such as decorative cornices and balusters. Styrofoam is easily contoured with a band saw. Surface forming may be done with a knife, a fine toothed rasp, or sandpaper. A contour template will aid in shaping the form uniformly. Where intricate surface shapes may be desired, the hot wire method of cutting styrofoam is often used. This involves the construction of a simple device to hold a heavy piece of resistance wire that is contoured to the desired configuration. The wire is connected through a voltage regulator to a 120 v. current so the wire temperature can be maintained at around 180° F. This should not be attempted without first consulting an electrician to determine the proper size and length of resistance wire and the type regulator required. As the styrofoam is passed across the hot wire, the wire melts a cut in the material.

Covering Scenery

The materials required for covering flat scenery are: the fabric, usually No. 128 unbleached muslin because it is economical and heavy enough to be serviceable; a pail of hot scene glue and a glue brush; a staple tacker with ⅜″ staples, or #8 carpet tacks; a utility knife with a sharp blade and three or four scrap pieces of 1" × 3" × 5" long. A hammer may be needed to drive staples down tightly against the fabric.

When covering flats, the frame should be laid face up across a pair of sawhorses and inspected carefully to be sure that there are no unclinched nail points. A length of muslin that is two inches longer than the flat frame should be torn from the bolt and laid over the frame with one selvedge extending an inch over one of the stiles; the excess material on the opposite side will be trimmed off later. With the fabric in this position, a staple or tack is placed in the four inside corners of the frame to hold the fabric in place. In doing this, one should only draw the fabric tight enough to pull out the deep sag. The excess can then be torn off, leaving at least an inch outside the frame. All four edges of the fabric are then folded back to expose the stiles and rails of the frame.

Hot scene glue is now applied generously to one of the rails and the fabric drawn over it, pressing it down firmly so the glue will work into the weave of the material. The excess material provides a handhold to pull gently to remove wrinkles or puckers. This operation is repeated on the opposite rail, stretching the fabric just enough to draw out any large wrinkles. The stiles can now be glued and the fabric drawn over them. A swipe of extra glue may be needed at the corners. Using the wood blocks, all glued surfaces should now be rubbed to press the fibers well into the glue.

Though there are differing opinions regarding the placement of tacks to reinforce the glued surfaces of the flat cover, it is recommended here that tacks or staples should be placed six inches apart and $\frac{3}{8}"$ from the inner edges of the frame around the entire perimeter. In this way, if the cover should pull loose when it is sized, additional glue can be applied without losing the shrinkage. It is also a good practice to tack the outer corners. If glue fails to hold it is because the glue has cooled.

Trimming away the excess fabric should be done before the glue has set up. The material is trimmed away about $\frac{3}{16}"$ back on the face of the frame. By grasping the knife so the thumb rests on the edge as a guide, one

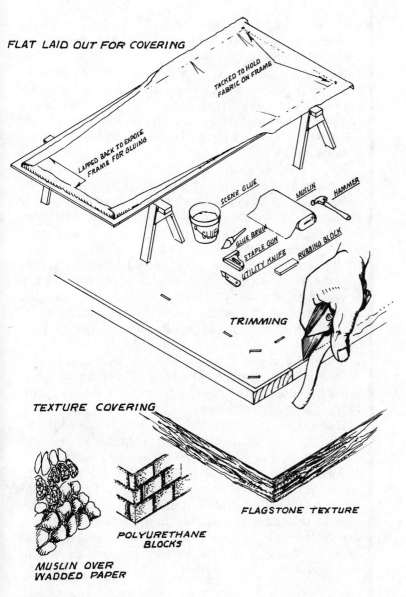

FLAT LAID OUT FOR COVERING

TACKED TO HOLD
FABRIC ON FRAME

LAPPED BACK TO EXPOSE
FRAME FOR GLUING

SCENE GLUE

MUSLIN   HAMMER

GLUE

GLUE BRUSH

STAPLE GUN

UTILITY KNIFE   RUBBING BLOCK

TRIMMING

TEXTURE COVERING

FLAGSTONE TEXTURE

POLYURETHANE
BLOCKS

MUSLIN OVER
WADDED PAPER

Figure 4–22. Covering scenery.

can trim rapidly. The knife blade must be very sharp to cut the fabric rather than to drag it loose from the soft glue. Any dribbles of glue on the fabric or frame should be sponged away, then the flat should be set aside to allow the glue to dry thoroughly. These same covering procedures apply generally to all open framework scenic units. (See Figure 4–22.)

It is often necessary to cover solid wood surfaces, either to provide a base texture that matches surrounding fabric covered surfaces, or to cover imperfection in the wood surface. In these situations, scene glue is applied to the wood and the muslin smoothed over the surface.

Steps, platforms, and wall surfaces are often covered to simulate stone or heavy timbering. This can be accomplished in various ways. Heavy flagstone can be simulated by covering the face of steps or platforms with strips of muslin 18″ to 24″ wide which are dipped in scene glue, squeezed out, and applied to the surface of the unit in irregular wrinkles and strata to appear like the stone texture. When the glued muslin dries, it is very hard and ready for painting. Tree bark and other heavy textures can be created in this manner. Strips of burlap and coarse netting can be glued to flat surfaces to make other textures. The effect of field stone can be achieved by wadding newspaper and covering it with dipped muslin; regular cut quarry stone can be simulated by adhering 1″ thick polyurethane shapes to the face of flats with latex cement.

If structural framing is to be covered with dyed fabric, rather than material to be painted, the fabric is dyed before it is attached to the framework. Since fabric treated in this manner will transmit light, the framework may be joined on edge rather than flat, with the fabric attached to the back of the frame. The dyeing preshrinks the material so it must be stretched very tightly and fastened to the frame with staples or tacks, instead of glue. Gluing is avoided because any smears of glue will render the fabric opaque.

ASSEMBLING SCENERY

It was noted earlier that the elevation drawings should indicate the way in which set pieces are to be joined. Some units may be lashed together, others may be hinged; several flats may be joined by cleats or battens on the back to make up larger units, and some corners may be formed by setting screws through the face of one unit into the edge of the next.

Methods of Assembling

A set made up of 15 or more flats which were all joined with lash lines would be extremely flimsy and unstable. At the same time, if the set has to be shifted during the performance, lashing can be the easiest means of separating the units, so lashing is used to join segments of scenery which can be moved in units. For example, a right stage wall unit is usually lashed to a fixed two-dimensional tormentor at the downstage end, and the upstage end is lashed to the back wall unit. If the back wall contains a portion which sets back, it may be convenient to divide the wall into three segments with the setback lashed to the two flanking segments.

It is possible for two stagehands, with a little practice, to move a single wall segment that is 10' to 12' long without other assistance. If we assume the right stage wall is flat and made up by joining three 4' 0" flats, this segment may be assembled by laying the flats face down, making certain that the bottom rails are all even. A 1" × 3" batten, 12' long, is laid over the top and bottom rails and fastened down with 1½" screws: Two screws should be placed on either side of each joint and at the ends of the batten. A screw should also be set into the center of each rail, but since the batten rests on the corner blocks, a scrap of ¼" plywood should be inserted beneath the screw to prevent bowing the rails. A third batten should be fastened in the same manner along the toggle rails. This is known as battened assembly. (See Figure 4–23.)

Using this same wall as an example, it is sometimes more convenient to handle a single wall segment of this size if it can be assembled more compactly. This can be accomplished in two ways: (1) By battening two of the flats together and attaching the third with back flap hinges on the front, the overall size of the segment when folded is reduced to 8'; or (2) all three flats can be

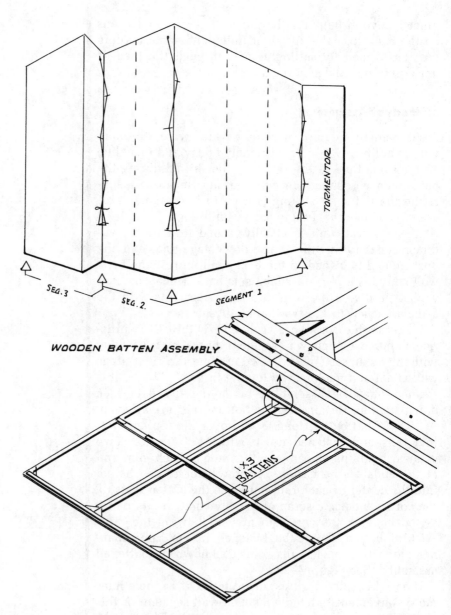

Figure 4–23. *Batten assembly.*

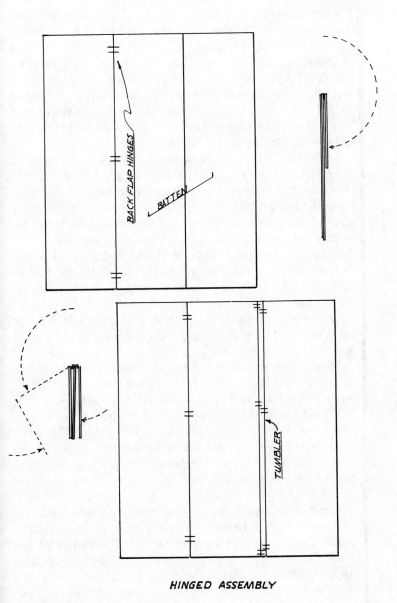

HINGED ASSEMBLY

Figure 4–24. Hinge assembly.

hinged together so that the side units fold over the center. The top flat will not fold over completely, however, because of the thickness of the flat beneath it. This problem can be overcome by inserting a 1" × 3" running the full height between two of the flats. This is hinged with back flap hinges to both flats, thus creating a spacer called a *tumbler*, which will allow the three flats to fold flat one on the other. These methods of assembly are often referred to as book folds and threefold units.

Ordinarily, three 2" back flap hinges are sufficient to hinge flats together, unless the stiles are badly warped. The top and bottom hinges should be located no more than 9" away from the ends of the flats, and the third should be in the middle. The stiles should be fitted together snugly, applying some pressure if necessary. The hinges are fastened with ¾" No. 9 flat head wood screws. Care should be exercised to align the hinges with the pins parallel to, and directly over the joint between the two flats. (See Figure 4–24.) Screws are easier to start accurately if a shallow hole is predrilled for starting the screw threads. An 8d nail may also be used to form a starting hole.

Jogged corners and corners that must be sturdy are often assembled with screws rather than stage hardware. The two units to be joined are fastened while standing, with the upstage unit butted into the downstage flat so the crack between will not face the audience. Four 1½" screws are required, one near the top and bottom, the other two evenly spaced in between. Such joints may be noted on the elevation as butt screw joints. (See Figure 4–25, a.)

Long wall segments, even though they are made up of flats battened together, require bracing for stability. Stage braces may be used at or near the center of the wall. Brace cleats are mounted on the toggle rail or stiles approximately 8' above the floor. Brace jacks that can be constructed in the shops are also efficient. These are attached to the set wall with loose pin hinges. (See Figure 4–25, b.)

Walls that have been hinged tend to bend at the hinges unless a stiffener batten is placed across the span of flats to add rigidity. If the set is to be shifted, it must be

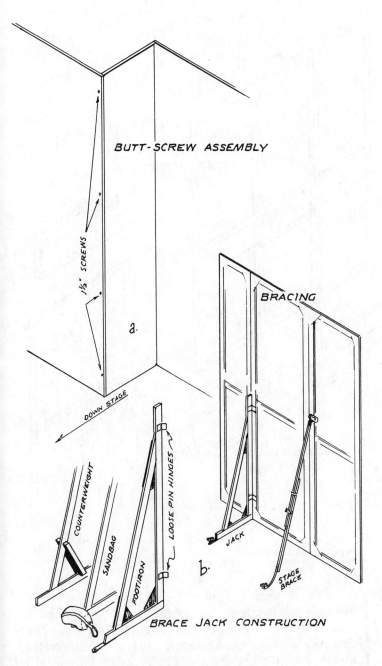

BUTT-SCREW ASSEMBLY

1½" SCREWS

a.

DOWN STAGE

BRACING

COUNTERWEIGHT

SANDBAG

FOOTIRON

LOOSE PIN HINGES

JACK

STAGE BRACE

b.

BRACE JACK CONSTRUCTION

Figure 4–25. Screw assembly and bracing.

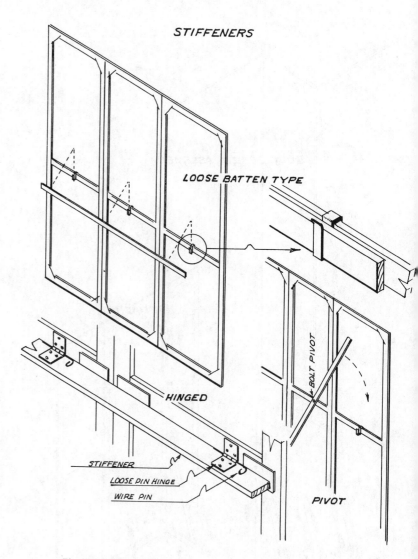

STIFFENERS

LOOSE BATTEN TYPE

HINGED

BOLT PIVOT

STIFFENER

LOOSE PIN HINGE

WIRE PIN

PIVOT

Figure 4–26. *Stiffeners.*

possible to remove the stiffener quickly, so several methods of attaching them are used. One method involves the use of keeper hooks attached to a long batten that hooks over the toggle rails; a second method attaches a batten with loose pin back flap hinges to the toggle rails (the pins are pulled when striking the set piece); a third method fastens a batten to the stile of one of the flats with a carriage bolt so the batten can be turned horizontally to engage in keeper hooks. (See Figure 4–26.)

It should be noted that nails are never used to join flats or attach stiffeners. Nails will not hold unless they are clinched, making it difficult to dismantle the units, as well as inflicting damage to the set pieces.

SHIFTING AND FLYING SCENERY

Directors, designers, and technicians often spend as much time planning the shift plot for a large multiscene production as they do on the actual preparation of the show. Scenery and properties must be set on the stage, as well as struck from it. This must be done quickly and quietly, everything must be in precisely the right place, and there must be no confusion about where each piece is to be stored offstage. This is only possible if every technician is fully alert and cognizant of the entire shifting operation.

Methods of Shifting Scenery

Running a unit of scenery involves more skill than merely grabbing hold of it and shoving it around. Running a single flat requires less strength than balancing skill. Most flats are 12′ to 16′ high, so they have a great tendency to topple unless they are held nearly vertical at all times. Also, flats should be pulled rather than pushed. This can be done by grasping the stile with one hand around 30″ above the floor, with the other hand as high on the stile as comfortably possible to hold the flat upright. The leading edge is raised an inch or two off the floor so that the opposite end of the bottom rail slides on the floor. If the unit of scenery is made up of two or more flats, two or more stagehands will be needed to shift the scenery. Stagehands should always wear white cotton gloves when shifting painted scenery to avoid leaving finger smudges on the painted surfaces. (See Figure 4–27, a.)

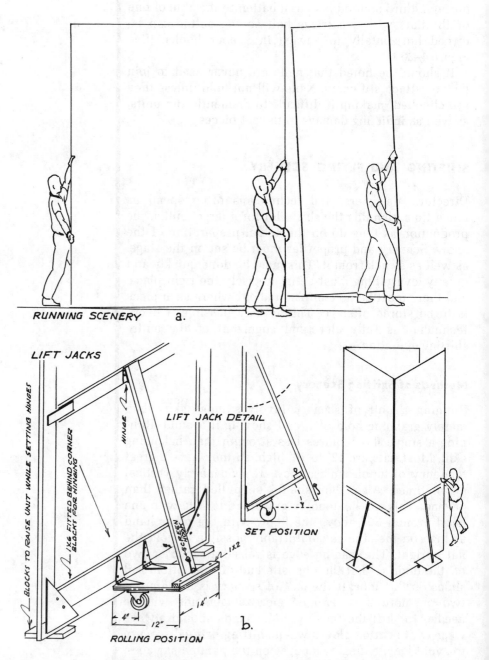

RUNNING SCENERY   a.

LIFT JACKS

LIFT JACK DETAIL

BLOCKS TO RAISE UNIT WHILE SETTING HINGES

1X6 FITTED BEHIND CORNER BLOCKS FOR HINGING

HINGE

SCREEN

1X2

SET POSITION

ROLLING POSITION

4"   12"   14"

b.

Figure 4–27. *Running and shifting scenery.*

Large segments of scenery which may contain door or window units become quite heavy. There are at least three techniques for shifting heavy units that cannot be run effectively. If the segment can be assembled with hinges so that it will fold, even part way so it will stand by itself, simple *lift jacks* that will raise the unit off the floor onto casters make it possible to roll the unit. These jacks are hinged to the back of the flats near the base. The casters are mounted on a ¾″ plywood platform in such a way as to act as a fulcrum for lifting the flat. A hinged brace holds the platform in position while shifting, and allows the flats to sit on the floor when not engaged. (See Figure 4–27, b.)

A second method uses a constructed *tilt jack*. and is often used where the wall segment is battened solidly. The tilt jack is a triangular unit mounted with casters which is bolted to the back of the set piece so that when the unit is tilted back the casters come to rest on the floor; thus the unit is rolled while tilting back. (See Figure 4–28, a.)

The third method involves the use of a rolling scaffold to which the set piece is bolted permanently. When the segment is in position, it remains ½″ to ¾″ off the floor. This type of shifting device is called an *outrigger* and is often used for shifting groundrows and partial three-dimensional units.

Stage wagons are the most efficient shifting devices, provided they are not so heavy that they are hard to start in motion. All scenery and properties can be moved intact so when the wagon is in set position, the scene can begin. There are problems, however. This equipment takes up a great deal of space in the wings; it is often difficult to lock in position so that it will not move when the actors step on it; and both swivel and stationary casters tend to be erratic and difficult to guide on and offstage in a prescribed path.

Scenery mounted on wagons will seldom withstand the pressure required to pull or push the wagon. Ring plates or heavy eye bolts mounted on the base of the wagon into which pull ropes or pull rods can be hooked, provide the best means of guiding it. (See Figure 4–28, b.) Where the casters are beneath the wagon, it is often im-

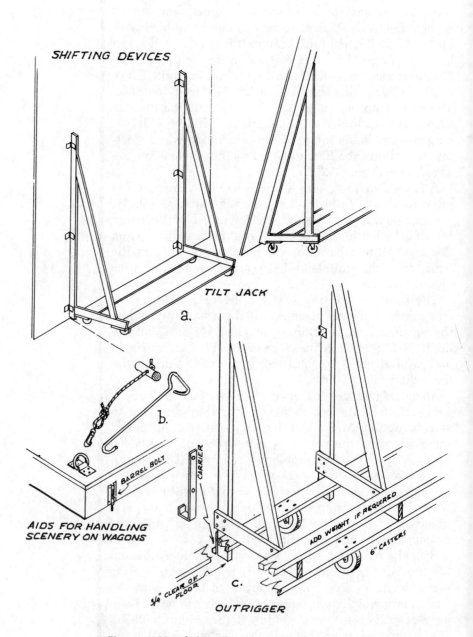

SHIFTING DEVICES

TILT JACK

a.

b.

AIDS FOR HANDLING
SCENERY ON WAGONS

BARREL BOLT

CARRIER

ADD WEIGHT IF REQUIRED

6" CASTERS

3/4" CLEAR OF FLOOR

c.

OUTRIGGER

Figure 4–28. Shifting devices.

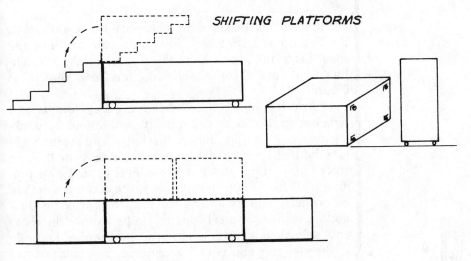

Figure 4–29. *Moving platforms on casters.*

possible to set the brake on locking casters. Mounting barrel bolts on the wagon skirt so that the bolt can be slid into a hole in the stage floor is one of the best methods of locking the wagon in place. A plunger rod that extends through the floor of the wagon to operate the caster brake can be rigged, but the plunger must remain above the level of the floor, which is seldom practical.

Shifting heavy platform and step units can be accomplished by mounting casters on the upstage side rather than the bottom. To shift the unit, it is tilted over on the casters. Platforms may have casters on the bottom too, and step units or other adjoining platforms aid in holding them stationary. Step units with rolling platforms are often constructed with the top tread flush with the top of the platform, in which case the step unit can be hinged to the platform top so it can be swung over on the platform, thus making it possible to move both units. (See Figure 4–29.)

Rigging Scenery to Fly

Every stage technician should be able to recognize and tie basic rigging knots and know which will be the most

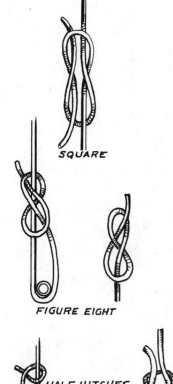

SQUARE

FIGURE EIGHT

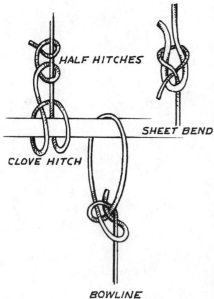

HALF HITCHES

SHEET BEND

CLOVE HITCH

BOWLINE

Figure 4–30.
Common rigging knots.

effective for particular jobs. These are the square knot, the figure eight knot, the clove hitch, the bowline, the sheet bend, the prusik knot, the stopper hitch, the lashline knot, the sheep shank, and the bow knot. (See Figure 4–30.)

The square knot is used when tying a cyclorama to a pipe batten. It can be tied quickly, and untied by yanking one end sharply across the knot. The figure eight may be tied in the end of a lashline to prevent the line from pulling through the lashline eye, or tied as a running knot (slip knot) that is less apt to come loose than an ordinary slip knot. The clove hitch is used to tie a cotton, manila, or steel rope to a pipe batten; the loose end is finished off with a half hitch or wrapped securely to the standing end with friction tape. The loose end of steel rope may be secured with a cable clamp. The bowline is a nonslip knot tied to form a loop and is used for tying cotton or manila lines to pipe battens. The sheet bend is like the bowline except it is used when tying two lines together of unequal size. Both the prusik and stopper hitch are used when attaching security lines or weight carrying lines to another. The prusik uses a doubled line which makes it possible to add a sandbag to counterweight an unbalanced load. The stopper hitch is used to attach a safety line to a load bearing line during flying operations. The lashline knot is used when lashing scenery because the knot can be released by pulling the end of the rope. The sheep shank is used to shorten a rope and is particularly useful to shorten a lashline so it will not drag on the floor during shifts. The bow knot is used when tying tie-lines at the top of a border or leg to a pipe batten.

The hardware used for flying scenery must be attached to the unit where the weight will be distributed equally and where joints will not be separated by the weight of the unit when it is raised. Relatively light units of scenery may be raised from the top, but heavier units can be lifted more safely if the stress is exerted near the base. Standard hanger irons should be bolted to the stiles so that there will be no pressure on the top rails. The hanger irons may be located just below the corner block, or laid over the block. Since the lower end of the hanger will extend below the corner block, a plywood strap should be tacked to the stile so the iron will rest flat and the bolts can be drawn tightly. 1½″ × ¼″ stove bolts or carriage bolts should be used for fasteners.

Bottom hanger irons hook beneath the bottom rail and must be fastened with bolts. If the rigging lines are to remain attached, a standard hanger iron should also be mounted at the top of the unit so the fly-line can be run through the ring to hold the unit upright. However, if the fly-line is to be removed while the set piece is on the floor, a large hook formed from ¼″ × 1″ strap iron must be mounted on the top rail 6″ to the right or left of vertical so that tension will keep the line within the hook until it is slackened. (See Figure 4–31, a.)

Three methods are used for attaching fly-lines to wooden battens for soft drops. The simplest is to tie the wood batten directly to a pipe batten which will hold the drop straight and in trim. This can be done with short lengths of No. 12 (⅜″) cotton sash rope inserted through a series of ½″ holes spaced approximately six feet apart along the batten and tied around the pipe with square knots. Where the drop batten is flown lower than the pipe batten, bridle ropes of ⅜″ manila rope will prevent the flexible wood batten from sagging. Bridle ropes should be precut long enough so the point at the top of the triangle is approximately 4′ above the batten after they are tied in place. These ropes can be wrapped around the batten by cutting a small hole in the drop fabric, or put through holes in the batten, as described above, and tied with two half hitches. Short lines are tied with clove hitches to the pipe batten and the other end with a bowline so the loop passes around the bridle line. The third method uses drop holders which may be used with bridle lines or with trim chains. They are quick and easy to install and eliminate the need for drilling holes in the battens, or making holes in the drop. (See Figure 4–31, b.)

One of the complications of handling flown scenery is to make certain that each time the unit is lowered, it will be in precisely the same trim position. This is particularly difficult in theatres that still have hemp rig-

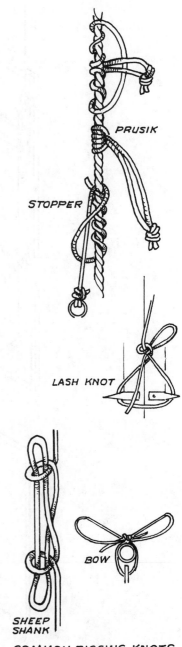

PRUSIK

STOPPER

LASH KNOT

BOW

SHEEP SHANK

COMMON RIGGING KNOTS

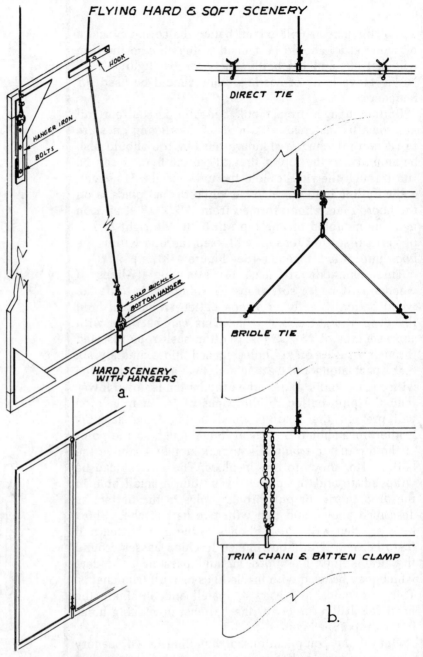

FLYING HARD & SOFT SCENERY

HOOK

HANGER IRON

BOLTS

SNAP BUCKLE

BOTTOM HANGER

HARD SCENERY
WITH HANGERS

a.

DIRECT TIE

BRIDLE TIE

TRIM CHAIN & BATTEN CLAMP

b.

Figure 4–31.
Rigging hard and soft scenery.

ging where three or more individual lines control each flown unit. Rope sets can be clamped together using a device called a *clew* which prevents the lines from slipping out of trim. A heavy cotton cord inserted in the lay of the handline at the point where the line passes the lock rail or pin rail may also be used as an effective means of marking the trim level without hampering the rope's passing through a pulley. An endless trim clamp is another device that may be attached to individual lines. Often called a *knuckle buster,* this device is clamped around the handline just above the lock on the lock rail of a counterweight system when the flown piece is in its low position. (See Figure 4–32.)

In conclusion, the primary concern when building, assembling, and handling scenery must be twofold: (1) structurally, all units must be well built and technically functional; and (2) even though speed is generally a requirement when shifting and flying scenery, the safety of the actor and of those who will be handling the shift must have precedence.

A limited budget may make it necessary to rely entirely on materials that are salvaged and improvised hardware, but this should not affect the way in which these materials are used, or the effectiveness of the scenery that results.

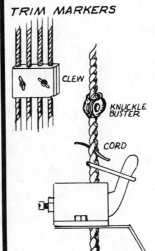

TRIM MARKERS

CLEW

KNUCKLE BUSTER

CORD

Figure 4–32.
Trim marking devices.

SUGGESTED READINGS

Burris-Meyer, Harold and Cole, Edward. *Scenery for the Theatre.* Boston: Little, Brown, 1972.

Cornberg, Sol and Gebauer, Emanuel L. *A Stage Crew Handbook,* rev. ed. New York: Harper & Row, 1957.

Gillette, A. S. *Stage Scenery: Its Construction and Rigging,* 2nd ed. New York: Harper & Row, 1972.

Parker, W. Oren and Smith, Harvey K. *Scene Design and Stage Lighting.* New York: Holt, Rinehart and Winston, 1963.

Ramsey, Charles G. and Sleeper, Harold R. *Architectural Graphic Standards,* 5th ed. New York: Wiley, 1956.

Selden, Samuel and Rezzuto, Tom. *Essentials of Stage Scenery.* New York: Appleton-Century-Crofts, 1972.

Selden, Samuel and Sellman, Hunton. *Stage Scenery and Lighting.* Englewood Cliffs, N.J.: Prentice-Hall, 1959.

PAINTING THE SET AND PREPARING SCENERY FOR PAINTING

After all the scenery for a production has been built and covered and the larger segments assembled, it is often helpful if the set pieces can be set in position or joined so that a final inspection of fitted parts can be made before the painting starts. There is a great advantage in having an offstage area to do this, but if painting must be done on the stage, there are some preparatory steps that must be done first: All stage curtains must be flown out or drawn back and covered with shrouds of clean muslin; the stage carpenter and designer should supervise the marking of the exact position of the set pieces on the floor with chalk or masking tape; and a large polyethylene drop cloth should be laid over the floor area where work is to be done. The remaining steps in completing the setting: pasting, sizing, and painting are all messy activities.

PREPARING SCENERY FOR PAINTING

Flameproofing

While some theatres may not be affected by strict fire regulations, it is a good practice for every theatre to treat combustible articles to retard fire. No flammable material can be made 100 percent fireproof, but material treated with a solution that will only char, rather than flame up when held to a lighted match is usually acceptable to fire inspectors. Flameproofing solution can be purchased from scenic suppliers, or one can prepare a solution by combining 1 lb of sal ammoniac, 1 lb of borax and 3 quarts of water. These ingredients can be obtained from chemical suppliers and the grocers. A few ounces of acetic acid added to this solution will counteract its corrosive effect on metals.

Flameproofing is usually applied to flats as soon as the glue holding the cover is thoroughly dry. Units should be sprayed or brushed on both sides, including the framing, and allowed to dry thoroughly. If used scenery has been washed, it will be necessary to flameproof these pieces also.

Dutchman

A dutchman is a term used to describe a strip of cloth

pasted over the exposed joint between flats which have been battened or hinged together. These strips serve to prevent offstage light from filtering through, as well as to cover the joint so the wall or platform appears to be continuous. It is obvious that it would not be practical to dutchman two units that are hinged or lashed on the back, but where the hinges are on the front, the strip is pasted over the hinges. (See illustration.)

The paste for applying dutchman, the prepartion of which was given in Chapter 3, p. 88, should be heated and remain hot during the application. If the units have been covered with new fabric, the dutchman strips should be torn from new fabric also; if the cover is from salvaged material, similar fabric should be used for dutchman. Strips should be torn 5″ wide in full length strips if possible. Using a wide board or heavy cardboard five or six feet long as a pasting pallet, one can brush the hot dutchman paste onto the back of the strip, working from the center to the outside edges. Starting at the top of the joint, center the strip in position over the crack and press the edges out smooth. A staple driven at the top edge on either side of the joint will aid in holding the strip while you work down the length of the joint. The strip should be stretched downward to remove any wrinkles, and the edges worked out so they do not curl under. After the strip is applied, it should be wiped down thoroughly with a clean, damp sponge to remove any excess paste. The fabric should be trimmed off at the bottom with a sharp knife. The dutchman must dry completely before any further work can be done. Where the dutchman is applied over hinges, a staple just above and below each leaf of the hinges will prevent any likelihood of the strip buckling forward when the unit of scenery is folded. A patch of unpasted material laid over each hinge will prevent the hinges from rusting and clogging the slots of the screw heads.

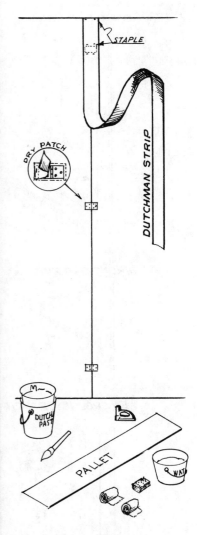

DUTCHMAN OVER JOINTS

Patching

Scenery that is handled carefully should rarely have tears or holes in the covering, but some are inevitable where pictures must be hung, or where special assembly

BACK PATCHING

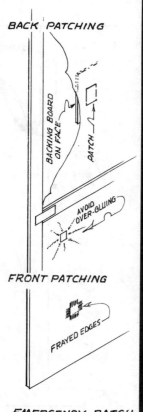

FRONT PATCHING

EMERGENCY PATCH

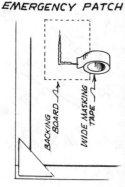

requires the insertion of screws through the fabric. These small holes seem insignificant until it is necessary to have backing lights behind the setting. (See illustration.)

Patches may be added to the back side with small squares of fabric. These are applied by placing a small dab of scene glue on the patch, and while someone holds a flat board over the front side of the hole, the patch is smoothed over the hole from the back. Care must be exercised to avoid using too much glue or spreading it over the surrounding surface because it will cause puckers in the covering.

Where it may be necessary to apply a patch to the front surface, the edges of the patch can be feathered by fraying out the threads around the edges of the patch. Gluing should be light and any excess sponged off, wiping away from the center of the patch to fan out the frayed edges.

An accident during performance may result in a torn covering. It is risky to attempt a permanent patch which most likely would stain the painted surface. If the tear can be closed, wide masking tape applied to the back will hold the material in place temporarily. The bulge around the tear can be removed by spattering the back of the spot lightly with clear water. This will reshrink the material, and, hopefully, the mend will not be noticed.

Sizing or Priming

Most scenery, particularly hard scenery, will take the base paint coat better if the surface has been sized first to shrink and fill the pores of the fabric. Sizing is a diluted glue solution prepared by mixing hot animal glue and water in proportions of 16 parts water to one part glue. Approximately one gallon of Danish whiting per 16-quart pail is stirred into this solution which serves as a filler. This mixture will be very thin and requires no further preparation. It is applied by painting it on with a large priming brush, covering all fabric covered surfaces. The whiting is nearly transparent, so some painters add a handful of yellow ochre pigment to tint the solution to avoid missing spots in the coverage. When the size coating is completely dry, the fabric will be drawn taut. One should avoid a stronger glue solution because it is apt to shrink the fabric so tightly that the frame will warp, or the cover pull loose from the frame.

If the finished painting is to be done with dyes, rather than opaque scene paint, a mixture of 8 ounces of cooked laundry starch in a 16-quart pail of water will shrink the fabric without filling or glazing the surface. Prepared wall sizing can be purchased from paint stores in gallon cans. This can be diluted 50 percent or more, but it is more expensive than sizing prepared in the shop. After the prime coat has been completely dried, the base coat of paint can be prepared.

PAINTS, PIGMENTS, AND DYES

There are three kinds of opaque water base paints suitable for painting scenery. These types are preferred to oil base paints because they dry without luster, and oils and thinners of other kinds of paint mixtures are highly flammable.

Casein Base Paints

Casein paints are made by combining pigmentation with a phosphoprotein of milk which is a strong adhesive. Although casein paints may be thinned with water, after the paint has dried thoroughly, it is insoluble in water. This paint is packaged in quart, gallon and five gallon cans. The range of hues includes earth colors, as well as the very brilliant colors. Also available in black and white, caseins can be intermixed to produce any tint or shade. Caseins are particularly desirable on settings that will be used out-of-doors and those that will be toured because the paint is water resistant and may be touched up to match the original colors, unless they have become faded by the sun.

Caseins may be applied with brushes, rollers, or sprayers. Since they dry flat, brush marks do not show and strokes may be made in all directions. There is virtually no separation of mixed pigments, although paints used in a spray gun should be strained to remove any particles that might clog the gun. Caseins dry quickly, and become completely waterproof in about eight hours. Brushes are cleaned in warm soapy water, rinsed thoroughly, and hung to dry. The same care should be given pails and spray equipment.

Acrylic Base Paints

Using acrylic resin as a pigment binder, acrylic base paints for scenic use have recently been developed that offer several advantages over caseins. The range of colors is extensive enough for most scenic work. Colors are prepared in concentrated form to be mixed with a concentrated vinyl acrylic emulsion or white base, then mixed with water. The result is high opacity, excellent coverage, and a finished paint surface that has no luster.[1]

Perhaps the greatest advantage of acrylic scene paint is that it does not spoil or cake in the bottom of the pail, and pump dispensers or calibrated syringes can be used to measure the color concentrates economically. Warm soapy water is required for cleaning brushes and utensils.

Latex Base Paints

Latex paints are packaged in cans and ready-mixed. Pigmentation is combined with water and emulsified rubber which acts as the binder. Latex paints are used primarily for interior and exterior domestic use, and the range of colors are limited to tints. While bright toners are available in a few hues, darker shades are seldom adequate for producing wood tones or brilliant colors. This type of paint is very thick, so to improve its workability on fabrics it may be diluted with water without greatly affecting its opacity. Surfaces painted with latex tend to have a slight luster and overpainting on an already dry surface often dries slightly lighter than the base coating. After this paint has dried completely, it

---

[1] Roscopaint, a product of Rosco Laboratories, Inc. Port Chester, N. Y.

cannot be washed off, so usually it is necessary to re-move and replace flat coverings after three or four coats have built up. Nevertheless, where only one or two shows are produced each year, it is often more economi-cal to use latex paints than it is to lay in a supply of dry pigments, maintain a supply of glue, and provide storage, even though it is less expensive. Latex paints can be purchased at any local paint store.

Latex can be applied with brushes, rollers, or spray guns. The paint has excellent covering power and may be overpainted without colors bleeding through, unless the paint has been thinned so much that it becomes transparent. Brushes and equipment can be cleaned with warm soapy water.

Dry Pigment and Glue Base Scene Paint

The least expensive and most widely used scenic paint is prepared in the scene shop. Almost a complete range of colors are available in dry pigment form that can be dissolved in water. A few of the very high intensity colors are prepared in pulp form because they are dif-ficult to handle as powders, but these may be inter-mixed with dry pigments in the preparation of the paint. However, dry pigments must have a binder added; otherwise, the pigment will dust off the surface once the water has evaporated. A glue and water sizing, about 16 parts water with one part hot animal glue, makes a workable binder that will hold most pigments. Some of the darker shades, particularly browns, reds, and greens, require the addition of more glue to prevent their rub-bing off, but too much glue will cause crazing—fine hair cracks—in the painted surface.

It is seldom necessary to stock the complete range of pigments. A few pigments may be found in local paint stores, but the intensity of these rarely matches that of pigments prepared especially for scenic uses. Every technician should acquire firsthand knowledge of the more commonly used pigments, their names, and their general characteristics. The descriptions which follow places the pigments in three general categories: earth colors, high chroma (intensity) hues, and neutrals.

EARTH COLORS:

> *Source:* Highly refined and finely ground oxides, chiefly iron, commonly found in clays and earth deposits

Yellow Ochre or French Ochre

> Characteristics: A medium light dull yellow that is slightly golden; mixes readily with other pigments; added to white, it produces straw tint; added to blues, it dulls or grays the blue to dull gray green

Raw Sienna

> Characteristics: Slightly deeper than ochre and more toward the orange; grays blues without greenish quality; with white, produces pale yellow orange

Burnt Sienna

> Characteristics: A deep rust red or red brown; mixed with black, produces red mahogany color; excellent for dulling greens and blues; added to white, gives pinkish tan

Raw Turkey Umber

> Characteristics: A dull earthen brown with a greenish tinge; with white, a dull ivory; used with all colors to dull the chroma; used straight for graining weatherworn wood

Burnt Turkey Umber

> Characteristics: A deep chocolate brown; excellent for dark oak wood grain; mixes easily but requires more glue

Van Dyke Brown

> Characteristics: A very dark brown with little hint of red; excellent for walnut wood effect; difficult to dissolve in water without adding denatured alcohol to size water; add extra glue to size water

Venetian Red

> Characteristics: Bright brick red; with white, gives a pinkish tan; with black a dull red brown

HIGH CHROMA PIGMENTS:

Source: Mineral oxides

Chrome Yellow Light

> Characteristics: A brilliant yellow often described as canary yellow; very light value; with green, produces yellow greens; with blues, produces fairly high chroma green; with red, oranges

Chrome Yellow Medium

> Characteristics: A brilliant yellow more to the gold; high value; with green produces warmer yellow green; with blue, warmer green; with red, yellow orange

English Dutch Pink

> Characteristics: Contrary to its name, a rich golden yellow pigment similar to raw sienna but much higher chroma

American Vermilion or Chelsea Vermilion

> Characteristics: A brilliant red that is slightly toward the orange; mixed with ultramarine, will give dull lavenders; with chrome yellows, medium high chroma orange; tends to drop out (separate) in mixture and overbrushing will produce red splotches

Chrome Green Light

> Characteristics: A high chroma green often described as leaf green, slightly toward the yellow; mixes easily, but requires frequent stirring to prevent settling

Chrome Green Medium

> Characteristics: A deep green that is near spectrum green, but somewhat lower chroma; mixed with ultramarine blue and black, produces dark evergreen

Italian Blue

> Characteristics: A deep turquoise blue; mixed with chrome yellow light, produces bright yellow greens; will stain skin if paint is mixed by hand

Ultramarine Blue

Characteristics: A brilliant blue purple; mixed with white and a small quantity of yellow ochre, produces a good general sky color; an all round mixing color

Celestial Blue

Characteristics: A deep, near spectrum blue; with white, produces excellent sky blue; with yellows, deep greens

NEUTRAL PIGMENTS:

Source: Mineral oxides, char residue and earth deposits

Permanent White

Characteristics: A white pigment derived from oxide of tin; an opaque white

Danish Whiting

Characteristics: A pure whiting composed of calcium carbonate that is highly soluble in water; used as a paint extender and semitransparent white pigment; also in sizing and putty

Ivory Drop Black or Bone Black

Characteristics: A warm black pigment used in water soluble paint mixture; do not confuse with lamp black used in oil base paint which will not dissolve in water

These pigment colors dry several shades lighter than they appear after they are mixed with sizing; therefore, the pigment mixture must be matched with the desired color before sizing is added. While this is not totally reliable either, it is better to start by matching the dry powder mixture than to attempt to obtain a match after they have been wet with the sizing. When the approximate color has been reached, a small quantity can be mixed with size water and allowed to dry to test the color before the entire batch is mixed. These dry pigments are so intense that the best procedure is to start by putting the approximate quantity of Danish whiting in the mixing bucket that will be required for the paint job, then to stir in the pigment colors in very small quantities until the desired shade is reached. The whiting will lighten the mixture, but the addition of permanent white may also be needed to get the proper tint. The sizing will almost completely displace the whiting so there will be very little increase in volume. Where dark wood tones are desired, the addition of whiting will result in a chalky appearance, thus it should be omitted unless that color quality is desired.

Scene paint is best applied with a brush. Drying time usually requires at least an hour, depending on the humidity. No attempt to texture or overpaint should be made before the base coat is thoroughly dry. All brushes and equipment should be washed in cool water immediately after using.

Scenic Aniline Dyes

Aniline dyes are completely different in character from pigments. The dyes derived from vegetable and mineral sources are crystalline and dissolve completely in water. There is no residual pigmentation deposited on the surface, thus the dye becomes a part of the material, rather than a coating on the surface, as with pigment paints. While the liquified dyes can be mixed to get intermediate shades, lighter tones are produced by diluting the dyes with additional water and deeper tones by increasing the dye concentration. Scenic anilines are available in the same range as dry pigment colors, with the exception of white.

Anilines are prepared for use by mixing a very small quantity in boiling water to make a concentrated solution, usually ¼ to ½ teaspoon of dye to a cup of water. Small amounts of the concentrate are added and mixed in another vessel, preferably a plastic pail, containing clear cold water until the desired shade is reached. If several colors are to be painted next to one another, enough dextrine glue solution or boiled laundry starch can be added to the water to make it slightly tacky. This will retard the spread of the dyes. Each color should be tested on a matching scrap of fabric and allowed to dry thoroughly. Make certain that sufficient quantity of each color has been prepared because it is nearly impossible to match colors exactly a second time.

Aniline dyes can be applied with brushes, or where only a single color is needed for a gauze or scrim, the fabric can be dipped after it has been dampened with water. To make the dye fast, a 5 percent solution of acetic acid added to the dye will aid the chemical union of the dye with the fabric. The dye must be washed out of the brushes completely or it will bleed out in other paints. When working with strong dye concentrates, the dye can be drawn from the bristles by soaking the brushes overnight in a thick mixture of whiting and water.

SCENE PAINTING TOOLS

The most important tools the scene painter uses are brushes. These will range in size from small soft bristle brushes required for minute details to large wall brushes that are nearly 2" thick and 7" wide. In addition, the painter will need a straight edge for painting line detail, a chalkline for laying out long trim lines, sponges and rags for texturing, stencil paper, and a variety of other materials to achieve special effects.

Brushes and Painting Aids

It has been noted that the paints used in scene painting are all prepared with water base rather than oils. It is, therefore, important that the brushes used for scene painting do not deteriorate in water, or that the bristles become limp or curl. Two factors determine the quality of a good brush: (1) the bristles which are set in hard wood must be vulcanized in rubber or other adhesive which will not permit the bristles to pull loose under prolonged soaking; and (2) the bristles must be nylon and aligned in compact rows set closely together to hold a large quantity of paint without excessive dripping. Low quality brushes may only have a row of bristles around the outer edge and one down the center of the block. These hold sufficient paint, but release it down the handle, or in puddles, when brought in contact with the painting surface. The metal ferrule surrounding the bristle block must be rustproof and securely fastened, particularly on flat brushes because the ferrule holds the handle in place.

Brushes that will be used in shellac or oil base paints cannot be used interchangeably with those used in water base paints. No amount of cleaning will restore a brush so it will be suitable for both purposes.

Priming Brushes

For applying size and base coatings, a large priming brush is the most efficient. Priming brushes are available in widths from 4" to 7", although most painters find 5" and 6" the most workable. These brushes are usually 1½" thick across the ferrule and the bristles at least 4" long. (See illustration.)

Lay-In Brushes

A lay-in brush is flat and is used for fill-in or general painting where a priming brush would be unmanageable. These are available in both long and short bristle. Short bristle brushes may be 3" to 6" wide and ⅞" thick, with the bristles' length approximately 3". The long style brushes range from 3" to 5" wide, 1⅛" thick, with bristles around 4⅜" long. The shorter brushes are better for working in corners and over heavy surface textures because the bristles have more spring, but the longer brush carries more paint.

Lining Brushes

Every scene painter probably has a favored brush for laying in fine lines. Some prefer a brush that is slightly oval, others work best with a thin, flat brush. Actually both styles are practical. Where curved lines are required, the oval brush that has a round handle gives better control; for straight lines, a flat brush works well with a straight edge. Stock scenic lining brushes have

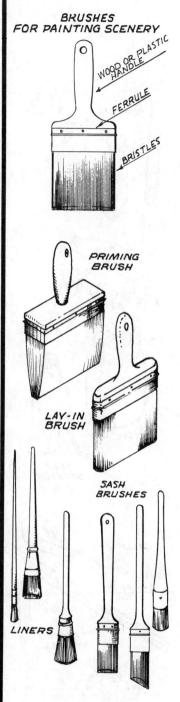

BRUSHES
FOR PAINTING SCENERY

WOOD OR PLASTIC HANDLE

FERRULE

BRISTLES

PRIMING BRUSH

LAY-IN BRUSH

SASH BRUSHES

LINERS

bristles that are fanned out slightly and trimmed at the tip to form a thin edge. These are available in the following sizes:

STENCIL BRUSHES

SPRAY GUN

TANK SPRAYER

CHALK LINE

STRAIGHT EDGE

TRACING WHEEL

SPONGE

#2   ½″ × ⅜″
#4   ¹³⁄₁₆″ × ⁹⁄₁₆″
#6   ¹⁵⁄₁₆″ × ⅝″
#8   1⅛″ × ¾″
#10 1¼″ × ⅞″
#12 1⁷⁄₁₆″ × 1¹⁄₁₆″

For flat lining brushes, tapered sash brushes, available at local paint stores, work exceptionally well for straight lines. These are constructed like any flat brush except the ends of the bristles have been trimmed at an angle. Sash brushes come in widths from 1″ to 2″, and in thicknesses from ¼″ to ⅜″.

After both flat and stock liners have become worn, they can be used for foliage painting; however, an oval foliage brush or an oval sash brush—they are nearly identical—is superior for leaf detail.

Stenciling Brushes

Where a design is to be stenciled, laid in with the aid of a cutout pattern, for wallpaper or prints on draperies, a short stubby brush is required which will apply the paint without causing it to spread beyond the pattern. The bristles of a stencil brush must be short and relatively stiff and not become limp when wet with the paint. The brushes are round, the bristles will range from ½″ to 1″ in length, and the diameter may be from ¼″ to 1¼″, depending upon the size of the stencil detail. (See illustration.)

Paint Spray Guns

It is seldom practical to spray paint an entire setting because the mist tends to settle on everything in the surrounding area, and the rapid drying paint creates a clogging problem in the equipment. At the same time, with practice, subtle shading and tonal effects are possible with a sprayer that cannot be obtained by other methods of painting. Two types of equipment are used most commonly: the spray gun and compressor; or the portable tank type that must be pumped by hand.

Other essential tools needed by the scene painters include a chalkline to snap long trim lines, and a straight edge for painting straight lines. A roll of brown wrapping paper and a tracing wheel for making transfer patterns is frequently needed. Pounce bags of coarse muslin filled with chalk dust or dry pigment are required for dusting in patterns. A good stencil knife and heavy oilboard or stencil board will be needed for wallpaper stencils. Large natural sponges that have been cut flat on one side and an assortment of soft rags are useful for texturing.

SELECTING COLORS AND PREPARING SCENE PAINT

Most beginning stage technicians have a very limited knowledge of color, either as an esthetic experience or a physical science, unless they have had a background in painting and design or physics. The physical properties of color and light affect what the spectator sees when he views the stage. The organization of color into a composition of harmonious relationship between dominant and subordinate areas of color affects not only the visual response of the spectator, but also enhances the esthetic wholeness of the production as well.

The Language of Color

Already, references have been made in terms which are unique to describing the characteristics of pigments: hue, chroma and intensity, light and dark, and tint and shade. These are descriptive terms that are part of the language of color; they are terms used by painters, decorators and designers to describe the subtleties of color. Another reference was made to a spectrum blue. This is a physicist's term to define the hues as they appear in a band when a ray of sunlight is refracted by a prism. Physicists have discovered that each of the spectrum hues has a wave length, with red having a much higher frequency than blue. This carries us deeper into technology than is necessary at this time, except that if we should decide to paint the backing unit behind an archway blue, the distance behind the arch will appear deeper than if we paint it pink. The reason is that the lower frequency blue appears to recede, while the higher frequency red seems to advance, thus appearing closer. When advancing and receding hues of high intensity are juxtaposed, a visual vibration is created which can literally cause physical discomfort for the viewer.

The artist/painter whose work will be viewed in a gallery must be concerned primarily with skillfully mixing pigments on the pallet and applying them to the canvas so they appear well under white light. The scene painter must also be concerned with how to mix colors that will appear well together, and also how to make them appear to be or actually be changed when seen under the colored lights used on the stage. Aside from physical limitations that may affect one's capacity to sense color, we must assume that all sensations of color are dependent on two factors: (1) the pigmentation in or on the surface observed; and (2) the spectral hues present in the light which illuminates that surface and reflects from it. Therefore, the spectator at the theatre sees color as a reflection of light from the surfaces on the stage.

The color components in sunlight are such that all pigment colors show as individual hues. When the sunlight is separated by means of a prism, it will be noted that there are red, green, and blue bands, with yellow, blue green, and violet bands where the colors seem to overlap. By introducing a filter to block out each hue individually, red, green, and blue remain the only ones that are not mixtures of the others. Hence, these are considered to be the primary light colors. Using three spotlights, each covered with one of the primary color filters, focused on the same area of a white screen, the circle of light will be white. When the spotlights are separated so that only a portion of each circle of light overlaps the other two, where the three overlap will appear white. Where the separate beams overlap around the outside, there will be an area of yellow, blue green, and lavender, as well as small segments of red, green, and blue where there is no overlapping. By introducing into the area of white light a card painted with spots of the three pigment primaries—red, yellow and blue—each appears normal. However, if the blue spotlight is turned off, leaving only the red and green, the white light area becomes yellow, and the blue painted area appears black because there is no longer blue in the light to stimulate the sensation of blue. While this explanation describes an exercise in the physics of light, this phenomenon is used by both the scene painter and lighting designer to affect the color sensations experienced by the audience. (See Figure 5–1, a.)

In mixing pigments to prepare paint, the primary hues, red, yellow, and blue, are so designated because they can be intermixed to produce all of the other hues. Since pigments lack the purity of light, a mixture of the primaries will not produce white, nor will the mixture of yellow and blue, for example, result in a green as high in chroma as those described earlier. To lighten a pigment mixture, white must be added. Black is added to darken a mixture. In the language of color, neither white nor black are considered hues; thus white, black, and the intermediate grays are referred to as neutrals. The following definitions are helpful in describing the dimensions of color:

Hue: Used in reference to a specific color: the hue red, orange, blue, green, etc.

Value: Used to describe the level of lightness or darkness of a hue as it relates to a scale of grays between black and white, and/or many hues used together to form a scheme of color.

Chroma: Used to describe the scale of purity between the brightest and dullest extremes of a single hue or of several hues used together to form a scheme of color.

As an example of how these color dimensions may be used, a pale pink can be described as a high value, low chroma red, which indicates that a great deal of white was added to the red to raise its value, but which also

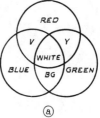

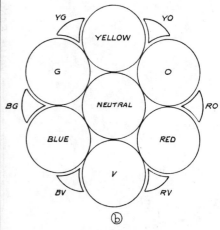

Figure 5–1.

Light and pigment primaries: light and pigment primaries, and value scale.

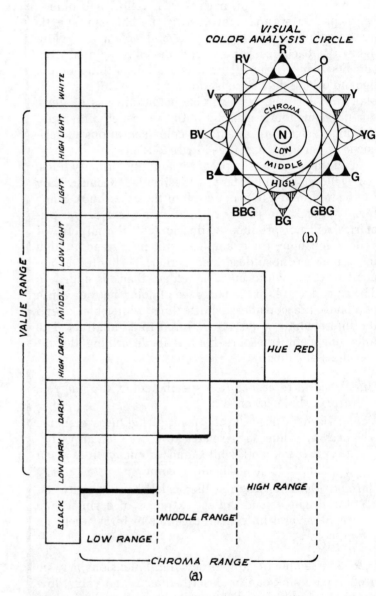

Figure 5–2.
Value/chroma ranges and visual color analysis circle.

affected its chroma, changing it from pure to a very low level of brilliance. To describe pure red, the value level of the brightest red pigment is only about four steps above black, or slightly below the middle of the nine step value scale.[2] If we desired a low chroma red at middle value, it would be necessary to add both black and white in order to achieve that level of value. (See Figure 5-2, a.)

The paragraph above would appear to indicate that chroma is controlled mainly by adding white and black. Actually, this method of manipulating the bright-dull character of a color is avoided in scene painting because the addition of a great deal of white and black results in the colors having a chalky, lifeless quality. A circle diagram with the pigment primaries spaced equidistant around the circumference with the secondary hues located in between and a neutral spot in the center, serves to show the relative position of each hue. Hues which are directly opposite each other are called complements. By mixing any two complements together, each tends to neutralize the other, hence a neutral spot in the center of the circle. A small amount of green pigment added to red will reduce the chroma of the red, just as purple added to yellow will dull the yellow. Managing chroma in this manner produces low chroma colors that have considerably more vibrancy than when black and white are used. (See Figure 5-1, b.)

It should be expected that the set designer will have prepared a color sketch or painter's elevation to guide the preparation of paint colors. Nonetheless, an understanding of how color organization is achieved can greatly enhance the scene painter's sensitivity, but since there are conflicting theories about how this can be done, the following statements pertaining to color organization are generalizations based on several theories:

1. Select a *dominant hue*, or closely associated range of hues in which one hue predominates. Example: yellow with yellow red (orange) and yellow green.

---

[2] Based on the theories of Albert Munsell and Denman W. Ross as conveyed by Richard G. Ellinger, *Color Structure and Design* (Scranton, Pennsylvania: International Texbook Company, 1963), Chapters 3 and 4.

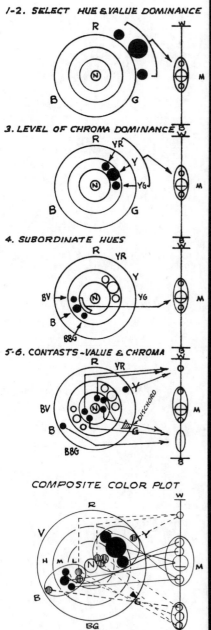

1-2. SELECT HUE & VALUE DOMINANCE

3. LEVEL OF CHROMA DOMINANCE

4. SUBORDINATE HUES

5-6. CONTASTS -VALUE & CHROMA

COMPOSITE COLOR PLOT

2. Establish a *dominant value* level, light, middle or dark. Example: middle value yellow with major areas of yellow red and yellow green adjusted to same value.

3. Establish a *dominant chroma* level, low, middle or high. Example: middle yellow with major areas of yellow red and yellow green adjusted to chroma.

4. Select a *contrasting hue,* or closely associated range of hues that are complementary or near complements to the hue dominance. Neutral grays may be used as substitutes for contrasting hues. In either case, the area given to contrasting hues must be subordinate. Example: blue-blue green to blue-blue purple as hues opposing the yellows in examples above.

5. Introduce a *contrast in value* with accents of light and/or dark in both the dominant and subordinate hues, or with neutrals. Example: dark browns and dark blues, and light yellows and pale blues. Areas must be subordinate to the value dominance.

6. Provide *contrasts in chroma* by introducing small areas of high and/or low chroma in both the dominant and subordinate hues. Example: bright yellow flowers in a bright blue vase. High chroma colors command attention and should be confined to small accents.

7. Distribute the dominant and subordinate hues to provide rhythmic *repetition* of value and chroma relationships. Example: Repeat the color of a chair upholstered in blue in a painting or drapery background. Repeat the wall color with a matching cushion on the sofa. This should be done intentionally, without being too obvious.

8. Do not hesitate to introduce an occasional *discord.* A discord is an accent color completely outside the hue range of both dominant and subordinate hues. Example: in the limited color organization referred to thus far, a splash of bright green in a plant or drapery pattern would be a discord, but not out of place. The area must be small, but chroma can be high.

It should be noted that in the examples cited with the above generalizations, the range of colors was restricted to three closely related hues and their complements. It should also be noted that the choice of complements was derived from the arrangement of colors on the light color circle, rather than the pigment color circle because when combining hues into an organized scheme, they will be observed as sensations of reflected light. Thus, the pigment circle is useful when mixing pigments together to produce intermediate hues, but the light color circle is most reliable when combining hues that will appear well together. The examples used also suggested that the dominant hue was yellow, or on the warm side of the color circle. It could just as well have been one of the blues from the cool range of hues, or one further restricted by limiting the range to only two opposing hues. The important concept is that dominance must be established on one side or the other and not split between the two. (See Figure 5–2, b.)

Mixing and Matching

Matching the colors which appear on the elevation or sketch provided by the set designer can be quite difficult, and sometimes perplexing. If the color renderings have been done in transparent water color, the white paper showing through the color cannot be duplicated in scene paint, only the effect can be reproduced. If the painting has been done with opaque water color, the task is somewhat easier, but the pigment colors used to make these kinds of paint do not always match those the painter has at hand.

By close scrutiny, it should be possible, in most instances, to identify every color on the sketch with one of the dry pigments, particularly those within the warm range. The cool range may be more difficult since there are so many different blues and greens. Once the basis of the color is identified, it is a good practice to prepare a sample—no more than a teacup full—keeping an account of the proportions of each pigment used to arrive at the desired color. From the sample, mix a small amount with size water to a creamy consistency and paint a small area on muslin. After the swatch has air dried, compare it with the color sketch, then make adjustments in the dry sample and test again until the match is attained. This suggestion may be helpful: Colors on a small sketch or elevation that may seem correct, when blown up to the full scale of the actual setting, often appear much more intense than intended; either paint a larger sample for the designer to check before mixing the entire batch, or reduce the chroma one step to compensate for the large area.

As noted earlier, a great deal of whiting is used with the lighter colors to extend or add bulk to the paint. The whiting is put in a dry container first, then small quantities of the pigments are added. It should be re-emphasized that dry scenic pigments are very strong. A handful of pigment is often enough to tint a pail of paint. This dry mixture should be mixed thoroughly and both visual and wet tests should be made to ascertain the proper color. Frequent tests should be made when mixing greens, Italian blue, and the bright reds which tend to come out stronger than the dry mixture would indicate.

Size water is then added to the dry pigment and stirred in rapidly with a wooden paddle. Enough size should be added at the beginning to wet the pigment thoroughly, then additional size stirred in to make a heavy cream mixture. Stirring should continue until no lumps remain in the mixture, then the paint should be boxed —poured back and forth between two pails—at least five or six times to assure a complete mixture of all the pigments. Additional size can be added to dilute the mixture if the paint seems to drag when brushed, but it should be heavy enough to cover the surface with an opaque coating.

There is no precise criteria for determining the exact quantity of paint that will be needed to paint a setting. If a box setting is to receive a base coat, and there are approximately 18 flats, including door and window flats, one and two-thirds to two 16-quart pails of paint will cover the set with a single coat. One thing is certain: It can be disastrous to run out of paint before the job is completed. Mix a little extra and save out a gallon of the dry mixture. This will take care of shortage and be available for touch-up. Leftover dry mixtures should not be wasted. They can often be combined with others, or pigments can be added to make paint for backings, texturing, and trim colors.

The quantity of paint needed for line work, texturing, and trim may vary from a cupful to a gallon. It is often convenient to have a supply of buckets, coffee cans, and smaller containers on hand for this purpose.

No attempt should be made to save the paint prepared with pigments and size more than a day or two because it will spoil. Spoilage can be retarded somewhat by adding a few drops of phenol (carbolic acid), Lysol, or a preparation of 8 oz. phenol and 1 oz. of sweet oil. This latter preparation smells better, but it will not prolong the life of the paint. Where a setting is painted with the ready-mixed paints, the quantity of paint needed will be approximately the same, but these paints can be stored in closed containers indefinitely.

PAINTING THE SET

Scenery can be painted either when it is flat on the floor or standing upright. When painting scenery on the floor, it is usually necessary to walk on the surface of the scenery which stretches the sized cover, unless wide boards are laid across the stile for the painters to stand on. Care must be exercised to prevent paint from forming puddles which will dry slowly, leaving dark rings or spots. Most painters will agree that it is best to paint the set pieces while they are standing, first, because it is less strenuous; and, second, because it is possible to stand back from the work for frequent inspections of the paint application and consistent control of the medium.

A counterweighted paint frame that can be raised as painting progresses provides one of the more convenient devices for painting flat units. A scaffold with two or more levels mounted on casters, called a "boomerang," is also excellent for working on flat surfaces that stand on the floor. Stepladders are inconvenient because they must be moved constantly, but they are more maneuver-

PAINT FRAME

"BOOMERANG"

PAINTING FLAT

FROM A LADDER

BOXING:
POURING BACK AND FORTH TO MIX

Figure 5–3. Methods used in painting scenery.

able where painters must work around corners and irregular surfaces. If ladders are used, they must be stable and have provisions for setting or hanging paint containers.

Painters should not attempt to work with a completely filled bucket. Several smaller containers that have stout bails will permit the distribution of paint between painters, as well as make it more convenient to box the paint, which should be done frequently to keep the paint well mixed. (See Figure 5-3.)

Painting Procedure

If there are major divisions of color on the surfaces to be painted, lines marking these separations should be made with a chalkline or charcoal before the base coating is started. Since there will be some dripping, the uppermost color should be laid on first, from top to bottom. Where excessive dribbles occur, they should be wiped away with a damp sponge because when the base coat is spread over them, they soften and cause streaks.

The large priming brush is best for applying the base coat over large areas. These brushes carry a great deal of paint and are relatively heavy, but it is important that the paint be applied rapidly and with a minimum of spattering. A crisscross or horizontal figure eight stroke causes less dripping, and since the paint will dry flat, the stroke pattern will not show. When painting over the wood of the frame beneath the covering, the paint stroke should be parallel to the wood to avoid leaving a heavy ridge of paint where the brush passed across the board. It is imperative that once painting has begun on a large surface, it be done quickly and to completion so that none of the edges of adjoining areas dry before the area has been filled in. Painting over a dry area to blend it in with a freshly painted one constitutes a second coat which will dry a different shade. (See Figure 5-4.)

The base coat on smaller areas, such as woodwork, wainscot, and thicknesses is usually applied with a lay-in brush which is easily controllable in small areas.

MOTTLED SCUMBLE

GRADED SCUMBLE

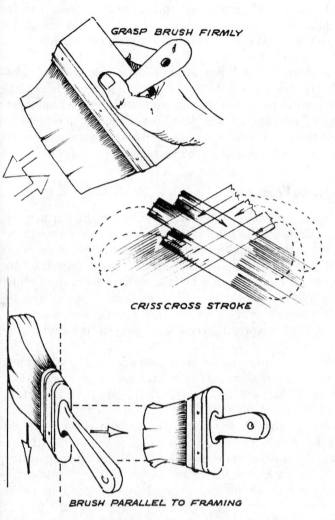

GRASP BRUSH FIRMLY

CRISSCROSS STROKE

BRUSH PARALLEL TO FRAMING

Figure 5–4. *Brushing techniques for general coverage.*

This type of brush can also be used to work the paint into heavily textured areas, but should not be abused by stroking it edgewise more than necessary.

Immediately after the painter has finished working with a brush, it should be washed in cool water, working all the paint from the bristles, particularly near the ferrule. If paint is allowed to dry in the brush, the glue in the paint dries under the ferrule which causes a swelling at the base of the bristles, breaking the vulcanized bond.

Painting Techniques and Textures

Many techniques are employed by the scene painter to create textural effects, as well as reflective and absorptive textures that will respond to the lighting of the set. These effects may be applied as a base coat or over the base, often combining several techniques.

Scumbling

Scumbling is a method of blending two or more colors while both are still wet on the surface to produce a mottled effect, or a transition from one tone into another.

One method is to prepare two colors that are closely related in value and chroma. The hues may be shades of a single hue, or of adjacent hues. For example, a red brick wall usually has a variety of shades of red, rather than a single color overall. Mixing venetian red with a small quantity of raw sienna and white, and venetian with a small amount of ultramarine blue and white, will give two shades of brick red, one cooler than the other. These two shades are blended on the surface by using a priming brush in each hand, brushing on an area of one color, then an area of the other, blending the two with the brush where the colors meet. By repeating the procedure in an irregular pattern, and varying the sizes of the areas, a suitable undercoat for brick work will result. It is important to work rapidly so the edges of one color do not dry before the second has been blended in.

A second method blends the color from dark at the top to lighter tones at the bottom. The hue may be the same, but the value of each successive color to be blended is lightened. For example, to create the effect of a dingy plaster wall, raw umber would provide a suitable pigment. By adding a small amount of chrome green medium and ultramarine to the umber, it can be dulled and darkened for the top color. A second value level can be made by the addition of white, and a third by combining white and umber for the lighter value. Using a vertical brush stroke, the dark tone is brought

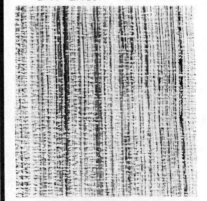

DRY BRUSH TEXTURES

CROSS-HATCH

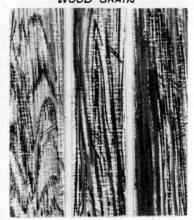

WOOD GRAIN

down two or three feet from the top and lower near the corners. The second value is then blended into the first and brought down midway on the wall. Finally, the lighter value is added, extending to the floor. A pail of sizing in which the brushes can be dipped to add moisture for blending can be helpful. The painter must work quickly and strive to keep the transitional levels of the value changes consistent throughout. (See illustrations.)

Dry Brushing

To produce a dry brush effect, the brush is dipped only a short way in the paint, then wiped out on the edge of the pail to remove most of it. By using a very light stroke, the paint is deposited in fine lines left by the individual bristles. With practice, this technique can reproduce the grain pattern of most woods, the effect of broomed plaster, and of diagonal and cross-hatched wallpaper. The brush is twisted and turned for graining, or guided along a straight edge where uniform pattern is desired. The brush must be kept uniformly dry. A sheet of smooth cardboard slipped between toggle rails or corner braces may prove helpful in avoiding an imprint of the rails made when the brush sweeps across them. (See illustration.)

Spattering

This is a texturing technique produced by tapping a lightly loaded brush on the palm of one hand so that small droplets of paint are spread over the surface of the scenery. The object is to spread the droplets evenly without pattern or large blobs, which will occur if the brush is too wet. The best effect is achieved when the spots are no larger than $3/16''$ across, and done from a distance of three or more feet from the surface of the scenery.

A fine spatter in a dark receding color will give the pitted surface quality of brick, stone, and concrete. A light spatter with a shade of higher value than the base coat will suggest highlights. Spattering may also be used to enhance the general tonal quality of a setting, as well as to aid color control in lighting. A general spatter in one or more colors that are closely related in hue, value,

SPATTER TEXTURE

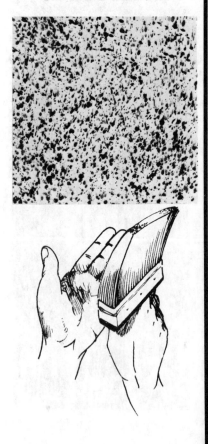

and chroma to the base coat can be applied to relieve the flat, uninteresting surface quality of a solid wall color. The upper third of wall surfaces are often spattered heavily with a dark tone that sweeps lower in corners and gradually diminishes at lower levels. The darker tone at the top absorbs the light so that the illumination appears to be concentrated on the actors. An allover spatter with pastel tints of the primary colors over a neutral gray base color makes it possible to manipulate the color of the set by changing the color emphasis in the lighting. (See illustration.)

Ragging, Flogging, and Rolling

Coarse textures can be produced more effectively with rags or sponges than with a brush. A large natural sponge which has been cut in half so it has a flat surface can be dipped in scene paint and dabbed on the surface to give an effect of rough plaster or stucco. If this is done well, the results can be quite pleasing, but most beginners tire quickly of this job and begin dabbing in patterns so the results often look like chicken tracks. By using a 30″ square of washed muslin instead of a sponge, repetitious patterns can be avoided. The cloth is dipped in the paint and squeezed out, then the crumpled cloth is pressed lightly on the surface to leave an imprint. After each print, the cloth is recrumpled so the pattern is continually changing.

Flogging also uses a similar cloth, burlap or netting, but the paint saturated material is slapped (flogged) against the surface to produce a larger, more exaggerated pattern. The color may be darker or lighter than the base coat. This technique can be used for Spanish stucco, stone texturing, tree bark, and marbleizing.

Smaller, more controlled texture can be made by rolling the saturated rag across the surface. Using light guidelines to assure rolling the cloth straight, this technique can be effective for wallpaper. (See illustrations.)

Lining and Panel Detail

Lining details are done for two purposes: to decorate the surface; or to simulate variations in the surface, such as panelling or moldings.

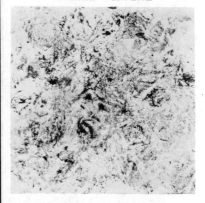

RAGGED TEXTURE

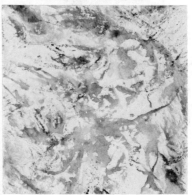

FLOGGED TEXTURE

ROLLED TEXTURE

The details for surface decoration should first be laid out on brown kraft paper, then perforated with a tracing wheel and sanded lightly on the back to produce a pattern. The design is transferred by dusting over the design with a pounce bag. The outlines of the design should then be laid in solidly with a pencil or charcoal and the excess chalk dusted away. (See illustration.)

The secret of painting lines that are uniform in thickness is to exert uniform pressure on the bristles of the brush—light for thin lines and heavy for thick lines—and to work with the brush held nearly vertical to the painting surface. The consistency of the paint will depend on the medium, but it may be thinner, hence the brush must be wiped out quite well to avoid dripping. Curved lines require a narrow brush with a round handle which may be rotated in the fingers as the line progresses. For straight lines, a 1" to 1½" liner or flat sash brush will work satisfactorily. (See illustration.)

Where detail is to appear raised or lowered in relation to the surface, form is defined by highlights and shadows, rather than by outline. Therefore, the painter must establish a light source that is real or imaginary in order to determine where the shadows and highlights will occur. On a raised surface, the highlight will be on the side of the form nearest the light, while on a lowered surface there will be shadows on the side nearest the light source. Once this is determined, the colors and value of the shadows can be prepared. When paneling on a light background, soft gray tones that contain a hint of the complement to the base color, and one or two levels of value darker, will suggest shadows. On dark backgrounds, the shadow may be lower in chroma and value of the same background color. To give greater definition, a lighter value of the shadow color may extend around the highlight side of the form, but the edge of the highlight should be brought out with a narrow line that is very light; white or pale yellow is sometimes used. A very thin dark line may also be used to define the edge of the shadow.

Paneling must be marked in carefully with pencil or charcoal. Where paneling is low on the wall, the shadows will be at the top and one side; where the panel is raised, vice versa. A straight edge tool should always

PERFORATE PATTERN

SOFT BACKING BOARD

SANDPAPER BACK

POUNCE WITH CHALK BAG

PAINT IN WITH NARROW LINER   a.

CHALK LINE

b.

LINING WITH STRAIGHT EDGE

be used when laying in straight lines, but one should avoid overloading the brush to prevent the likelihood of paint running under the tool. If panels are to be wood grained, the dry brush texturing is usually done after the line work is completed. A masking paper held over the lines will prevent the dry brushing from obliterating them. (See illustration.)

Stenciling

A stencil is an open pattern cut in a piece of paper or other paint resistant material which will mask the areas surrounding the design. Its major use in scene painting is to aid in applying a design or pattern that must be repeated, such as a border decoration or design for wallpaper or draperies.

Regular stencil board stock, which is heavy and treated so it will not deteriorate, can be bought at larger paint stores. The design is cut out with a stencil or X-Acto knife, leaving adequate tabs to hold the design together and support the delicate parts of the pattern. If the stencil is given several coats of clear acrylic spray or shellac, the edges are less apt to curl. Where large areas of stenciling will be done, it is usually wise to cut a spare to replace the original stencil which may wear out. Since the paint builds up rapidly on the surface of the stencil, it should be sponged off frequently. A stencil design with several colors will require a separate stencil for each color.

The sharpest definition of a stenciled design is achieved with a stencil brush. The paint for stenciling with the stubby brushes must be thickened to an almost pulp consistency and applied with short pounce strokes that move from the masking surface toward the open areas. An allover pattern can be very busy, unless the value contrast between the background and pattern colors is very close. Hand stenciling with a brush can be very tedious and can require hours of work. (See illustration.)

Where only a single color is desired, a dry brush technique can be effective. A lay-in brush is used, but great care must be exercised to avoid brushing the paint beneath the cut-out areas of the stencil.

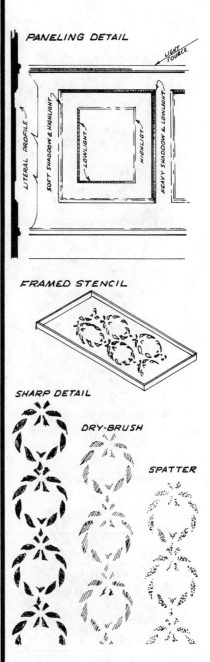

PANELING DETAIL

LIGHT SOURCE

LITERAL PROFILE

SOFT SHADOW & HIGHLIGHT

LOWLIGHT

HIGHLIGHT

HEAVY SHADOW & LOWLIGHT

FRAMED STENCIL

SHARP DETAIL

DRY-BRUSH

SPATTER

Spattering the paint through the stencil produces the softest effect because there are no hard edges. The design shows up as subdued pattern in which some detail is lost, but this technique is excellent for faded quality.

With a spray gun, the amount of paint flow must be reduced and sufficient masking must be added to prevent the spray from spreading beyond the stencil. This technique gives a sharp pattern but saves little time.

Detail Painting

Painting the details for groundrows, foliage borders, and wings of hard scenery may involve one or more of the techniques just described, but the methods of preparing the paint may vary from small amounts of pre-mixed color to mixtures prepared on the spot with dry pigment and size water. Where the shape of the units are contoured and consist of a combination of muslin, with Upson board or plywood, a size coating with enough additional whiting to opaque the mixture will tend to unify the surface textures. Both Upson board and corrugated paper should be sized back and front to minimize the tendency of these materials to curl.

For structural details such as brick or stone, a base coat and texturing is done before surface detail is begun. Line work to define the pattern of bricks, for example, should be laid out with a chalkline to mark the spacing of the horizontal courses. The outline of bricks is then painted with a lining brush using gray or a darker tone to represent the mortar. A few random bricks dry brushed in deeper tones will add interest and relieve the monotonous repetition of the pattern. Where a set will be standing for only a few performances, brick lining can be done with ordinary blackboard chalk. The lines are drawn on with chalk, then rubbed with a cloth wrapped around the forefinger to smudge the chalkline. A straight edge is necessary. This technique is fast and works equally well for ashlar stone patterns. (See illustration.)

Groundrows, borders and wings which are contoured to depict trees, shrubbery, and foliage or rows of buildings, require the preparation of many small amounts of

BRICK TEXTURE

STONE TEXTURE

FOLIAGE TEXTURE

paint and several brushes. The drawing is laid out to conform to the contours by gridding or pounce pattern. The colors needed may be prepared in small containers which the painters apply to designated areas of the design, blending colors together where color gradations are needed. Some painters prefer to work with a palette of dry pigments, mixing their colors as they go by first dipping the brush in size water, then in the pigments, blending them on an aluminum or porcelain palette. The latter method gives the painter a greater range of color possibilities, but with either method one must remember that the wet colors will be much lighter when they dry.

Although the designer's color sketch and details of the unit should provide a suggestion of how the finished work should look, it would be futile to try to give verbal instructions in the techniques of scenic painting. However, these suggestions may prove to be helpful guidelines:

1. The distance between the audience and the painted unit is usually great enough that colors tend to merge, and forms that seem to be sharply defined at close range appear less distinct. Both color and form can be exaggerated somewhat to compensate for the distance.

2. Reinforce the vibrancy of the color by introducing small areas of the complementary hues, even though they do not appear that way in nature. Small touches of bright red, blue, and purple in the shadows beneath a cluster of green leaves will make them seem more alive than if dark green and black were used; the eye will mix these colors at a distance.

3. The effect of great distance can be achieved by raising the value of each color, and lowering the chroma, as well as eliminating small details. After the painting is thoroughly dry, brushing lightly over the surface with a pale Italian blue aniline dye will give a misty quality that suggests distance.

4. A wet sponge to wipe away color can be used effectively to create highlight areas that are often impossible to achieve with a brush.

Wing units sit closer to the audience and therefore

WASH BLENDING

PAINTED WINDOW DETAIL

require closer attention to detail. Architectural pieces are usually designed in forced or exaggerated perspective and require careful measurement or a pounce pattern for the layout. The general procedure for base and texture colors can be followed, but details such as cornices and trim moldings may be painted rather than actual. The movement of light over the curved surface is the most difficult effect to produce. If the molding is topped by a fillet or forward sweeping curve that casts a shadow, the darker shadow is painted in as a thick line, then followed immediately—before the paint dries —with a wide line using clear water, overlapping the shadow line. The water causes the shadow color to run, blending into the wet area. A clean sponge can be used to draw up the excess water should it threaten to spread beneath the straight edge. (See illustration.)

Wing units are often fitted with practical doors, in which case the painting is handled the same as painting for any other door unit, but windows are very often painted in completely. If the window has no function other than that of a window, the details of the framework, highlights, and shadows are laid in and painted as though it were a panel. The most difficult feat is to create the effect of the glass panes. Since most interiors appear dark beyond the draperies when viewed from the outside, details of the interior are usually omitted and painted as a dark void. Details of the drapery or shutters can be painted in as they would appear from the outside. A suggestion of the glass can be made by a few diagonal flashes of light gray across the panes and by overpainting around some of the corners with gray aniline dye to suggest exterior reflection and shadows of the muntins on the drapes.

Where a glow of light through the window is needed for a night scene, the framing, muntins, and drapes are painted with opaque paint, and the void area suggesting the interior is painted with aniline dye which is semitransparent, permitting offstage light to pass through.

Wings that are cut out to suggest tree forms involve the same procedures used in painting the detail of a groundrow. A relief from the flat painted quality can be achieved by building up surface textures on the heavy tree trunks with occasional strips of burlap or netting glued to the surface to suggest the coarse bark. After the base bark color is painted in, dry brushing over the surface with a darker tone will bring out the coarse texture of the glue on materials. Both chroma and value levels are usually kept low, with a few highlights and darks added to accentuate the form. The upper foliage masses are usually kept dark and in very low chroma, lightening and brightening the hues somewhat in the lower areas. Details of leaves should be minimized to a few suggestions around the lower edges of the foliage.

PAINTING SOFT SCENERY

Painting a soft drop is difficult, even though it is one of the oldest types of scenery. A large work area is required; it makes demands on the painter's skill and it involves many hours of working time. These are reasons enough for discouraging many small theatre groups from using them.

Enlarging and Transferring the Design

Enlarging the designer's rendering to full scale by gridding over a drawing was described briefly in the preceding chapter (page 148), but even this method can result in distortions on large scale designs. By enlarging the drawing on a full scale paper cartoon first, it is possible to make corrections before the design is transferred to the fabric. A cartoon is made up with several strips of kraft paper taped together. The cartoon is then perforated with a tracing wheel and the design pounced on with a chalk bag. It is usually necessary to reinforce the chalked lines after the paper has been removed. Where there is adequate floor space, the drop may be spread over a paper or cloth floor covering and tacked to the floor on all sides. The painters, wearing white cotton slippers, then walk on top of the drop painting in the design with small brushes fitted into the end of slender bamboo poles that are four or five feet long.

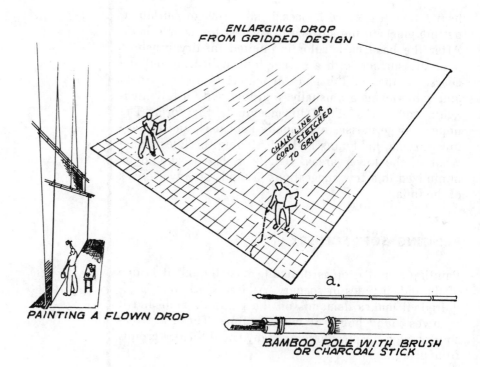

ENLARGING DROP
FROM GRIDDED DESIGN

CHALK LINE OR
CORD STETCHED
TO GRID

PAINTING A FLOWN DROP

a.

BAMBOO POLE WITH BRUSH
OR CHARCOAL STICK

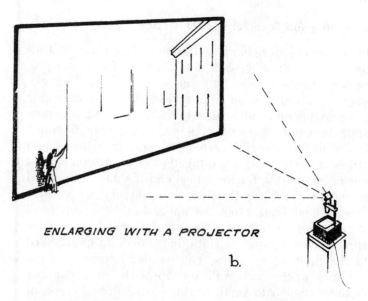

ENLARGING WITH A PROJECTOR

b.

Figure 5–5. *Methods of enlarging and painting drops.*

As frightening as this may sound, enlargement detail can be done this way with little likelihood of distortion of forms. The eye can observe the total effect better when standing erect than when crawling about on hands and knees. (See Figure 5–5, a.)

An overhead projector that uses a transparency slide provides another means of design enlargement. An inked line drawing of the drop design is prepared in either ½″ or ¼″ scale. The drawing is then Xeroxed on an 8½″ × 11″ clear acetate sheet. If the design is too long for a single slide, it may be necessary to make two, a separate slide for each half so the projection may be matched at the center. One or two projectors may be used to project all or half of the design at a time. Projectors are set at a distance that will enlarge the design to full scale. While working in the dark, with only light from the projectors, the design is drawn on with charcoal. The level of the projectors should be at the horizontal center of the drop; otherwise, some distortion will occur. (See Figure 5–5, b.)

Painting Drops

The drop should be sized before the design is transferred if opaque paint is to be used, or with a starch size if the drop is to be painted with aniline dyes. A drop that will be stored by rolling it on a batten, or that will be used for a touring production, which will require that it be folded, should be painted with a medium that will not crack or flake off under these conditions. Flexible glue used in the size mixture for opaque pigment retains its flexibility. It is prepared like animal glue and its strength for paint preparation is comparable.

For the best results, a drop should be flown while it is being painted, working from the top down. To avoid dribbling paint on the lower part of the drop, the drop may be hung on two adjacent battens, the top attached to the downstage pipe and the bottom to the upstage one. The front pipe can be raised or lowered to bring the drop surface within working height while the back one is adjusted to keep the rest of the drop out of the way. A wooden batten of 2″ × 4″ stock laid in the swag will keep the fabric taut: A metal batten is apt to leave rust stains that will not cover with the painting. The paints should be prepared in sufficient quantities to cover each color designated area. Where there will be abrupt color changes, the upper color should be dry before proceeding with the lower one to prevent the colors from running together. Darker colors and hues of higher intensity tend to bleed through lighter ones, so the lighter colors painted over darker ones should be laid on with a minimum of brushing.

Painting a drop with scenic aniline dyes is no more difficult than with opaque scene paints, and in some respects, less time consuming. The consistency of the dye solution is like water and must be brushed vigorously enough to work it into the fibers of the drop fabric. Nevertheless, a small quantity of dye solution can be spread over a large area. Since the dye is absorbed into the fabric more readily than scene paint, which dries on the surface, drying time is slower and there is greater tendency for colors to run together. Running can be retarded by adding dextrine to the dye solution, but overlapping colors may still be troublesome. One method that has proven to be effective in preventing the running of colors is to lay in the outline of the entire design with a narrow line (¼″) using a middle value of gray latex or casein paint. This serves to delineate the design, as well as to form a waterproof barrier between the colors.

The dyes should be prepared in rustproof containers, preferably enamelware pans or plastic pails which can be covered to prevent evaporation and impurities getting in the dye between work sessions. The dyes will stain the hands and clothing so necessary precautions should be taken.

Dyes can be blended by mixing them on the surface, and a color can be blended out by diluting the color with clear water. Since no white is mixed with the colors to lighten or subdue their brilliance, a careful control of the chroma must be exercised so the drop will not become too strong in color. After the basic colors of the drop have been applied and allowed to dry, dark line details can be painted in but, of course, lighter additions are not possible unless another medium is used.

Drops done in a cartoon style—outline rather than full painting—are often more appropriate for melodrama and fragmentary settings. These can be painted while in a flown position, but where a straight edge may be needed to lay in straight lines, painting the drop on the floor is usually more convenient. The floor area must be immaculate and should be covered with a canvas or muslin floor cloth to absorb any moisture and paint that may penetrate the drop. In this case, a floor cover of polyethylene should not be used because it is nonabsorbent, and will greatly retard the drying time of the paint which can cause staining. One advantage of painting a drop flat on the floor is that the fabric can be tacked down, which prevents the fabric from shrinking irregularly. However, it is nearly impossible to paint on the floor without soiling the surface of the drop unless everyone makes a special effort.

The procedure for painting a scrim drop is the same as for the cloth drops, except scene paint should be used instead of ready-mixed paints or dyes if there is any intention of reclaiming the scrim for another production. Most of the scenic pigments will wash out if the scrim is sent to a commercial laundry.

Muslin drops painted with scene paint can also be washed to retrieve the fabric. This can be done most successfully where there is space to lay the fabric face down, like a smooth grassy area, so that the material can be first soaked on the back side. With cold water and brooms, the paint can then be scrubbed from the front surface. The heavy pigment will come off easily. Although some color will remain, the material is reusable for covering platforms, mâché work and groundrow units. (Washing scenery on the lawn will not damage the grass or soil.)

Oil, Shellac, and Spray Paints

Thus far, no reference has been made to paints with oil, lacquer, or acrylic bases, except to note that they are flammable. There are numerous small paint jobs where these kinds of paints are practical.

Wood trim painted with the flat scene paints looks dull and flat because it lacks the luster of finished wood. To add luster, a coat of flat varnish or white shellac that has been thinned one-quarter with denatured alcohol, will produce a sheen without having a high shine. Both shellac and flat varnish will darken the base flat coat beneath, and any graining effects are lost almost completely. This can be compensated for somewhat by lightening the base color, or by mixing the dry pigments with flat varnish to produce the desired textures.

Metallic colors, gold, silver and bronze, which have been premixed with bronzing varnish, lose their metallic luster when painted over flat paint or on absorptive fabrics. Metallic colors in spray cans react the same way, except on hard surfaces. To use the metallic bronzing powders on scenery, they are mixed with dextrine. The dextrine is mixed with water in sufficient quantity to make an amber solution, heated in a double boiler, and cooled. The bronzing powder is stirred in to make a creamy consistency. This will paint on and retain its full luster without tarnishing.

Shop built furniture usually looks more authentic if the wood is stained with an oil rubbing stain, then waxed. The stain is painted on with a brush then wiped off with a cloth. 24 hours should elapse before applying wax. Wiping rags used with stain must be placed in a closed metal container because if they are left in the open air they will ignite by spontaneous combustion. An effective wood stain can also be made with a concentrated solution of aniline dye and water. After the water has evaporated, the surface can be polished lightly with steel wool and waxed.

The spray cans of acrylic (Krylon) paint have limited use, except for painting properties. They must be used in a well ventilated room and surrounding areas should be covered to catch the paint mist that fills the air. Besides being expensive, these types of spray paint should not be used on flats or scenery that will be washed.

A final word applying to all painting activity: brushes and paint containers should be washed thoroughly after each use; small quantities of paint should be disposed of immediately and not allowed to dry in the pail; dry pigments should be stored in moisture proof bins or containers that can be closed; and dry pigment powder should be swept up; otherwise, it will track throughout the theatre. Brushes that will not be used for an extended length of time should be wrapped in paper to prevent the bristles from becoming separated and misshapen.

SUGGESTED READINGS

Ashworth Bradford. *Notes on Scene Painting,* ed. Donald Oenslager. New Haven: Witlock, 1952.

Burris-Meyer, Harold and Cole, Edward. *Scenery for the Theatre.* Boston: Little, Brown, 1972.

Ellinger, Richard G. *Color Structure and Design.* Scranton, Pa. Intext, 1963.

Gothic Color Company. *Scenic Artist's Handbook,* a brochure by Gothic Color, Dept. L-3, 727 Washington Street, New York, 10014.

Munsell, A. H. *A Color Notation.* Baltimore: Munsell Color, 1941.

Munsell Color. *Munsell Book of Color.* Baltimore: Munsell Color, 1942.

DRESSING THE SET

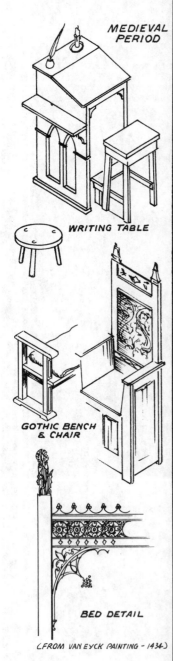

MEDIEVAL PERIOD

WRITING TABLE

GOTHIC BENCH & CHAIR

BED DETAIL

(FROM VAN EYCK PAINTING - 1434)

essing the set is a responsibility assigned to a property crew who will be guided in their selection of properties by the set designer and director, but an effective crew should possess a knowledge that will enable them to proceed on their own where specifications are lacking. The scope of such knowledge must include a variety of technical skills, including simple tasks like hanging curtain rods and pictures, to complicated construction jobs which may include making furniture, modeling, casting, and creating draperies. In addition to these skills, dressing the set also involves the coordination of styles and periods of furniture, draperies and bric-a-brac, even providing the proper glass for serving wine. It is helpful to possess a storehouse of trivia: to know that pictures were usually hung higher on the wall during the nineteenth century because the furniture was taller; that crocheted doilies were used to protect marble and hardwood tops of late Victorian tables around the turn of the century; and that antimacassars came into vogue with overstuffed chairs to prevent oily hair from staining the upholstery.

Obviously, to include all the information implied in the above paragraph in this text is impossible because there are volumes of material. The point is that it is necessary to research the subject or period if you do not have the necessary knowledge. The materials that will be included in this text are elementary guides for selecting period furniture and related accessories, for drapery construction and window treatment, and for property construction with various media.

FURNITURE AND ACCESSORIES

Egyptian, Greek, and Roman

Most information available pertaining to furnishings of these periods comes from the artifacts that remain. Friezes and sculpture dating back before 3000 B.C. verify the use of stone and wooden benches, thrones, tables, and dining couches that were elaborately carved. Some pieces were massive, but other pieces like the wooden chairs from the Tomb of Tutenkhamon (circa 1500 B.C.) were delicately carved and inlaid with gold.

Furniture of this period is not reproduced today; therefore, such pieces must be constructed. The lines of the very early furniture were basically severe. Chair legs were often contoured like the front and back legs of an animal, with feet carved like a claw. The chair backs were nearly vertical with pierced or carved detail. Throne chairs had low arms with carved heads of animals, birds, or serpents at the front. Other furniture seems to have been four-legged tables with carved detail, backless benches, tripod braizers, and stools.

The later periods, from 600 B.C., were furnished with less severity. The wooden furniture of Egypt, Greece, and Rome had become lighter and more graceful. Side arms terminated in scrolls or swept out in graceful curves. The shapes of pitchers, wine jars, and serving dishes are classic and illustrations of these can be found in every history of Greek and Roman art. Lyres, bows and arrows, and Greek shields and armor are depicted on many of the vase paintings.

The Middle Ages

The furniture for plays set during the Middle Ages must be improvised to a great extent, but a few clues can be found in paintings of the early Gothic Period. Simple benches and chairs with austere decoration typical of the period will usually suffice for such plays as *Saint Joan* by G. B. Shaw, or *The Lady's Not For Burning* by Christopher Fry. Wrought iron lamps, lanterns, and candle holders were common, and pewter mugs and plates are acceptable table service. The quill pen was the main instrument for writing and ink was held in a pewter ink well. Writing paper was parchment which might be rolled on scrolls or bound in a portfolio. Fireplace dressing included heavy andirons, pokers, and bellows. Draperies were heavy, coarse woven fabric with iron rings at the top which slid on a wooden or iron pole. (See illustration.)

By the end of the Renaissance, several styles of furni-

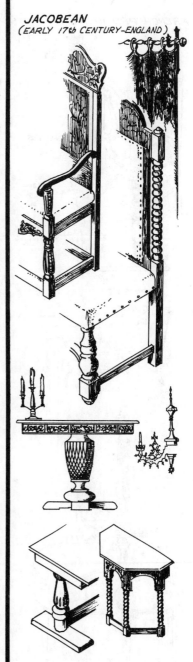

JACOBEAN
(EARLY 17th CENTURY—ENGLAND)

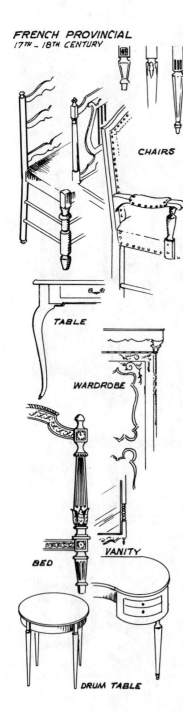

FRENCH PROVINCIAL
17ᵀᴴ – 18ᵀᴴ CENTURY

CHAIRS

TABLE

WARDROBE

VANITY

BED

DRUM TABLE

ture were developed that are still being reproduced. One that has been copied extensively is referred to as the Jacobean style, and associated with James I of England. Built of oak, this furniture was typified by heavy turned legs that were covered with carving, or corkscrew leg, arm, and back members with carved straight backs. Pedestal based tables were common, as were three or four leg tables. Upholstery on the backs of the chairs usually consisted of a center panel surrounded by wood. The more elegant styles had an upholstered seat, but a loose cushion was also used. (See illustrations.) Similar styles were also found in Spain and Italy. This heavy style adapts well to such productions as *A Man For All Seasons* by Robert Bolt, and *The Lion in Winter* by James Goldman.

Because Jacobean furniture is heavy and massive, the accessories should be consistent. Pictures on the walls should have heavy frames that are gilted, or deep-set in dark wood frames. Draperies should also be heavy, as though to keep out the cold, and be either rich brocade or plain colored in deep shades. The lighting of the early seventeenth century was candlelight. Candelabrum in silver or brass, as well as individual candlesticks or wall sconces were used. (See illustrations.)

Provincial Furniture

The term provincial as it applies to furniture and furnishings, describes the simpler cabinet work that was made by local craftsmen, rather than by the masters commissioned by the courts. Although there is no doubt that the court designs were the inspiration for many of the provincial styles, the workmanship was excellent and appealing. ". . . provincial furniture is fundamentally simple, uncomplicated in turnings and carvings, . . . [but] do not confuse it with the roughhewn rustic pieces."[1]

French provincial is one of the more familiar styles, first gaining popularity during the seventeenth century. During the reign of Louis XIV, and lasting through the period of Louis XVI, the heavy cabinet styles were re-

[1] Florence B. Terhune. *Decorating For You* (New York: Barrows, 1944), p. 17.

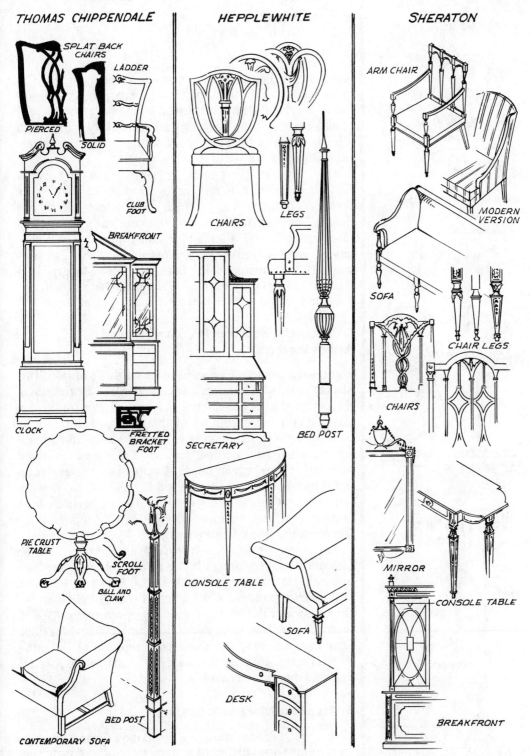

THOMAS CHIPPENDALE

SPLAT BACK CHAIRS

LADDER

PIERCED

SOLID

CLUB FOOT

BREAKFRONT

CLOCK

FRETTED BRACKET FOOT

PIE CRUST TABLE

SCROLL FOOT

BALL AND CLAW

BED POST

CONTEMPORARY SOFA

HEPPLEWHITE

CHAIRS

LEGS

SECRETARY

BED POST

CONSOLE TABLE

SOFA

DESK

SHERATON

ARM CHAIR

MODERN VERSION

SOFA

CHAIR LEGS

CHAIRS

MIRROR

CONSOLE TABLE

BREAKFRONT

Figure 6–1. Recognizable characteristics of Chippendale, Hepplewhite and Sheraton furniture styles.

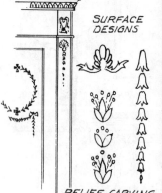

ADAMS BROTHERS

CHAIRS

LYRE
BACK

WHEEL
BACK

CURVED SLAT
BACK

SIDEBOARD   PEDESTAL
CUPBOARD

SURFACE
DESIGNS

RELIEF CARVING

Figure 6–2A. *Adams brothers.*

placed with lighter, more delicately formed pieces. The most recognizable features of contemporary interpretations are the fluted and turned legs, inset panels delicately curved at the corners, and upholstery fabric with allover patterns on blue, ivory, or mauve backgrounds. (See illustration.)

The American provincial style is commonly called Early American. It is best recognized by its distinctive turning and the wood which was either cherry or maple. The lines are severe on the very early pieces, but later, around 1700, slat, ladder, and bent wood Windsor chairs were popular. (See illustration.) The Pennsylvania Dutch furniture also falls into this category. It is known for its constraint, as well as for its painted surface decoration of conventionalized floral designs.

Chippendale, Hepplewhite, Sheraton, and Adams Brothers

Eighteenth century England produced this group of furniture makers whose work was recognized in their own time, and is still considered the best of the traditional styles. With the exception of the Adams Brothers who were designers, Chippendale, Hepplewhite, and Sheraton were superior cabinet makers. Their work injected new interest in curved lines, piercing, and surface carving. The furniture of this period is believed to have influenced a renewed interest in the classic style in both architecture and interior furnishings that marked the Georgian Era. (See illustrations.)

This same period in America is associated with the Colonial Period. Though many of the colonial furniture and cabinet makers received their training in England, and their designs were influenced by the English styles, they also developed their own interpretations. (See illustrations.) The Georgian style architecture, particularly in the South, and the classic replicas in the cities of the North, affected the taste for classic style furnishings and decorative carving.

Styles of the Nineteenth Century

Five styles of furniture were developed during this century that were distinctive, but generally considered, they were overly decorative and not as well designed as the work produced before. When Napoleon became Emperor of France, he commissioned a new style of furniture that would satisfy his vanity. The result was a style now known as French Empire. It is described as ". . . classicism debased with over-ornamentation in chased brass and ormolu mounts, heavy, cumbrous proportions, and trademarked with Napoleon's bewreathed N, stars and the bee symbol."[2] (See illustrations.)

Simultaneously, the Regency style appeared in England. Regency was equally ornamental and only a few pieces are considered worthy of reproduction today. The most notable piece of furniture is the Regency sofa which has graceful classic lines. (See illustrations.)

In America, Duncan Phyfe had gained recognition as a furniture craftsman. It is said that his early work ranked with that of Sheraton, but he too was influenced by the French and English trends. While his styles, which bear his name, were similar in many ways to the Regency, they are simpler and more sturdy. In decoration, the period in which Duncan Phyfe worked is referred to as the Federal Period. The primary motif was based on patriotic themes: wreathes surrounding the eagle clutching flags, stars, ribbons, and bells. These appeared in carved ornamentation, fabric prints, plates, and metal ornaments. (See illustrations.) Both Federal and Duncan Phyfe furniture styles are still reproduced by contemporary furniture makers and the two styles can be combined tastefully.

Victorian furniture is regarded by many to be the least practical, even though it has maintained its popularity among the decorators as an antique style that can be introduced as an accent piece. It is overly ornate with flowing curves that never stop until they reach the floor. Never particularly comfortable, this style is associated with the "gay nineties," rigid morality and gingerbread houses. (See illustrations.)

Twentieth-Century Furniture

The first 25 years of the twentieth century was a nondescript period. Victorian homes retained that style fur-

[2] Florence B. Terhune, op. cit., p. 45.

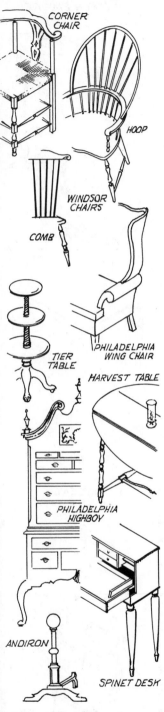

COLONIAL AMERICA

CORNER CHAIR

HOOP

WINDSOR CHAIRS

COMB

TIER TABLE

PHILADELPHIA WING CHAIR

HARVEST TABLE

PHILADELPHIA HIGHBOY

ANDIRON

SPINET DESK

Figure 6–2B. *Distinctive colonial styles.*

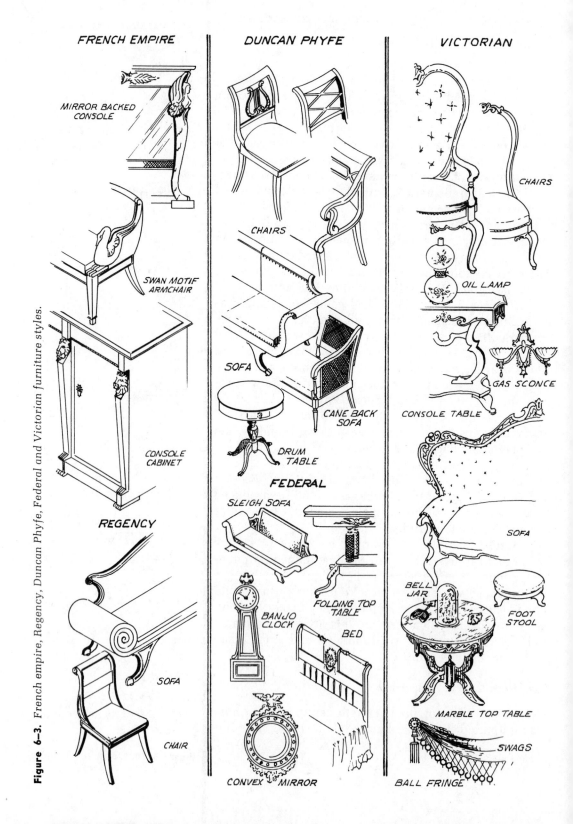

Figure 6–3. *French empire, Regency, Duncan Phyfe, Federal and Victorian furniture styles.*

FRENCH EMPIRE

MIRROR BACKED CONSOLE

SWAN MOTIF ARMCHAIR

CONSOLE CABINET

REGENCY

SOFA

CHAIR

DUNCAN PHYFE

CHAIRS

SOFA

CANE BACK SOFA

DRUM TABLE

FEDERAL

SLEIGH SOFA

BANJO CLOCK

FOLDING TOP TABLE

BED

CONVEX MIRROR

VICTORIAN

CHAIRS

OIL LAMP

GAS SCONCE

CONSOLE TABLE

SOFA

BELL JAR

FOOT STOOL

MARBLE TOP TABLE

SWAGS

BALL FRINGE

niture, while others clung to replicas of Chippendale or other period pieces. Perhaps the most prominent change was toward overstuffed chairs and sofas. The better designs adapted the lines of good period furniture, but there were also those that became massive and out of proportion to any other units of furniture that might be used with them.

When dressing the set in the contemporary mode, the practice of combining compatible styles is acceptable within reason. A modern glass cocktail table will not go well with Early American furnishings, but it can be used with a Duncan Phyfe sofa, for example. The larger pieces of furniture or prominent clusters of furniture will usually dictate the dominant style. The scale of the major furniture to the space and height of the setting can present a problem. A piece that looks fine in a small living room can appear lost when placed on the stage. This does not suggest that all pieces of furniture used on stage must be huge, but the arrangements must be planned so that a proportional balance is achieved. At the same time, the Swedish and Danish modern furniture, which concentrates its beauty on fine woods and structural simplicity, is most effective set in contemporary surroundings rather than in mixed traditions.

Wherever possible, the accessories used in conjunction with any of the periods of furniture should be consistent with the style, even though the play may be set in modern times. The exception mainly would be in the use of lamps, chandeliers, or similar functional fixtures that can be electrified to simulate oil, gas, or candle light, whereas contemporary lighting would emanate from electrical lamps which have been produced in brass, pottery, and other materials that will harmonize with the traditional furnishings.

Window curtains and draperies are often as difficult to provide as the proper furniture to dress a period set. One can rarely find ready-made draperies that are the proper dimensions for windows on the set; finding drapery fabrics that are suitable can be expensive and often impossible. The solution is to make drapes and apply the print design if necessary. This will be discussed under drapery construction later.

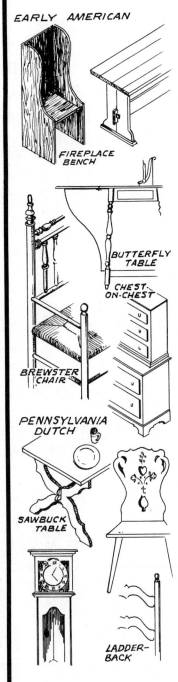

EARLY AMERICAN

FIREPLACE BENCH

BUTTERFLY TABLE

CHEST-ON-CHEST

BREWSTER CHAIR

PENNSYLVANIA DUTCH

SAWBUCK TABLE

LADDER-BACK

PROPERTIES DEFINED

Properties fall into three general categories: those that the actor carries, such as handbags, umbrellas, wallets, keys, suitcases, briefcases, books, letters, or packages, cigarettes, and lighters; those that the actor will use while on stage, such as newspapers, telephones, opening drapes, food that must be eaten, and clothing taken from a closet; and those that are primarily dressing for the set, which include furniture, pictures, flowers, draperies, and all other items, whether they are used by the actor or not. Properties in the first category are considered *personal properties*. Those that the actor must use while on the stage are *business properties*. When properties are used primarily for creating an environment for the play, they are referred to as *dress properties*.

Personal properties which are associated with an actor's costume, such as watches, armor, daggers, and jewelry, are usually provided by the costume department. However, if a handbag or hat is to be picked up by an actor offstage, or is left on the stage at the end of a scene, it is considered a personal property of a specific actor to be provided and handled by the property department.

Business props (properties) must be practical. That is, they must be functional, and if they are not actually what they appear to be, they must be reasonably good facsimilies. Window curtains that are to open must operate without fail; food that must be eaten must be edible and allow the actor to speak; and if there must be running water in the sink, the faucets must work and the water must drain without flooding the stage. In other words, the actor is highly dependent upon the technical efficiency of business properties.

Dress properties are actually an integral part of the set. In some instances, the dress props and the set may be one and the same insofar as the presence of a prop may suggest the locale. A placard with an arrow painted on it with lettering reading "To All Trains," may be the only scenic unit on the stage, a prop. Set properties are usually stipulated by the set designer, but here again, the categories may overlap. A bouquet of flowers brought on stage during the scene is at that moment a business property, but once in place, it becomes a part of the set dressing.

SOURCES OF PROPERTIES

Rented and Purchased Properties

Most small theatre groups rely heavily on borrowing properties, but inevitably some will have to be purchased outright, such as food, construction materials, drapery, and upholstery fabrics. Outside of the larger metropolitan areas that support established theatre companies, there are few shops where theatrical properties can be rented. Occasionally it is possible to negotiate with a dealer in used furniture to purchase an item at full price, then sell it back to him for a price considerably less after the show has closed. This is the same as a rental fee, but the rate is usually quite high. Unless an item is so unusual, too expensive to purchase, or impossible to construct, rental should only be considered as a last resort.

Items which are apt to be broken or damaged during the run of a show should be purchased outright, rather than rented or borrowed. These would include such things as vases, glassware, and even furniture if the business of the play calls for rough usage. Special effects equipment like flash pots, smoke machines, strobes, and black lights are often considered properties, and rental of this equipment is usually less expensive than purchase, unless it will be used quite frequently.

Before any purchases or rental agreements are made, there must be a policy established that will protect the purchaser, as well as the renter in regard to reimbursement, damage limits, and return goods. Some suggestions will be made in the section to follow.

Borrowed Properties

Community and educational theatre organizations depend on the community itself for most of their properties. Though many people are hesitant to loan furniture or other items to the theatre, they will often agree to do so if they can be assured that articles will be returned promptly, both clean and undamaged. Any piece of furniture borrowed for use on the stage, whether it is contemporary or antique, must be considered sacred from the moment it leaves the place of the lender until it is returned. If a piece is damaged, the chances are that the lender will refuse to loan anything again.

Recent federal regulations inhibit the willingness of local furniture dealers to loan articles for use in the theatre. A new item that is out of the store more than 24 hours must be marked down and sold as a used piece. This regulation does not apply to secondhand items, although most merchants will reserve the privilege of recalling an item at any time. This can be a real disaster if a production is in progress.

Unless the lender of furniture suggests otherwise, it is prudent to hire a bonded moving service to transport items to and from the theatre. They should be fully insured to cover any damages. To avoid any misunderstandings between the lender and the borrower, an agreement form similar to the one that follows will eliminate a number of problems.

Borrower/Lender Agreement

Borrower_____Date_____

Lender_____ Phone_____

 Address_____

_____Zip_____

The Borrower has been granted permission to use the items

listed below for the production_____

to be presented on the following dates:_____

_____

The Borrower will arrange for these items to be picked up on

_____, to allow for their use at dress rehearsals at a

mutually arranged hour, and to return the items to the Lender on

_____. While in the custody of the Borrower, these items shall be given the utmost care. The Borrower will accept full liability for breakage, soiling or theft. Should any items be damaged, soiled, or stolen, the Borrower shall not replace or attempt repairs without the express consent of the Lender, at which time the items shall be repaired or replaced, or financial restitution shall be made in accordance with the expert opinion of an authorized appraiser.

Item_____ Color_____ Finish_____
    Condition: Note all marks, scratches, cracks, soil, chips, open seams, etc. _____
_____
_____

Item_____ Color_____ Finish_____
    Condition: Note all marks, scratches, cracks, soil, chips, open seams, etc. _____
_____
_____

Item_____ Color_____ Finish_____
    Condition: Note all marks, scratches, cracks, soil, chips, open seams, etc. _____
_____
_____

Signatures: Lender_____ Date___/___/___/
    Borrower_____
    Managing Director_____

Items Returned___/___/___/
Verifying Initials
    Lender_____
    Borrower_____

Making Properties

Properties that are not available from any other source must be constructed in the property shop. This may involve simple tasks such as preparing documents and scrolls, or more complicated jobs such as rebuilding a piece of furniture, constructing a Roman chariot, or providing a portrait in oil of the leading lady.

Larger properties must be planned in detail and many times the construction can take several weeks. The technical skills required in property construction are so many and varied that it may become necessary to recruit outside assistance to direct the more specialized jobs. As noted earlier in this chapter, furniture building is a highly skilled art, yet there are a few pieces that can be made in the theatre shops. The same is true of sculpture, but a good property person can produce wonders with plaster, wire, a bucket of paste, and a pile of old newspapers.

PROPERTY CONSTRUCTION

Food Properties

Food props for the stage fall into two groups: those that must actually be consumed by the actors, and those that are seen by the audience and appear edible, but are never actually served. Since most edible foods cannot be preserved any length of time without refrigeration or some storage, they must often be purchased fresh for each performance. Some edibles cannot be used on stage, such as alcoholic beverages, which require realistic substitutes, and expensive cuts of meat that will not be consumed must be faked. The suggestions for workable substitutes for food properties described below are, for the most part, traditional, but they are still economical and effective.

BEVERAGES

Champagne: The nearly clear sparkly character of champagne can be simulated with ginger ale, but transferring it to a champagne bottle allows much of the gas to escape unless it is extremely cold and poured very slowly. If the ginger ale is room temperature when the cork is removed, it will generate sufficient bubbles in the glasses to be convincing. A small amount of red food coloring can be added to make pink champagne.

Whiskey: Bourbon whiskey can be simulated by adding a small amount of cola drink to ginger ale to produce the proper color, or most often, tea is used. Tea can be diluted to make the color lighter for Scotch whiskey. Some actors object to the carbonated mixtures if they are too sweet, and others prefer some sugar in the tea so it is advisable to consult the performers and arrive at an acceptable compromise.

Wines: Red wines are often difficult to simulate, especially the deeper red burgundies. Red food coloring added to tea will most nearly produce the proper colors. A few minutes of research into the colors of various wines and brandies, as well as the proper glass for serving them, will be worthwhile. White wines have a very pale straw tint that can be made with water and enough tea to give the proper coloration.

Beer: Beer is a medium straw color that can be produced with tea but the head of foam on top is difficult to fake. The easiest solution is to use opaque mugs.

Coffee: Most actors have no objections to real coffee, but a cola drink that has been allowed to go flat can be used if real coffee cannot be tolerated.

Ice Cubes: It is sometimes difficult to keep real ice from melting under the hot stage lights. 1" square cubes of Lucite (plexiglass) can be effectively substituted. These can be washed and used cver and over. They look and sound like real ice in a glass.

FOWL

Roast Fowl: Where a roasted fowl is served on a platter, it is usually a property piece that will not be

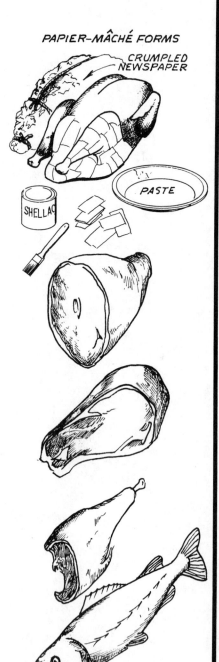

PAPIER-MÂCHÉ FORMS

CRUMPLED NEWSPAPER

PASTE

SHELLAC

carved or eaten. A convincing roast bird can be formed with crumpled paper, some stiff wire, and papier-mâché. After the mâché work is dry, it should be given two or more coats of white shellac that has been half diluted with thinner. The most effective paint is acrylic artist's colors thinned with matte medium. If actual servings are needed, thinly sliced pressed turkey can be laid along the sides of the platter and the bird fashioned to look as though some carving had taken place in the kitchen before the platter was carried on stage. Cold fried chicken is preferred by most actors where the fowl must be eaten. If possible, the meat should be loosened from the bones. Chicken should be purchased and prepared daily so that it will be moist and easy to handle.

MEATS

Roasts: Like fowl, most large cuts of meat should be formed with papier-mâché. In a play like *The Taming of the Shrew,* for example, where the meat is strewn across the floor, the pieces should not sound like a board dropped on the floor. If the mâché is done with pieces of muslin and latex cement instead of paper, the proper thud may be expected. Edible meats can be cold cuts or ground meat patties shaped like the appropriate cuts of meat. Steak can often be simulated with slices of dark brown bread that have been trimmed to suggest the form.

VEGETABLES

Cooked and Raw: There is actually no good substitute for real vegetables and the spoilage is minimal. Boiled potatoes are easy to prepare and handle. They are usually more easily managed by the actor if they are diced in about half inch squares. Where nondescript food is to be ladled into bowls, cooked cereals are manageable and palatable.

FISH

Cooked and Raw: Uncooked fish is often introduced in comic situations. It can be molded or formed with styrofoam or polyurethane and then mâché covered with a thin fabric and latex cement. The surface markings can be painted with acrylics or dyes and shellacked. Edible fish can be substituted with thinly sliced bread trimmed to the appropriate shape.

EGGS

Boiled and Fried: There is no effective substitute for boiled eggs. They are easily prepared and handled. Fried eggs may be simulated by placing half an apricot on a thin slice of white bread that has had the crust trimmed away.

FRUITS

Fresh and Artificial: Fruit that must be consumed should be fresh. Where it is to be used for set dressing, the plastic artificial fruit makes the best substitute. It is quite expensive, but it can be stored indefinitely.

Flowers and Plants

Many plays that are set as interiors and exteriors require plants, flowers, vines, and hedges. Fresh growing plants require constant care and the theatre, which may be dark during the day, is hardly conducive to their healthy appearance. For this reason, most live plants have been replaced with artificial ones that look authentic and require no special attention. There are plant forms, however, that must be constructed.

Vines that cling to the side of a porch or roses that climb on a trellis are properties, even though the units will be moved as a part of the setting. Flowering plants along a walk, or three-dimensional hedge rows falls into this same category. Although large trees, piles of rock, and tree stumps may be a part of the functional scenery, they too are properties even though they may be built by the carpenter shop, rather than in the property department. In other words, there is bound to be some overlapping of responsibility. Two-dimensional ground-rows that are in painted detail are usually built by the

VINES AND SHRUBS

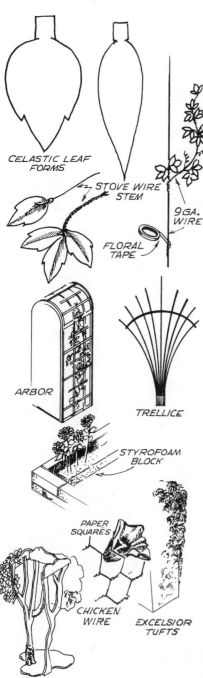

CELASTIC LEAF FORMS

STOVE WIRE STEM

9 GA. WIRE

FLORAL TAPE

ARBOR

TRELLICE

STYROFOAM BLOCK

PAPER SQUARES

CHICKEN WIRE

EXCELSIOR TUFTS

carpenter and painted by the scenic artist, but those with projecting foliage and flowers are considered properties.

VINES

Climbing Vines: The main vine stems are formed with 9 ga. wire which is usually laid out straight until the smaller stems and tendrils are attached. Stems are attached by coiling lighter gauge wire—12 ga. or 14 ga.—tightly around the main stems. Leaves may be formed with heavy green paper in varying shades of dark green, or cut from medium or light weight Celastic, which is more durable and easier to attach to the wires. Colored crepe paper can be used for leaves, but it is very soft and difficult to handle.

Paper leaves may be glued to the wire with Duco cement or white glue, wrapping the leaf tab around the wire. (See illustration.) Celastic leaves are dipped in softener or acetone, held up to allow excess softener to drip off, then pinched firmly over the wire. The leaf should be shaped and allowed to dry.

The vine stem must be wrapped with floral tape, which is a ⅜″ wide self-adhesive tape, by spiraling it around the wire, or by wrapping a one inch band of brown crepe paper around the wire and shellacking it to hold it in place. After the leaves and stems have been painted, the wire can be shaped by hand to give it a vinelike appearance.

FLOWER BOXES AND TRELLISES

Flower Boxes and Floral Edging: It may be assumed that the flowers will be plastic, although there are those who are adept at making paper flowers. The flower box may be constructed of pine or Upson board panels that are glued together with white glue. The plant stems may be held erect by crumpling a length of ¾″ chicken wire in the bottom of the box to support the stems, or sticking the stems into a 2″ block of styrofoam laid in the bottom. The plastic flowers usually have leaves around the blooms, but additional greenery may be required to fill in the space. This is available in plastics also, but sprigs of hackberry leaves which may be purchased at the florists will last several days without moisture. Lemon leaves are also good fillers.

Floral borders along the edge of a porch or walk can be made up in much the same way as a flower box, but a simulated brick or low lattice edging will usually be necessary to hide the wire or styrofoam that supports the stems.

Trellises: The design of the trellis will be in keeping with the style of the set. If the form of the trellis is straight, stock lattice is generally used for the construction. This can be woven or nailed together with small cement coated nails. Sweeping or fanned trellises will use the same materials, but if the curves are too extreme, the lattice can be made more flexible by soaking it in water for several hours. This will also toughen the wood so that it will not break so easily. (See illustrations.) Ornamental iron trellis work can be simulated by ripping ⅛" strips from very straight grained pine. These thin strips must be soaked in water then formed within a rigid frame of 1" × 1" or 1" × 2". The scrolls are secured to the outer frame with 3d cement nails, and where they touch within the frame they can be joined with several wraps of fine stove pipe wire.

HEDGES AND BUSHES

Hedge Rows: Where hedges form a background, they may be made as groundrows with contoured Upson board and painted. Three-dimensional hedges, like those that Sir Toby, Sir Andrew, and Fabian hide behind in *Twelfth Night*, can be made by cutting a branch structure of ¾" plywood, boxing out the top with a light frame to support a chicken wire body, and stuffing squares of crepe paper into the openings of the wire for the textured surface. (See illustration.) A rectangular frame covered with used muslin or corrugated paper can also be used for the texture base. The texture can be built up with excelsior dipped in scene paint that has had additional glue added to make it very tacky. This is put on the prepainted undersurface in tufts to suggest the irregular foliage texture. (See illustration.)

FLOWER AND PLANT ARRANGEMENTS

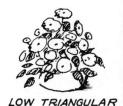

Cut Flowers: Fresh cut garden flowers are most attractive additions on any setting, but the selections must be made from varieties that will remain open under the artificial lighting. Most lilies, for example, will close when brought inside, although chrysanthemums, zinnias, and daisies will hold up for several evenings' performances. Most bouquets of fresh flowers are more attractive if fern, lemon leaves, or other greenery is used to supplement the natural leaves.

Since fresh flowers are seasonal, they are often difficult to obtain, which makes artificial blooms more practical and actually less expensive in the long run. Paper flowers are rarely available and can be objectionable because they rustle when handled.

LOW TRIANGULAR

The Japanese excel as flower arrangers, but where less exotic arrangements are desired, florists often provide illustrated brochures which can be helpful guides for those who have had little experience in working with flowers. The secret of attractive arranging is to vary the length of stems so the blooms form an interesting cluster, and to introduce enough greenery to give a contrast of pattern and color.

Flowers set so that they become a part of the background may be fairly tall. Those that will be used on low tables in front of playing areas should be low arrangements that will not block out the actor's face or interfere with actions. (See illustrations.)

VERTICAL

Plants: Larger sized growing plants such as ivy, philodendron, or ferns are showy and add a decorator touch to the set. Several pots of different varieties may be necessary to create enough mass color to project effectively. If plants of this type are borrowed, check with the owner as to the frequency of watering, the amount of light, and the temperature at which they must be kept. Plants that are to

LOW INFORMAL

be displayed in a planter should not be removed from their pots: The planter should be constructed to accept the pots.

Banners and Draperies

Flags, banners, and swags of silks are an important part of many theatrical productions because they add glamor and pomp. They may display a coat of arms or insignia, or only bright pieces of fringed cloth to add color. Except for a lavish production, real silks and satins are very expensive, and no more effective than less expensive materials, such as taffeta, batiste, or even muslin. The major mistake one can make is to use a rich fabric and an inexpensive substitute side by side with the intention of displaying equal quality. If part of the banners are to be made of muslin, then all others should be of the same material.

Designs can be applied to the fabric with scenic aniline dyes or surface appliqué using patches of material. The aniline dyes will penetrate taffeta and batiste so the pattern will show from both sides; however, the back will be in reverse. The anilines on muslin will not penetrate the heavier fabric with sufficient intensity to be viewed from either side. The most workable alternative is to combine the two methods, dye and appliqué, by applying the design to an overlay patch that will be duplicated for both sides and appliquéd to both surfaces of the main banner.

The reason for using aniline dyes instead of scene paint is to retain the softness of the fabric. Scene paints will stiffen and pucker the fabric. The anilines should be mixed from the concentrates, as described in the preceding chapter (p. 209), with sufficient dextrine added to prevent the colors from spreading. Because the dyes are transparent, the color of the fabric will affect the results. Where pure color is desired, the design should be applied over a white background.

Designs which are to be applied by the appliqué method should be carefully basted in place, then either sewn by hand or with a sewing machine. If sharp outlines are desired to accentuate the design, the pattern

FLAGS AND BANNERS

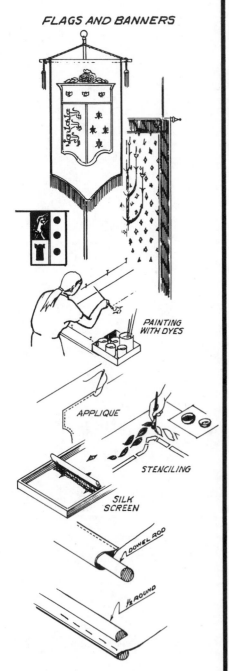

PAINTING
WITH DYES

APPLIQUE

STENCILING

SILK
SCREEN

DOWEL ROD

½ ROUND

may be outlined with a decorative machine stitch, or outlined with a broad-tipped permanent marker. (See illustration.)

Designs may be applied to banners and flags with stencils if there will be several alike. Silk screen fabric inks applied with stencil brushes are more satisfactory than other paints for this technique. A final finishing touch of fringe along the bottom edges of banners can add elegance, as well as weight so they will hang well. A wide variety of cotton, rayon, and metallic fringes are available at the fabric shops.

Draperies are not too difficult, but attention must be given to style, period, and pattern. If the fabric is commercially printed, the pattern will be repeated at certain intervals, making it necessary to match the patterns of each panel throughout the entire room. With draperies that are practical—to be opened or closed—it is important that the heading, or top hem, be reinforced with a stiffening band so that it will not lop over and the pins or rings that hold the curtain do not tear out when the drape is drawn. To control the draping of the fabric so that it will hang in uniform folds, pleating is usually required, and either lead weights or small chain must be used in the bottom hem so the folds will hang soft and straight.

Most period drapes were opened by hand or tied back with a cord or band of fabric. The drapes were hung on wooden or iron poles and slid on wooden or brass rings sewn to the top hem. They were closed by either flipping the drape from the center, or by slipping a hook attached to a long pole into the lead ring to push the drape back. Most modern draperies are hung on traverse rods with the pull cord at one side.

The amount of fabric required for draping a window is basically the same for traverse, tie-back or rod-hung curtains that will hang straight. Since most window openings are framed with a wood facing, the length measurement should be made from the top edge of the facing. There are two correct lengths for straight draperies: three inches below the window sill, or 1½" off the floor. This is considered standard, although deep set windows, or windows in a bay with a seat would, of course, be exceptions. To the length measurement, an allowance for hems must be added, usually 4″ at the top and bottom.

To determine the width of the fabric necessary to cover the window, there must be adequate allowance for fullness and vertical seams. As a rule, 100 percent fullness allowance for each panel of drapery is considered to be the minimum for pleating. For example, if the window opening is 36″ wide, and you wish to extend the drapes 8″ beyond the opening on either side so when the drape is open most of the fabric will stack outside of the opening, adding 36″ + 8″ + 8″ = 52″. Thus, if the drape is to part in the center, two panels 52″ wide will be required. Where the fabric may be only 45″ wide, additional material will be needed to make up the necessary width, and particular attention must be taken to match the pattern repeat. It is very likely that an extra ⅔rds yard will be needed for each set of panels in order to match the pattern.

One of the more common problems in making draperies is cutting the fabric straight. The fabrics are usually stretchy and even after careful measuring, it is often difficult to cut the material straight. Most drapers prefer to lay the material out flat on a large table and make length measurements along the selvedge where the fabric is least stretchy. To assure a straight cut, a weft thread is pulled out across the entire width of the material. This leaves a line that is straight with the material. Vertical cuts are measured from the selvedge, or by following the pattern repeats, rather than a pulled thread. Where it will be necessary to match the pattern along a seam, if precisely ½″ is allowed for the seam there will be little likelihood of mismatch.

After the vertical seams have been basted and stitched in, the material should again be laid out flat to form the top and bottom hems. Unless a patented pleater tape will be used on the top hem, a three inch width of buckram should be enclosed in the top hem to stiffen and reinforce the heading. This can be done with a sewing machine as illustrated. (See illustration.) If pleater tape is to be used, a regular hem is stitched in and the pleater tape is sewn on top. A hem along the sides of each panel

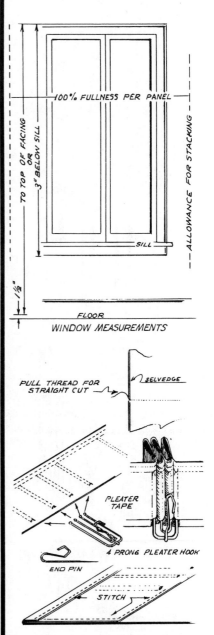

DRAPERY CONSTRUCTION

100% FULLNESS PER PANEL

TO TOP OF FACING OR 3″ BELOW SILL

ALLOWANCE FOR STACKING

SILL

FLOOR

WINDOW MEASUREMENTS

PULL THREAD FOR STRAIGHT CUT

SELVEDGE

PLEATER TAPE

4 PRONG PLEATER HOOK

END PIN

STITCH

DRAPERY PLEATS

CARTRIDGE
PLEATS

BOX PLEATS

FRENCH PLEATS

FLAT

SHIRRING

will give a finished appearance. Side hems should be sewn in before the top hem is stitched; if the side hems are pressed flat before the top hem is sewn, there will be less bulkiness where the hems overlap.

Of the several types of pleats, cartridge pleats, box pleats, and French pleats are the most common. Pleats are usually formed three inches apart. Cartridge pleats are formed around a buckram tube which gives the pleat a cylindrical appearance. Each tube is approximately ⅝" in diameter and 4" long. These must be sewn in by hand.

Box pleats have a flat double fold that is pressed down, but only stitched down at the bottom. (See illustration.) The edge to edge distance between pleats of this type should be no more than 1½", and the center to center distance should not exceed 3½", unless the fabric is exceedingly heavy. Draperies that are box pleated will take up a great portion of the window when stacked.

French pleats have a triple fold that is pinched together about 4½" below the top. Seven inches should be allowed for each set, with 3" between each set. This style pleat can be made most easily by using the pleater tape described above. A four-pronged drapery hook is used that slips into pockets in the tape. This method is a boon to the property crew because after the drapes have been used, the hooks can be removed so the drapery can be cleaned and stored flat.

As a general rule, the bottom hem is left until a final measurement can be made after the drapes have been hung on the rods. Often the bottom hem is basted in so that length adjustments can be made in the event the fabric stretches, or used on a different length window in the future. Should it become necessary to press drapes to remove wrinkles, they should always be ironed on the back with a warm iron. Many drapery fabrics are synthetic and will draw up under a hot iron. In no case, press in the folds. To form the drape so that it will fall in uniform folds, the finished drape should be laid out flat, then carefully gathered in folds as though it were stacked on the rod with the pleats bunched together. Working from the bottom, the material should be folded back and forth in straight lines to conform to the pleat folds, then loosely tied or pinned in this position with 4″ bands of muslin about every 18″ along the length of the bunched material. This is called *tabling*, and if there is space, the drapes should be left this way several days. Otherwise, they may be hung on the rods, leaving the bands in place until the last minute. (See illustration.)

Drapes which will be tied back may be pleated in the same manner as described above, but each panel should be wide enough to overlap at the center at least six inches. Stationary drapes can be attached to a drapery board with a stapler, rather than using a regular rod and, where a lace or marquisette glass curtain will hang behind the drape, a similar method can be used effectively. (See illustration.)

Sheer curtains are most effective when shirred rather than pleated. The material is tightly gathered on a rod inserted in the hem, or stapled in closely bunched flat pleats. (See illustration.)

One often finds it difficult to locate drapery fabrics with the appropriate color and pattern. Two alternatives may be followed: (1) to choose a fabric in a plain color that harmonizes with the general scheme, or (2) to dye and/or print fabric that meets the specifications of the design. The latter will take time, but the results are often the most satisfying. Unbleached muslin that has been washed to remove the sizing and to shrink the material, is sufficiently heavy for drapery fabric. It only needs to be washed in warm water and then hung flat to drip dry. If a color other than white is desired for the background, the material can be stretched over a frame and aniline dye can be brushed on while the fabric is still wet.

Three methods of applying the pattern may be used: freehand painting following a pounced pattern; stenciling the design in with textile dyes; or applying the design with silk screen print method. Where the design is to be painted by hand, the pattern is first laid out on paper, then perforated and pounced on the fabric. The material should be laid out and tacked to a large work surface. The design is painted in with aniline dyes, using small bristle brushes.

To stencil a drapery pattern, separate stencils will be

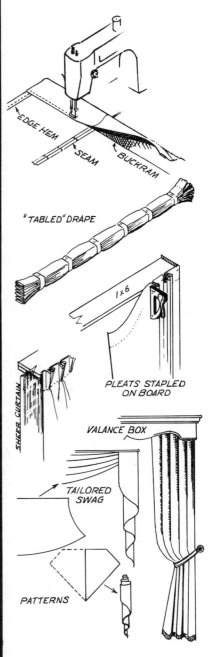

DRAPERY CONSTRUCTION

EDGE HEM SEAM BUCKRAM

"TABLED" DRAPE

1×6

PLEATS STAPLED ON BOARD

SHEER CURTAIN

VALANCE BOX

TAILORED SWAG

PATTERNS

needed for each color. Aniline dyes may be used, but because the dye mixture is so thin, the prepared textile dyes are often more satisfactory. These dyes can be mixed to any desired shade and extender added to make the paint go further. Textile dyes or paints for stencil and silk screen techniques are available at most large art suppliers.

Silk screening is the fastest method, but requires special equipment. The design is cut in a lacquer film, then adhered to a fine silk organdy that has been tightly stretched over a wooden frame. The backing paper is then removed from the film, leaving the cut-out design on the surface of the silk. After all areas outside of the design have been blocked out with lacquer or masking tape, the frame is positioned on the fabric to be printed. Textile ink is then spread along the top edge of the frame and wiped across the silk with a squeegee, forcing the dye through the silk onto the fabric. The frame is then shifted to the next position and the squeegee drawn across the silk. Where more than two colors are desired—the background and the print—other colors may be painted in with aniline dyes, or an additional screen prepared for each of the other colors. (See illustration, p. 262.)

Swags, flounces and valance boxes are often added as a part of window dressing in addition to the draperies. While contemporary window treatment is apt to be plain, interiors which reflect the eighteenth and nineteenth centuries often use fringes and ruffles, as well as swags to make the windows the center of attention. The elegant lace work that marked the Victorian period is practically impossible to find and very expensive. The best source is usually a trunk that has long been forgotten in someone's attic. (See illustration.)

Furniture and Fixtures

Even though most of the furniture that is used to dress the set may come from sources that will loan or rent their furniture, there will always be some pieces that must be built. The furniture for John Proctor's house in *The Crucible* can only be described as "rustic" since the audience should feel that he probably constructed it himself. The simple lines of this early Puritan era should not be difficult to reproduce. Slat-end benches and tables, straight back fireplace benches, stools, and open cabinets can all be built in the shop.

The sweeping lines of a sedan chair, or the Siamese benches for *The King and I* can be more challenging for the designer than for the property crew to construct. The most difficult tasks are often the repair and refurbishing of old worn-out pieces of furniture in order to modify them or make them usable. Occasionally it may be necessary to construct a period reproduction when a suitable substitute cannot be found. Only a few problems that may be considered the most typical can be shown to illustrate possible solutions to furniture construction. (See illustrations.)

Benches and Chairs

Of seating furniture, benches are the simplest to build and have the most uses as business and rehearsal properties. Any furniture on which the actor sits must be sturdy, but it must also appear sturdy to the audience. If the audience becomes anxious because the bench on which three people are seated looks as though it may collapse at any moment, their attention is diverted from the play. The strength of a bench is in its two components, the top or seat, and the legs that support it. The width of a bench top is seldom more than the width of a 1″ × 12″ board, which will carry the weight of several people if adequate support is put beneath it.

The ¾″ thickness of the top will not appear out of proportion to the weight it must carry if the bench is no longer than 30″, but longer benches will appear stronger if the edges of the 1″ × 12″ are framed with a 1″ × 2″. (See illustration.) If the completed bench is to simulate stone or marble, the edging may be even wider stock. The edging should be fastened to the top with 1½″ wood screws.

The supporting legs may be single square legs, or wide legs that splay outward at the bottom. Single legs require a skirt for support, but wide legs are usually fast-

SHOP BUILT FURNITURE

RUSTIC FURNITURE

SEDAN CHAIR

ORIENTAL STOOL

PEDDLER'S CART

SHOP BUILT FURNITURE

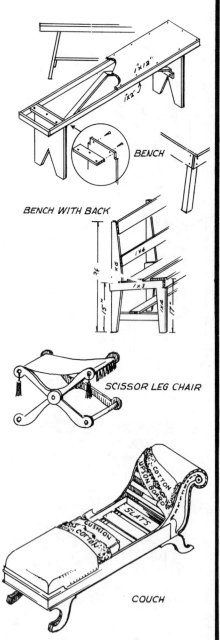

BENCH

BENCH WITH BACK

SCISSOR LEG CHAIR

COUCH

ened to a cleat on the bottom of the seat. Horizontal ties between the legs are usually necessary. (See illustrations.) Single legs may be made of $2'' \times 2''$, $2'' \times 4''$ or $\frac{3}{4}''$ stock that has been glued together in two or more layers. Classic style stone benches are usually constructed with double contoured legs separated with spacers, then covered with muslin. Since stone benches seldom had a tie between the legs, a pair of sill irons across the bottom must be used. Standard bench height is 17".

Benches with backs must have wider seats than those without backs. If the bench is to be open across the back, the back supports may be a continuation of the back legs, or attached separately to the legs. For the sake of comfort, the back of a bench should slope back slightly, and the back edge of the seat should be slightly lower than the front. This applies to most benches except the Early American fireplace seats which had flat seats and upright backs. The seats for a backed bench should be a minimum of 16" deep. If side arms are added, they should seldom rise more than 6" above the seat.

Chairs are generally the most difficult pieces of stage furniture to build, although it is occasionally necessary to construct a throne or sedan chair. The simpler styles of Grecian chairs that have neither backs nor arms can be cut from $\frac{3}{4}''$ plywood and joined with $1\frac{1}{4}''$ rods. Since they are not a great deal different than the modern scissor legged deck chairs, they can be made with heavy canvas seats, painted decorations, and tassles.

Basically, a sedan chair must have two heavy side rails for two or four bearers and a pallet or canopied chair between. Structurally, these are quite simple: It is the braids, fringes and tassles that make them theatrical properties.

Couches and Sofas

Built-in couches are often called for to fill in a bay or other units of scenery. While such units might properly be constructed by the building carpenters, the upholstered cushions and backs are usually considered a job for properties. Spring filled cushions from abandoned sofas can often be found at upholstery shops for little or no cost and make excellent padded foundations for built-in units. If the springs are not too bulgy, the cushions can be covered over with burlap and tacked to the base. A layer of upholstery cotton can be used on top of the burlap before the upholstery is applied. If the shape of the couch is irregular, the upholstery padding can be cut from 4″ polyurethane. This can be covered as loose cushions or as a complete unit. Upholsterer's cotton stuffed into the corners will prevent the corners from crushing down when the upholstery is applied. (See illustration.) A certain amount of tailoring is necessary to make the upholstery cover. Piped or corded seams give the most finished appearance, but boxed edges are quite presentable and can be done by an amateur. The material for the top and bottom is cut out with ½″ seam allowance on all sides. These are laid on the cushion wrong side up. The material for the edges is cut out with the same allowance for seams and wrapped around the edge of the cushion. The tops are basted to the edges on three sides so that the cover fits snugly, and the cushion is then slipped out the open side and the cover machine stitched and turned right side out. After the cover has been slipped over the cushion, the fourth side is closed with hand stitching.

There is seldom a need to build a free-standing sofa unless it must be a unique style that cannot be found elsewhere. Like any other construction project, a detailed construction drawing is the preliminary step. The illustration (p. 268) done in cut-away detail shows the basic assembly that might be adapted to several styles.

Tables and Cabinets

Rectangular, four-legged tables are simple to construct, although the beginner may experience some difficulty in making them sturdy. Tables that will be used for writing or dining are nearly always 30″ high. Card tables and typing tables are 27″ high. The strength of any table is in the base, the skirt and legs. If this part of the table can be made sturdy, the entire table will be steady when the top is added. Methods of base assembly are shown. (See illustration.)

Cabinets, bookcases, and cupboards are relatively

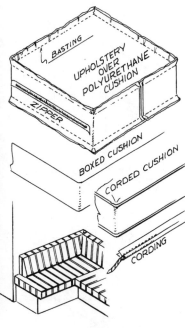

CUSHION COVERS

BASTING

UPHOLSTERY OVER POLYURETHANE CUSHION

ZIPPER

BOXED CUSHION

CORDED CUSHION

CORDING

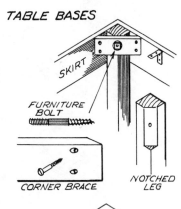

TABLE BASES

SKIRT

FURNITURE BOLT

CORNER BRACE

NOTCHED LEG

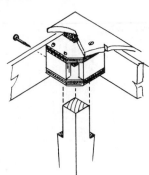

CABINETS

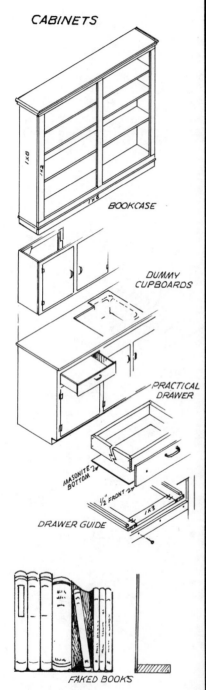

BOOKCASE

DUMMY
CUPBOARDS

PRACTICAL
DRAWER

MASONITE
BOTTOM

½ FRONT

DRAWER GUIDE

FAKED BOOKS

easy to build, but like steps and platforms, they require considerable lumber and are, therefore, expensive. Most pieces can be assembled from stock sizes of material and a few short cuts are often possible that can save money.

Cabinets, for example, are not always practical. It may only be necessary to open one door or drawer: the rest can be faked. Wall cupboards are the same: the business of the play may only require the removal of a cup and saucer or a stack of papers. In such cases, the cabinet framework may be constructed of small frames covered with muslin or Easy Curve, except for the practical opening. Hardware is mounted on the surface and the detail of other openings is painted in. There are a few standard dimensions to be considered if the units are to appear authentic: Kitchen cabinets that sit on the floor are 36″ high and 24″ deep; bar counters are usually 42″ high, unless they have fixed stools, in which case they are nearer 48″; and hanging cupboards are normally 12″ deep, varying in height from 12″ to 30″. Where cupboards are hung above a working counter, there should be 18″ between the counter and the bottom of the cupboard.

Cabinet doors may be made with a 1″ × 2″ backing frame with plywood or Easy Curve on the surface, or with a single piece of ¾″ plywood. The important thing is that the door panel must lay flat in the opening, otherwise it will not close properly. Doors which fit flush in the opening will require cabinet butt hinges. Door pulls and catches are standard and can be purchased locally.

Drawers can be very aggravating if they jam or lop when opened. This can be avoided by building in drawer guides, but the drawers must be constructed so they will slide easily. A tray or light framework on which the drawer will slide can be built into the cabinet in a few minutes, and will generally work better than slotted guides or commercially built units. (See illustrations.)

Practical bookshelves that are to hold real books are simple to construct, but they must be sturdy enough to support weight if real books are used. Shelves of this type need not be more then the depth of a stock 1″ × 8″ (7½″). The distance between shelves for standard books is 9", but larger volumes, such as law books, may require 12" to 14" between and 11½" depth. Shelves that are longer than 36" will require a center support. The simplest method of supporting shelving is to rest each end on a 1" × 2" cleat screwed to the sides of the case. (See illustrations.) Combination units such as secretaries or corner cupboards may also be constructed and finished so that they can be saved for future use. The glass doors usually found on cabinets of this type can be made as light wooden frames reinforced with light metal corner brackets or plates. The glass effect is achieved by tightly stretched blind cord across the back of the frame to simulate leaded glass.

Since most of the books on a shelf will be dressing for the stage, rather than for practical use, faked book backs are often used to fill the shelves. These may be cut in sections from Easy Curve and painted to simulate the book backs. By attaching a 1" × 3" board to the back, they will stand upright on the shelves. (See illustration.)

Three-Dimensional Properties

It was noted in an earlier part of this chapter that properties may often be part of the scenery. For example, a rock form that may be a part of the setting may also be considered a piece of stage furniture if the actor will sit on it. The building carpenter may be involved in the construction of such a piece, but very likely the property crew will take over the final modeling and handling of it during performance.

The construction of irregularly shaped forms is actually less difficult than it might seem. If the actor is to sit or stand on the rock surface, there must be sufficient flat area, and the supporting structure must be strong enough to bear the weight. Literally, such units of scenery are modeled platforms or benches in the shape of a rock. (See Figure 4–21, p. 178.)

The preliminary step in constructing a rock form is to lay out the material for the base on which will be scribed the contour. Since the contoured base will form a base for the supporting legs, there must be sufficient space for their attachment. Scrap pieces of $1'' \times 12''$ fitted and cleated together will be satisfactory, although there may be instances where plywood might be needed for strength. The stock for the weight bearing surface can be laid out in the same way, then the legs contoured and fitted so that they act as supports as well as ribs over which chicken wire or screen will be formed to create the irregular shape of the sides. The spacing between the ribs will depend on the contour, but there should be a rib at each major projecting point.

After the chicken wire has been shaped over the form, a final covering of papier-mâché, burlap or other material is pasted over the wire to create the textured surface. Papier-mâché is the least expensive and lightest weight covering, but it is brittle and susceptible to surface damage. Two methods of preparing the paper and paste for mâché may be used. The first is to tear newsprint into small bits and soak it in water until it becomes a pulp. Enough prepared wheat paste is added to the pulp so that it will stick together and this is spread over the wire form. Since a great deal of the pulp will drop through the wire, a layer of flat pieces of newsprint that has been pasted on both sides can be put over the wire first and allowed to dry partially before the pulp is applied. The second method uses only flat paper strips built up five or six layers thick. This produces a slick surface, as opposed to the roughness of the pulp method. Coarse surface texture can be added by mixing strong glue sizing with coarse sawdust, granulated vermiculite, or similar aggregates troweled or dabbed over the surface.

Coarse burlap (gunny sacking) can be dipped in hot scene glue and laid over the chicken wire, retaining the wrinkles to suggest rock or bark texture. The same can be done with strips of unbleached muslin where the coarser texture is not desired. When these materials dry, the surface is quite hard. Where weatherproof covering may be desired for outdoor use, Celastic or fiber glass may be used. Both are expensive, but they are very durable and unaffected by moisture.

Smaller three-dimensional objects, such as statuary, urns, and relief carvings may be done in several ways, depending upon how the object is to be used. One method is to model the form in clay or plasticine and then make a plaster mold from which the final pieces can be cast in plaster, poly-foam, or Celastic. Objects that are modeled in full-round will require a mold that is in two or more sections, but a one piece mold may be used for flat relief casting. In the first place, the advantage of a mold is to be able to make more than one object by recasting, whereas if only one piece is needed, time will be saved if the original model can be used as a base for mâché.

As an example of the steps necessary in making a casting, assume that two identical crests are needed for set properties. The first step is to model the form in clay or plasticine, starting with a slab of clay an inch or more in thickness. If the contour is symmetrical, a paper pattern can be cut and laid over the slab as an outline guide. The outline is cut, slanting inward from the base to avoid an undercut. The design is then modeled in the surface, or built up with thinner layers on the surface. After the design is completed, if moist clay has been used, the clay should be allowed to dry partially to a leather hard state, or if plasticine, the next step can be pursued immediately. Next, the entire model should be painted with liquid latex, building up at least five coats, allowing each to dry before adding the next. The latex will dry as a layer of pliable rubber and will serve as a parting agent for the plaster layer to follow.

To prepare for casting, a wood fence or wall is assembled that is at least 1″ larger than the model in every direction, and 1″ deeper than the thickest part of the model. The inside of the frame should be heavily coated with vaseline and set in place surrounding the model. Since this wall will be removed later, the joints should be screwed together.

The plaster is prepared as follows: In a plastic or porcelain lined vessel place enough cold water to fill the mold frame to the top of the model. (This must be estimated, but be generous rather than run short.) In another container, measure out an equal amount of quick-set gauging plaster or plaster of Paris. Sprinkle the dry plaster slowly into the water, stirring gently

CASTING IN PLASTER

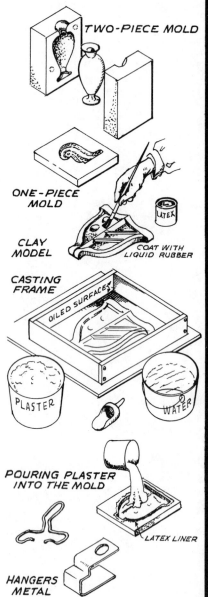

TWO-PIECE MOLD

ONE-PIECE MOLD

CLAY MODEL

COAT WITH LIQUID RUBBER

LATEX

CASTING FRAME

OILED SURFACES

PLASTER

WATER

POURING PLASTER INTO THE MOLD

LATEX LINER

HANGERS METAL

until all of the plaster has been dissolved. Sprinkle in additional plaster without stirring until the plaster forms small floating islands on the surface, then stir to mix and allow to stand until the mixture starts to thicken, not more than fifteen minutes. When a shallow furrow remains on the surface when a finger is drawn through the mixture, it is ready to pour into the mold. Slosh a small amount into smaller details first, then pour the remainder quickly because the plaster will set very rapidly. The sides of the frame should be bumped with the fist or a mallet to jiggle any air bubbles to the surface, then the mold should set for five or six hours before attempting to remove the outer frame. At this point the plaster will be hard enough to lift the mold off the model, but the casting should dry three or four days before further casting should be attempted. The latex liner should be removed and set aside until the mold is dry. The container in which the plaster was prepared should be wiped out with old rags or paper towel. Under no circumstances should plaster be washed down the sink because it will harden in the drain!

To make the final casting, the latex liner is replaced and the plaster prepared in the same way but only enough to fill the liner. A metal hanger should be prepared to embed in the wet plaster beforehand. This should be a heavy wire loop or a metal strip bent so that it will not pull out. The hanger is pressed into the wet plaster. To reduce the weight of the casting, some of the plaster may be scooped out of the back before it hardens.

After the new cast has set in the mold two to three hours, the mold can be lifted off by turning it over. The latex will peel off, and after cleaning in water, it can be replaced and a new casting started. When the castings are completely dry, they may be lightly sanded with fine sandpaper to remove rough areas, and shellacked. If the plaster is to remain white, the surface design can be accented by brushing a touch of raw sienna mixed with shellac into the corners and crevices. (See illustration.)

Sculptured forms are usually built up by constructing a skeletal form of wood with rounded segments to give the form definition. Screen or chicken wire is then formed over the wooden armature which can be covered with papier-mâché, Celastic or surgical gauze. The detailed parts, the head, hands, and feet may be modeled and cast in plaster; or, the higher density styrofoam is compact, yet soft enough to carve with a knife or shape with a hot wire. After the basic form has been roughed out with a knife, a little practice with the hot wire cutter will prove to be quite effective for finer details and smoothing. A hot wire device can be made by shaping a 7″ length of 14 ga. soft iron wire to fit into an electric soldering gun. The wire can be bent to any configuration and the heat melts the styrofoam so there is no crumbling as there is with carving. After the modeling is completed, a layer of surgical plaster gauze can be applied in small strips like mâché. The gauze is immersed quickly in water, then laid over the form overlapping each strip. This will harden in fifteen minutes, and after it is completely dry, it can be sanded lightly and painted with latex paint. Where the figure is to be draped, swags of muslin dipped in hot scene glue are easily worked into shape and will harden to look as though they were carved marble or stone. (See illustration.)

Special Effects

Many of the special effects that were once in the repertoire of every "prop man" have been replaced by special devices or recordings. Though all special effects are not in the realm of the property department, where special construction of effect props is necessary, the property crew should be able to handle them.

Running water effects or fountains that actually spurt water are not uncommon requests of the property crew. Both of these effects will undoubtedly require the assistance of a plumber, at least to supply the proper fittings because pipes or hoses will be necessary to bring water onto the stage. To plumb a sink, for example, a single faucet with water supply is usually adequate. This faucet should have a fitting for a standard garden hose which must be run to an offstage source. A member of the crew should be responsible for checking the flow before the scene begins to make certain that all

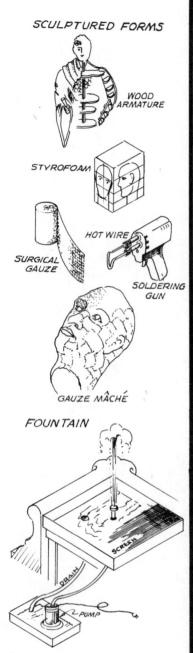

SCULPTURED FORMS

WOOD ARMATURE

STYROFOAM

HOT WIRE

SURGICAL GAUZE

SOLDERING GUN

GAUZE MÂCHÉ

FOUNTAIN

SCREEN

DRAIN

PUMP

the air has been exhausted from the line. If the sight-lines from the audience will allow, it may be possible to set a plastic dishpan in the sink to catch the water, otherwise it will be necessary to have a hose fitting attached to the sink drain so that the water can be caught in a pail backstage.

Rigging a fountain is more complicated. First of all, a galvanized pan large enough to contain the splash must be made to catch the water. Because the water probably will splash over the floor and set pieces, the top of the pan should be covered with fine window screen. The screen breaks the droplets and will prevent a great deal of the splatter. Second, the nozzle that emits the flow of water must direct the water so that it will fall within the pan. The size of the opening in the nozzle should be no more than ¼", but if the hole is too small, the stream may not be visible to the audience and is apt to be more erratic if there are changes in the water pressure. Third, the pressure in the main water lines changes whenever water is drawn, which may cause the fountain to spurt a stream of water six feet high one moment and one foot the next. A small electric water pump that recirculates the water is much more reliable and assures a relatively constant pressure. Remember that the painted areas surrounding the fountain must be either latex or casein to prevent the paint from running if it should get wet. (See illustration.)

Reasonably good sound effect recordings are available for almost every imaginable sound, but their effectiveness is directly related to the efficiency of the sound system and the placement of speakers. Also, unless there is a master technician editing and dubbing these "canned" sounds onto tape so that the cues are precise, many of the effects will be unsatisfactory. The heyday of "live" sound effects occurred during the 1930s when radio drama was popular, but several devices used at that time are still most effective, whether they are used "live" during performance, or recorded on tape to be played back on cue. (See illustrations.)

Visual effects, such as vases falling from a shelf or a picture frame crashing to the floor, are simple enough: A wire extending through the wall will dislodge the vase, and a pin that holds the frame can be withdrawn from offstage. Objects that float about can be manipulated with black filament fishing lines from above. Smoke effects can be produced by heating powdered sal ammoniac placed in a shallow pan over an electric hot plate, or in the cone of an electric heater. Heavy fog effects that hug the floor can be made by placing large quantities of dry ice in a vat of water. Fog that drifts above the floor can be created most effectively with a fog machine which ejects dense clouds of smoke produced from heated mineral oil. Fog machines can be purchased or rented and the oil—fog juice—can be purchased from scenic suppliers.

Bottles and glasses that must be broken can be a problem because of the danger of flying glass. The motion picture and television prop people have solved this problem by making glasses and bottles from candy glass —actually sugar and water heated to 260° F. as you would make rock candy. The syrupy mixture is poured onto a flat sheet, and when cooled it will harden into a flat plate of glass. It may also be cast in a well made two-piece mold. Santolite MHP, a plastic powder developed by Monsanto Chemical Company, can also be melted and cast as a substitute for clear glass.[3] This material has a higher melting point and is less apt to become sticky under hot lights than candy glass.

This section dealing with set dressing and property construction omits many things not because of space, but because the field is limitless. We are constantly learning new things about synthetic materials and the adaptation of them to the materials of the scene. Volumes have been compiled on the furniture of each period, on glassware, and on architectural interiors. However, knowledge about all of these things is not a substitute for ingenuity. Even ingenuity must be followed up with technical skills, many of which cannot be learned in the theatre. The arts and crafts, interior decoration, mechanical arts, physics, and architecture are only a few of the contributing resources which together make up the technology of the theatre.

[3] W. Oren Parker and Harvey K. Smith. *Scene Design and Stage Lighting*, 2nd ed. (New York: Holt, Rinehart & Winston, 1968), p. 277.

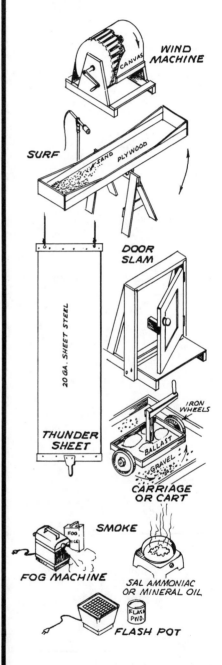

SPECIAL EFFECTS

WIND MACHINE

SURF

DOOR SLAM

20 GA. SHEET STEEL

THUNDER SHEET

IRON WHEELS

BALLAST

GRAVEL

CARRIAGE OR CART

SMOKE

FOG MACHINE

SAL AMMONIAC OR MINERAL OIL

FLASH POT

SUGGESTED READINGS

Aronson, Joseph. *The Encyclopedia of Furniture,* 3rd ed. New York: Crown, 1968.

Cescinsky, Herbert. *English Furniture from Gothic to Sheraton.* New York: Bonanza, 1968.

Gardner, Helen. *Art Through the Ages.* New York: Harcourt Brace Jovanovich, 1936.

Rogers, Meyric R. *American Interior Design.* New York: Bonanza, 1957.

Strange, Thomas Arthur. *French Interiors, Furniture, Decoration, Woodwork and Allied Arts.* New York: Bonanza, 1968.

Terhune, Florence B. *Decorating For You.* New York: Barrows, 1944.

The Connoisseur's Complete Period Guides. New York: Bonanza, 1968.

TECHNICAL ORGANIZATION AND RESPONSIBILITIES

For whatever reason an individual develops an interest in the theatre, it soon becomes apparent to that person that beneath what seems to be a spontaneous, and often undisciplined production, there is actually a tremendous amount of discipline, rehearsal, and organization necessary to make it that way. It is true that there are some forms of drama that attempt to avoid structure, for example the "happening," but these forms are, for the most part, experimental. Improvisation in any field of creative expression is admirable because it opens new avenues of expression that are not restricted by tradition, but at the same time, when artistic levels of production are achieved by this approach, it is more by accident than by intention. Thus, in spite of our liberated attitudes and receptiveness toward experimentalism in the theatre today, the technical structure of theatre production is still essential to achieve quality and artistry.

Technical organization is essential for several reasons: It distributes responsibility among those capable of performing the various tasks most effectively; it makes it possible for many facets of technical preparation to proceed simultaneously; and it contributes to greater efficiency by focalizing upon specific assignments. The coordination of the technical organization is usually the responsibility of a technical director who works with the director and set designer in planning the entire production. In nonprofessional organizations, the technical director may also design the settings, but in any case, the technical director must be completely familiar with all technical requirements of a production and assign crews to carry them out according to plan.

TECHNICAL ORGANIZATION

The Stage Manager

Among the personnel who make up the technical theatre organization, the stage manager is most closely associated with the director and the cast, even though his or her responsibilities include many phases of technical supervision during the run of a performance. For this reason, the stage manager is often designated on recommendations from both the director and technical director. Thus, the stage manager is considered an important link between the stage director and the technical director because it is through the stage manager that channels of communication are kept open.

The stage manager of a professional company is considered the chief liaison between the many departments of production, the producers, Actors Equity Association, and the other artists and labor unions involved. In addition, the stage manager is responsible for the play manuscript, noting there any changes that are made during rehearsals or the run of the show, and the technical operation of the production. "The stage manager is the center of the production . . . . As such, he should have a knowledge of the 'nuts and bolts' of the other specialities. He may not know a quarter-note from an oboe, but he should know in general how the orchestrator accomplishes his work, in terms of time. He may not have the faintest notion of how to tie a spanish bowline, but he must be able to grasp a master carpenter's explanation of a proposed short-cut and to discern how it will affect the artistic function of the show."[1]

Although the responsibilities of the stage manager of a nonprofessional production are far less complicated than those of a professional production in regard to personnel, tasks that relate to the running of a smooth performance differ very little. The list of duties described below is general, insofar as it is not associated with any particular production; however, the duties must be accomplished, whether the show will be a twenty minute one-act play for children, or a multiscene musical.

1. In conference with the director, designer, and technical director, determine the production plan with respect to schedule for rehearsals, location, and production dates.
2. With the director, determine the location, hours, and physical requirements needed for auditions for

---

[1] Bert Gruver. *The Stage Managers Handbook*, revised by Frank Hamilton. (New York: Drama Book, 1972), p. xxi.

the cast; check out sufficient numbers of manuscripts or playbooks for the auditions; mark each
with an identifying number and note in each any
cuts that the director may have made.

3. Post notices or prepare for the media, the announcement of auditions with all pertinent information,
including crew registration.

4. Prepare information forms to be filled in by those
who audition for roles in the production and/or
those desiring technical assignments; information
should include name, address, phone, previous experience, technical interests, and any other information the directors may desire.

5. With the director, determine how auditions are to
be conducted and arrange for assistants to help
with the organizing of procedures.

6. With the technical director, prepare special forms
for crew registration, including two or more prefer-
ences for assignment.

7. Following auditions, post the cast and crews, an
announcement of the first meeting, and a schedule
of rehearsals and work periods.

8. At the first meeting, check company roster for accuracy; present the general policies regarding the
use of the theatre, punctuality, discipline, and responsibilities.

9. Provide the directors and management with copies
of the company roster.

10. Before the first scheduled rehearsal, issue play manuscripts to each member of the cast and to the head
of each crew. Keep a record of manuscripts issued.

11. Prepare a stage manager's prompt book with adequate marginal space for notes, diagrams, and technical cues. Either attend, or have an assistant present at every rehearsal to record action blocking,
stage business, cues, and property requirements.

12. Arrange for furniture, or reasonable substitutes,
needed for rehearsal and be sure that it is properly
positioned before each rehearsal. Notify the technical directors and/or head of the property crew of
any changes or deletions.

13. With the director, determine the specific rehearsal

when hand properties, or reasonable substitutes, will be required and arrange with the head of the property crew to provide them, as well as an assistant who will set up and strike them at the end of each rehearsal.

14. With the technical director, arrange for special effects, such as door bells or telephone bells, needed for rehearsal cues. Effects of this nature are usually operated by the stage manager or an assistant.

15. With the head of the costume department, arrange for rehearsal costumes, if they are requested by the director. This would apply where full skirts or hoops might affect the actor's movement. Set up a schedule for fittings if necessary.

16. With director and technical director, arrange for first stage rehearsal. This is usually set aside as a technical rehearsal at which all set pieces, lights, costumes, and properties are brought together for the first time to familiarize the actors with the scenery, and the technical crew with the running of the show. An assistant should be at hand to take copious notes on every aspect of the rehearsal, and with a stopwatch in hand, time each scene, each shift of scenery, each costume change, and any other technical cues that would affect the running time of the production.

17. Establish and post a time schedule for dress rehearsals and performances when actors must be in the theatre. Make it mandatory that every actor report in on arrival and check the list religiously to make sure everyone is present.

18. Unless otherwise instructed by the director, schedule a meeting of the cast and crew heads immediately following each dress rehearsal for the purpose of going over notes taken by the directors and ironing out any technical problems.

19. After actors are in the theatre, they should be kept posted of the time at frequent intervals so that they will be ready to go on stage. If dressing rooms are equipped with intercom, this provides a convenient means of announcing the time, otherwise an assistant should be sent around. Usually the first call

is thirty minutes before curtain, the second fifteen minutes, and then every five minutes. Traditionally, the stage manager calls "places" for the opening scene ten minutes before the scheduled time for the curtain, which allows time for checking on everyone.

20. With the house manager and the head electrician, establish the routine and cues for opening each performance and each act. A starting time will have been established, but the house lights cannot be taken down while the aisles are full of patrons. When the house is seated, the house manager should notify the stage manager. After a final check to be sure the actors are in place, the stage manager signals the electrician to lower the house lights. House lights are usually lowered first to halfway, then on a signal from the stage manager, they are dimmed out all the way. This delay of a few seconds allows time for the seating of the last stragglers and for conversation among the audience to subside. Since the stage manager may not be able to observe the house, the electrician should confirm that the dimout is completed, and in turn the stage manager should announce that the curtain is being opened. If the stage lights are to come on after the curtain is open, the stage manager should cue the electrician when the curtain is open. At the end of the scene, a five second delay is usually allowed before the signal to fade the house lights is given. If the house lights are brought up too quickly, the applause is stifled.

21. With the director, before the final rehearsal, the routine for curtain calls should be worked out and rehearsed. A stage call should be sent out to all actors who are not in the closing scene at least five minutes prior to the final curtain.

22. Following the final curtain, the stage manager should remain on stage until all properties have been cleared, set changes have been made, and the work lights have been turned off.

23. With the directors, check on any changes that may be necessary after the opening performance. Such

changes should be communicated directly to the people involved and members of the cast should be notified if a special rehearsal will be required.
24. With the directors, determine a firm policy regarding the admission of visitors backstage after performances and assign assistants to supervise and enforce these policies.
25. Following the close of the show, check in all manuscripts and file the roster and attendance report with the business office.

Checking through the 25 duties of a stage manager just described, one sees there are very few that can be deleted, and it is easy to see how many added responsibilities might be necessary for a multiscene production. Many of the jobs can be shared with efficient assistants, and in some instances the director has an assistant who may take over some of the duties of the stage manager.

The Scenic Artist

The head of the scene painting crew has no counterpart in the "Broadway" professional theatres because Broadway scenery is constructed and painted in scenic studios on a job basis. However, there are many professional theatres that are self-contained and have facilities for building scenery and scene painting on the premises. Where union affiliation is required, the master scene painter must meet demanding standards with respect to skills and seniority, and assistants must work up through the levels of apprentice and journeyman before they are eligible to head a crew.

In nonprofessional and college theatres, the scenic artist is usually selected by the technical director and/or designer from the most qualified members of the technical volunteers. Hopefully, the scenic artist will have had sufficient experience in the preparation of paint and techniques of application to proceed with minimum supervision, otherwise it may be necessary for the technical director to give instructions along the way.

Although it would seem that the scenic artist's crew would have little to do until the construction of the scenery had been completed, there are tasks which must be performed very early in the schedule of construction activities. The following responsibilities are attributed to the scenic artist.

1. With the technical director, determine what the painting requirements for the setting will be and whether sufficient material and equipment is on hand to do the job.
2. With the designer, carefully examine the elevation details and color renderings to gain a thorough understanding of what is expected and which jobs should be completed first. This is particularly important where portions of the set may have to be flown and must be ready several days before the entire set will be moved on stage.
3. With the building carpenter, determine the anticipated completion schedule of newly constructed units, the need for scene glue, flameproofing, and sizing.
4. Prepare and have ready for use: hot glue, scene glue, and dutchman paste.
5. Check through all supplies: pails, brushes, pigments, dyes, dry glue, and whiting, and report the status of supplies to the technical director at least once each week.
6. If painted drops are called for, arrange for the fabric to be sewn together, for battens for the top and bottom, and for flying or laying out the material in preparation for work on it. If cartoon or projection methods will be used, preparation should begin at once so the design can be transferred as soon as the raw drop has been sized. Supervise the application of sizing and design.
7. With stage carpenter, determine when major set pieces will be ready for sizing and set up a schedule for the crew.
8. Supervise the preparation of base coat colors and check each with designer before painting begins.
9. Supervise the layout of all line work and surface details.
10. Supervise surface texturing.

11. Provide for touch-up paints to repair any damage to paint after set pieces are on stage. Look especially for unpainted edges and exposed screw heads.
12. Keep all brushes, containers, and work areas clean, and dispose of any left-over paints before they spoil.
13. Check over the set at least two hours before each performance and touch up if required.
14. Before the closing performance, provide the technical director with a list of all depleted supplies.

The Stage Carpenter

The technical organization in some theatres may not distinguish between the two phases of theatre carpentry, lumping all responsibility upon a master carpenter who oversees both construction and running of the production. It is suggested here that the differences between set construction and the assembly, and handling of scenery during the run of a performance are sufficient to warrant a separation of the two activities, with an efficient head in charge of each. Thus, the duties of the stage carpenter, aided by capable assistants, include initial assembly of scenic units after they have been built, setting scenic units on stage after they have been painted, rigging all flown units, and shifting all scenery during the run of a performance.

To head a stage crew, a person must be familiar with the rigging system and its operation, the stock scenery and how to maintain it, the scenery and how to assemble and handle it efficiently, and the organization and direction of shifts and movement of scenery during the production. The stagehands (grips) who assist the stage carpenter have a responsibility for the smoothness of a production equal to that of the actors: neither can be late on a cue. This is particularly true when the show has more than one scene, and shifts of scenery must be made during a brief blackout. Every individual must be at the assigned post and ready to move the instant the lights are lowered. It also means that grips assigned to work during production must be constantly aware of the production's progress, and under no circumstances should they converse among themselves or with the

RUNNING PLOT

Production   *The Little Foxes*   *Hellman*

Act *I*   Scene *1*   Right Stage   *Max*

Preset   *All*

On Cue _____

_____   Left Stage   *Mary*

Time _____

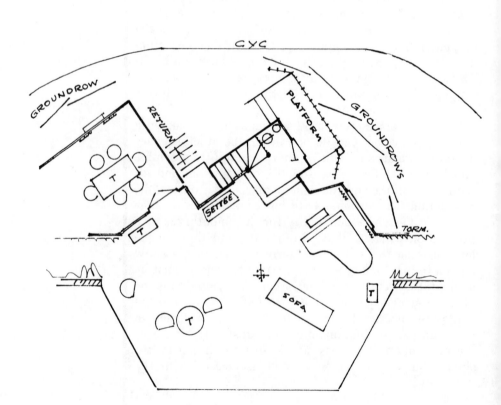

RIGGING SCHEDULE

Production _THE LITTLE FOXES - HELLMAN_

Act _I_ Scene _1_

Preset _ALL_

On Cue _____

Time _____

Distance	Set No.	Description	IN	OUT
	1.	HOUSE CURTAIN	✓	
1'-0"	2.	TEASER	✓	
5'-6"	3.	TORMENTOR	✓	
6'-0"	4.	CEILING PIECE - FRONT SET	✓	
7'-0"	5.			
7'-6"	6.			✓
8'-0"	7.			
8'-6"	8.			
9'-6"	9.	SKY CYC - FRONT	✓	
10'-6"	10.			
11'-6"	11.			
12'-0"	12.			
13'-0"	13.			
14'-0"	14.			✓
14'-6"	15.			
15'-0"	16.			
16'-0"	17.			
17'-0"	18.			
17'-6"	19.			
18'-6"	20.	CEILING PIECE - BACK SET	✓	
19'-0"	21.	ELECTRICAL - LEFT	✓	
20'-0"	22.			
21'-0"	23.			
21'-6"	24.			✓
22'-6"	25.			
23'-6"	26.			
24'-6"	27.			
25'-0"	28.			
25'-6"	29.			
26'-6"	30.			
27'-6"	21.			
28'-0"	32.	SKY CYC - BACK		
29'-0"	33.		✓	
29'-6"	34.			
30'-6"	35.			
31'-0"	36.			
32'-0"	37.			✓
33'-0"	38.			
33'-6"	39.			
34'-6"	40.			

----- DISTANCE BACK OF PROSCENIUM WALL -----

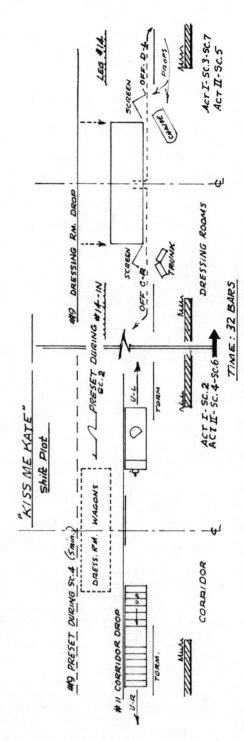

An example of a Shift Plot. Many diagrams of this type can be placed on a single work sheet.

actors unless it is absolutely necessary or relevant to the production.

A single set show minimizes the need for the stage carpenter backstage; however, it is poor production practice to excuse the entire crew. At least two members of the crew should be on stand-by to take care of emergency repairs, and the stage manager should be notified of their presence and where they are stationed.

Multiscene productions can be chaotic unless they are planned down to the last detail. A basic plan is usually provided by the set designer, but the final plan must be worked out by the technical director and stage carpenter and recorded in the form of a plot. The plot usually will include floor diagrams showing the position of each scenic unit, a rigging plot that will indicate numbers of each set of lines that will be used, the offstage position of each unit, and a roster of the crew and specific assignments for each shift. Copies of the plot should be provided for all members of the crew who should study and memorize their duties with the same diligence that they would for a role in the play. (See illustrations.)

The stage carpenter may be expected to assume the following duties:

1. Inspect and make an inventory of all stock scenery, including all flats, platforms, stair units, or other pieces of scenery, noting their dimensions and condition. A sketch of each piece may be required to describe it fully.
2. Make an inventory of all stage hardware; cleats, braces, hinges, casters, hanger irons, spare cable, and hemp lines, etc. Notify the technical director of any shortages which may delay production.
3. With the technical director and/or designer, study the production plan, elevations, and floor plans to become familiar with the setting and its requirements.
4. With the director and designer, assist stage manager in laying out the outline of the set on the rehearsal floor.
5. Scenery that is to be used from stock should be inspected and repaired if necessary. Minor structural

alterations should be made by the stage crew, but if rebuilding will be required, the units should be sent to the carpenter shop and brought to the attention of the building carpenter.

6. Assemble scenic units as indicated on the elevation and label each unit to correspond to the plan. Labeling should be done on the toggle rail with chalk, or on a file card attached to the toggle; never mark on the cover of a flat. Example, Act I-Rt (A-B-C), or Act III, L Platform, etc.

7. As units are assembled, set aside for paint crew to dutchman and size.

8. Clear all battens that will be needed for flying scenery and prepare cables and hanger irons. Flown pieces must be hung before other set pieces are set on the stage.

9. If painted drops are required, assist scenic artist in preparing battens and flying drop for painting.

10. After the stage floor has been scrubbed clean, lay the ground cloth or overlay in preparation for moving the set on stage.

11. With the designer or technical director, lay out the set outline on the stage floor. Preliminary marking is usually done with chalk. The scene painters may paint the line in with washable scene paint after the set is in position.

12. Carefully analyze the backstage area with the head of properties to determine the most efficient arrangement of scenery and props.

13. Make a running plot and assign the personnel for shifting and flying scenery.

14. If the shifts will be complicated, arrange with the stage manager for a technical run-through with sets and props before the technical rehearsal is called. Many technical bugs can be ironed out this way, particularly traffic congestion and timing that often makes a technical rehearsal last far into the night.

15. Clean—scrub if necessary—the stage area daily before rehearsals and performances. This must include the wings and upstage areas. Check before each performance 'that there are no obstructions, chairs, props, or debris, which will be in the way

of actors or stagehands who must move in the dark backstage.

16. Crew call should be no less than one hour before curtain time so there will be ample time to check all the operational details. It is generally considered good practice to reset the opening scene following the final curtain, rather than before the show because the audience may start entering the theatre before the job is completed.

17. When the show closes, it is the responsibility of the stage crew to strike the set. This involves removal of all scenery from the stage, dismantling all units, and with the assistance of the building carpenters, salvaging of all reusable materials. All drops and flown pieces of scenery must be removed from battens, and if counterweighted rigging has been used, each set should be rebalanced; otherwise manila lines should be neatly coiled over the belaying pins. Scenery to be saved must be stored.

18. All hardware used for set assembly is generally removed. Hardware should be sorted and returned to proper storage. Ropes and cables should be coiled and tied so they will not become tangled.

19. Permanent stage dressing, such as cycloramas, legs, and borders should be rehung.

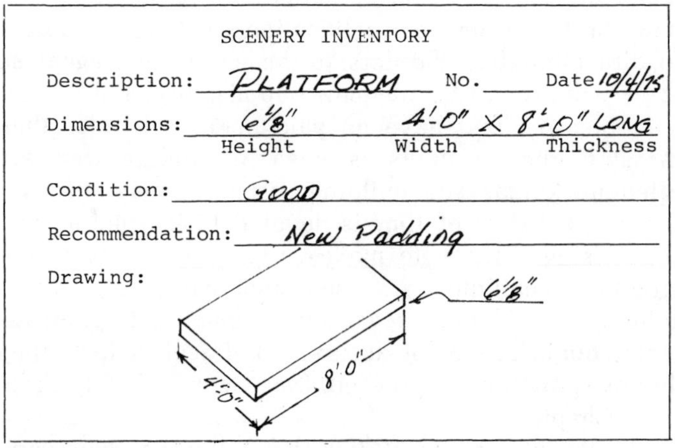

SCENERY INVENTORY

Description: *PLATFORM*　No. ____　Date *10/4/75*

Dimensions: *6⅛"*　*4'-0" X 8'-0" LONG*
　　　　　　　Height　　　Width　　　Thickness

Condition: *GOOD*

Recommendation: *New Padding*

Drawing:

Figure 7–1. *A typical inventory card.*

20. The stage floor should be thoroughly cleaned. If a ground cloth has been used, it should be cleaned, taken up, and stored.

Since the heaviest burden of cleaning up after a performance rests on the stage carpenter, organizing the strike is usually one of the responsibilities connected with this position. In college and community theatres, it is not uncommon for the entire company to share in the strike, which can be good since "many hands make light work," but organization is critical if chaos is to be avoided. If the planning of a strike establishes a sequence in which scenery is to be handled, there will be less likelihood of scenery damage.

The Building Carpenter

Maintaining tools and equipment and overseeing building materials are responsibilities a building carpenter must assume, in addition to constructing scenery. Thus, the head of the building crew, often referred to as the master carpenter, is in charge of the scene shop and the activities that go on in it. Above all, the crew head must be qualified to understand and interpret working drawings, be familiar with the basic tool processes and skills, and have a thorough knowledge of acceptable construction practices. Though the crew head may not be directly involved in ordering materials and supplies, it is important that his/her qualifications include the ability to direct intelligent orders to the purchasing agent so there will always be adequate supplies on hand.

In theatres that have no paid personnel other than the staff, the assistants assigned to building crew are often unskilled. The building carpenter may discover that a great deal of time is devoted to instructing and supervising activity to make certain that correct construction techniques are used, and that tool practices adhere to regulations regarding care and safety. Assistants should strive for accuracy and seek help if they do not know how to proceed. (See General Safety Practices, Chapter 4.)

The list of responsibilities that follows is basic and will apply to most levels of production activity.

1. Before any construction activity begins, make an inventory of all tools and equipment, including general supplies of nails, screws, bolts, staples, etc. Place an order for any shortages and retain a copy of the inventory and amend it as new tools or equipment may be added.
2. Check through the lumber stock and muslin or canvas stock to ascertain the amount on hand and place orders for stock where shortages appear likely.
3. With the technical director and/or designer, review the construction requirements for the production, and assign priorities to jobs so the general pace of production will not be delayed.
4. With the crew, lay out a plan of production, determine the distribution of jobs, the method by which tools will be checked in and out and the clean-up procedures. Janitorial work is usually done by the crew: first, because floor clutter and dirty equipment is conducive to accidents, and second, because working hours in the scene shop rarely coincide with regular janitorial service.
5. After construction work has begun, make a daily check on the condition of tools and equipment, and note particularly any shortage of supplies. As new supplies are delivered, check the stock against the amount ordered, and do not be hesitant to reject deliveries that do not meet specifications: This applies particularly to lumber that may be twisted or warped so badly that it will not be usable.
6. Keep the stock racks neatly stacked so that material will be accessible, and urge assistants to work from short-end stock wherever possible to avoid unnecessary waste.
7. Keep the scenic artist informed of daily requirements for scene glue or flameproofing so there will always be adequate supplies available. The carpenters may manage their own glue preparation, in which case a member of the crew may be responsible for keeping the glue pot full.
8. After all construction has been completed, the shop area cleaned, and the stock put in order, the work of the crew is complete until the set is struck. How-

ever, the crew head should be present at the technical rehearsals in the event any structural changes have to be made. The crew should remain on call.

9. The building crew must be present when the set is struck to dismantle all pieces of scenery that will not be stored, to salvage reusable stock, and to dispose of trash materials that cannot be used again.

10. After the strike is completed, all tools should be checked in and the inventory updated. Power equipment should be disconnected or the switches locked, and the tool cases locked. If the crew has been issued keys, they should be checked in.

11. The building carpenter should give a copy of the inventory to the technical director, noting any shortages that should be replaced, as well as the status of supplies that may be needed before the next production is scheduled.

The Property Crew

It was noted in the preceding chapter, devoted exclusively to properties, that the actor relies heavily on properties in the performance of stage business. In addition, the property crew is expected to provide those visual elements requested by the designer to dress the setting. The property master or mistress is therefore involved more directly with the running of the play than any of the other technical department heads.

The individual who heads the property crew must be a taskmaster insofar as tenacity and punctuality are concerned: Props must be in the proper place at the proper time. The property master must also be strict, and often authoritarian, with regard to the care and management of properties, many of which are borrowed and valuable. Hopefully, the cast and members of the technical crews will respect the property master's responsibility. Once properties have been brought on stage for a rehearsal or performance, a rigid "keep off" policy is in effect. This must apply to offstage, as well as onstage properties. In addition to acting as the guardian of properties, the crew will be expected to organize their work as follows:

1. Read and analyze the play, taking notes on properties actually listed, as well as those implied. Make
   a list of properties for each scene, noting whether
   they are personal, business, or dress properties.
2. Make a careful study of the designer's floor plans,
   elevations, and sketches noting style interpretation,
   arrangement, and changes. Some designers include
   a property plot in their plans which will indicate
   styles of furnishings, drapes, and bric-a-brac.
3. With the director and designer, confer on lists,
   changes, or deletions, and determine what properties or substitutes will be required for early rehearsals. The stage manager or an assistant should
   be included in this conference.
4. After a working list of props is confirmed, the information should be transferred to property plots
   and copies should be made for the directors and the
   stage manager. A plot is a chart listing each prop
   by description, category, location, and page reference. This will become a working prop list that may
   be changed as the play moves through rehearsals.
5. When rehearsals begin, one or more members of the
   crew should be assigned to provide rehearsal props
   and take notes on placement, additions, and deletions. This information should be relayed to the
   property master and the property plot updated.
6. Construction and procurement of properties should
   be organized and started immediately so that everything will be on hand for the first technical rehearsal.
7. A weekly progress report should be made to the
   technical director and/or the designer pertaining
   especially to articles that cannot be found and possible substitutions.
8. Assign the running crew and determine the duties
   each shall have during the performance run.
9. With the running crew, make a running plot that
   will be used by the crew to preset props before the
   show, and a checklist for setting up and striking
   the props for each scene.
10. With the stage carpenter, determine where prop
    stations can be set up backstage for the running
    props and personal props. Determine where larger

Property Plot

Production_____

Act_____ Scene_____   Date_____

Item	Per.	Biz	Dress	Preset	Location	Actor
Hall Tree			X	X	Up-L hall	
Three men's hats woman's hat & cape	X			X	Hall tree	Oscar, Ben, Leo, Birdie
Umbrella stand w/3 umbrellas			X	X	Up-L hall	
Hanging tapestry			X	X	Up-L hall	
Drapery-rose vel. lace curtains			X	X	Up-L bay window	
Chandelier—gas lighted			X	X	Center ceiling	
Grand piano w/bench 19th c.			X	X	Up-L bay	Birdie
Duncan Phyfe drum table			X	X	Down-R center	
2 Duncan Phyfe armchairs			X	X	R & L of dr. tbl.	
1 Lyre back Duncan Phyfe side chair			X	X	Up of dr. tbl.	
Victorian loveseat rose velvet			X	X	Up-center	
Victorian sofa gold brocade			X	X	Down-L center	
Victorian side table			X	X	Down-L	
Victorian oil lamp lighted			X	X	On table	
Victorian console table			X	X	Wall-R	
Crystal compote w/fruit			X	X	Table-R	
Crystal candle sticks w/white tapers			X	X	Table-R	
Dining table set w/ plates, goblets, napkins, silver			X	X	Dining rm. up-right	
Silver tray w/port decanter & 6 glasses	X	X			Off-dining rm.	Addie
Gold pocket watch	X				Vest pocket	Marshall

Figure 7–2. A typical property plot.

pieces or furniture can be stored. Also develop a plan with the stage carpenter whereby props can be moved on and offstage without interfering with scene shifts, and vice versa.

11. When the set is on stage, position all properties, furniture, tables, etc.; and place all set dressing. All floor units should be *spiked,* that is, marked with small strips of tape or paint, so that each piece may be reset in precisely the same place for each performance. For multiscene shows the spiking is done with a different color for each scene. Scenes that are changed in blackout are often spiked with luminous tape that will glow in the dark. Furniture positions may be changed during technical rehearsals, so be prepared to spike the new locations.

12. Before the technical rehearsal, set up prop stations —tables or carts—in the wings and arrange personal properties where they are readily accessible to the actors. Running props should be organized before the show and double checked to make certain everything is in the proper location. An assistant must be assigned to each prop station. A shielded work light can be helpful.

13. At the end of each act, props that will not be used again should be removed from the prop stations to reduce clutter and the likelihood of picking up the wrong article.

14. After each change of scene, the property master should signal the stage manager when all is in readiness.

15. Following the final curtain, all properties should be collected and returned to the property room, with the exception of furniture and those attached to the set. A careful check should be made to make sure that everything is accounted for. Furniture is usually moved together center stage and covered completely with clean dust covers. The clustering of furniture clears the stage area so the floor may be cleaned before the next performance. Offstage furniture must also be covered.

16. Crew call for each performance should be no less than one hour before curtain time so there will be

ample time to reset furniture and prop stations. If emergency repairs are necessary, the property master may set an earlier hour.

17. Immediately after the closing performance, the full crew must be on hand to strike all properties from the stage. This includes everything. The stage crew should not attempt to strike any portion of the set until the property crew is finished.

18. Furniture should be dusted and inspected carefully for soil or damage, then covered and stored, or set where it will be picked up for return. New properties that are to be kept should be listed on the property inventory before they are stored. Everything must be left clean, including the property room and the storage areas.

19. The property master must arrange for the return of borrowed or rented props immediately following the closing of the show. Such items should be delivered personally to obtain an acknowledgement of their return.

20. The property master should file a report with the technical director or production manager which confirms the return of all properties, along with any claims or problems.

The Lighting Crew

While lighting will not be included in this book because it is one of the advanced technical areas that requires study in depth to be of any significant value, the lighting crew and the work they perform in staging a production must be included in the technical organization. Heading the crew, the electrician must be more knowledgeable than the title would imply. A knowledge of circuitry is imperative, but the electrician must also be fully informed on the intricacies of the lighting control system, how to compute loads and resistance, how to use lighting instruments and color filters, and perhaps most important, how to control and manipulate the equipment to achieve a level of artistry that is compatible with the production as a whole. As theatre lighting technology has become more sophisticated, lighting design has gained equal status with scene design. The settings and lighting may be designed by the same person, but it is no longer uncommon for the lighting to be designed by another specialist.

The head of the lighting crew must be familiar with the light design symbols used by the designer, and be able to direct the crew in placing instruments to achieve the effects desired. After instruments have been placed, they must be patched into the dimmer circuits to permit flexibility of control, then focused and color filters put in place as specified in the lighting design. These are only preliminary responsibilities of the light crew head and members of the crew:

1. With the light crew, study the play script making detailed notes, scene by scene, of lighting changes, special cues, and probable sources of light.

2. With the light designer, analyze the design and the lighting effects, adding or deleting from the list already begun. Determine the requirements for control, the placement of specials, and color changes.

3. With the crew, check over every instrument that is to be used for faulty wiring, check the condition of connectors, check the freshness of lamps, and clean all lenses and reflectors. Lay out all stage cable and carefully check and test all connectors. The supply of color filter stock—gelatin and/or plastic—must be checked to make certain all colors needed will be available.

4. Place all instruments and plug into working circuits keeping a careful list of the number of each circuit. Many electricians record the circuit numbers on the designer's plot beside the instrument symbol.

5. With the crew, make a patch plot which will indicate the number of each circuit that will be patched into each dimmer. The plot should be planned for the greatest control possible without overcomplicating the actual manipulation of the dimmers during the performance. If the lighting design is plotted in areas, it is often helpful to group the controls for an area close together.

6. When the set is moved on stage, focus and insert

specified color frames. The designer often assists with focusing to check the angle and beam spread.

7. With the light designer, prepare cue sheets. This must be done with the script in hand so that each change is identified with stage business, line cues, or signals from the stage manager. Tentative levels for each dimmer, and the direction of fades can often be entered on the cue sheets before the technical rehearsal.

8. An assistant should be assigned to follow the script to warn of upcoming cues and to make notes of any changes in readings or cues. Two assistants may be needed on stage to plug in circuits following scene changes or make adjustments in focus or colors.

9. With the stage manager and house manager, plan the procedure to be followed in raising and lowering the house lights at the opening and closing of each scene.

10. Crew call for rehearsal and performances should be no less than one hour before curtain time. Every circuit must be checked to make certain there are no burned out lamps or other difficulties, and to replace color filters that have faded.

11. Check all instruments on the floor, or those attached to the set to be sure they have not been bumped out of position.

12. When the show closes, the general procedure is to remove all instruments and stage cable from the stage floor that would affect the striking of the set. Backing lights attached to the set must be removed, and as the stage is cleared, all other instruments should be taken down and stored. Instruments on the first pipe and ceiling beams are sometimes left in position, but color frames and filters are usually removed. Cables are coiled and stored.

13. All circuits should be unpatched, all dimmers set at full on position, and all switches turned off and the control panel locked.

14. The lighting equipment inventory should be checked to ascertain that everything is accounted for. The control room and storage areas must be left immaculate and locked.

15. The play script and cue sheets should be filed with the stage manager, and any shortages of equipment or supplies should be reported to the technical director.

The Costume Crew

The costume crew may work under the supervision of a costume designer who is a member of the theatre staff, and is often considered a separate department of the production team. In other instances, the costumes may be designed by the set designer, or the head of the costume crew. In any case, costumes and costume management must be coordinated with the production demands as a whole, just as properties, stage carpentry, and lighting must be, to achieve any degree of artistry.

It is the crew head who sets up the work schedule and organizes the activities of the crew. In the professional theatre, the stage manager is usually responsible for making dressing room assignments, but in smaller companies, particularly college and community theatres, the job is assigned to the head of the costume crew. This is a matter of convenience more than anything else because the crew has a definite place to hang costumes as they are completed. As a general rule, dressing rooms are locked when not in use, not only to protect the actor's personal effects, but to protect the costumes as well. If the actors are not issued keys, the costume crew must be on hand to open the dressing rooms before each performance and must assume responsibility for keeping the rooms clean and the costumes in order.

If the theatre maintains a wardrobe of stored costumes, one of the initial responsibilities of the costume crew is to see that it is kept in order and if costumes are taken out, that they are returned to their proper place. Most well organized wardrobes maintain a card file or inventory of all costumes, so as new items are added, they should be noted on the inventory.

The following is a list of responsibilities which are generally expected of the costume crew:

1. Check all supplies and sundry materials such as pins, sewing and machine needles, thread, etc., that

will be needed for general operation. Equipment should also be inspected and repairs made if necessary.

2. With the costume designer and/or set designer, determine the requirements of the production. From the sketches, select fabrics and colors, see which items can be taken from the wardrobe and which will be constructed.

3. With the director, set up a schedule for members of the cast to report to the costume room for measurements. Measurements should include head and hat sizes, neck, shoulder, chest, bust, waist, hip, inseam, and outseam. Other measurements include shoulder to center back, shoulder to wrist, shoulder to waist, waist to floor, and shoe size. These are measurements usually requested by houses that rent costumes.

4. After costume fabrics have been selected and gathered, patterns are developed and the work schedule set up for construction.

5. Post a schedule for fittings as the work proceeds. As each costume is completed, it should be pressed, labeled with the name of the character and the scene in which it is to be worn, then hung in the player's dressing room.

6. Rented costumes must be ordered several weeks in advance to assure delivery. The name of the play and scene, the name of the character, and the complete list of measurements must accompany the order. Also include the dates of performance and dress rehearsals, specifying the date that delivery must be made.

7. At the request of the costume designer and/or director, a "dress parade" may be called at which all costumes are worn to check appearance and fit, ensemble color groupings, and omissions. Take notes on any alterations or additions. This meeting should occur before the first dress rehearsal.

8. Assign assistants to serve as dressers, to assist actors who have fast costume changes, and if necessary, to arrange with the stage manager to have temporary dressing facilities set up backstage.

9. The crew head should sit with the director and designer during all dress rehearsals to take note of changes or alterations.

10. Following each rehearsal, each costume should be carefully inspected for possible repairs. Daily pressing is usually necessary to keep costumes looking fresh, and frequent cleaning may be required. This should be a daily routine throughout the run of the performance.

11. After final performance, all costumes should be taken out of dressing rooms. All costumes, except rented ones which are cleaned by the costume supplier, must be either dry cleaned or laundered. Costumes must never be stored in soiled condition.

12. A crew call should be made to return costumes to storage and the inventory amended to include new items.

13. Dressing rooms and the costume shop must be clean and all work materials stored.

14. A report should be filed with the head of the costume department or technical director, reporting the status of equipment and supplies.

There are obviously other areas of technical responsibilities that have not been discussed, partly because they are often included in the jobs of other crews, and partly because the nature of the assignment makes them unnecessary for some productions. One example is a sound crew. Many hours of preparation are often necessary to record and synchronize musical backgrounds and sound effects for some productions, while another may only require entr'acte interludes. Where scenic effects will be produced with projections, there obviously will be a need for a projection crew to prepare films or slides. Both of these areas are highly technical and require a crew that is familiar with the equipment and its use.

While the house manager and the ushers are not considered part of the technical organization, they cannot be overlooked in the production plan because they form an important link between the activities backstage and the handling of the audience. The house manager is often appointed by the managing director or the business office since the position may also include the collection of tickets, but in college or community theatres, the house manager is often appointed from members of the company who are not in the current production. In either case, efficient management of the house has much to do with the audience's receptiveness and the technical smoothness of good theatre.

The responsibilities of a house manager include: the selection of assistants to collect tickets; the assignment and training of ushers so they will be familiar with the seating plan and can seat the audience quickly with a minimum of confusion; and setting up of a system of handling emergency calls. With the stage manager, determine a routine for opening and closing scenes, the length of intermissions and signals that will be used to communicate when the house is in, and for the time when the auditorium doors can be opened before each performance. Finally, the house manager may have a responsibility of providing security guards for the corridors and one or more stand-by firemen to handle emergencies.

Business management, like house management, is a nontechnical assignment, but one which is closely linked to efficient technical theatre operation. The role of a business manager will vary greatly, depending on the kind of production group. In professional groups, the business manager is concerned with bookings, rentals of facilities, the purchase of goods and services, and union and equity relationships. In other words, the job is that of a general manager and often the producer as well.

A well organized community theatre which maintains a regular schedule of productions will generally be headed by a production manager who either appoints or hires a business manager to supervise box office income, ticket sales, and the payment of royalties and production expenditures. This means, of course, that a bank account must be set up, as well as an efficient system of accounting. Educational theatres seldom allocate monetary management to students. Nevertheless, a student business manager can perform an important service even without the authority to disburse funds.

Business management at any level connotes record keeping and efficiency. Though a student in this position may not be involved in preparing the operations budget and the handling of monies, there are responsibilities that the business manager can assume which will aid in maintaining liaison between the technical personnel and the front office. Procedures for handling financial matters differ greatly, so the suggestions that follow are general, and by no means all-inclusive:

1. Maintain a ledger or cash book with sufficient columns and pages for recording detailed purchase requests submitted by crew heads. There should be a column each for: the date of the order, the person or company from whom the purchase is to be made; the unit and total cost, and the date the order is received.
2. A simple order form on which crew heads can list the items needed can be helpful. This form must have space for the director or technical director's approval. The student business manager may be authorized to contact merchants to determine the best price, but some merchants are hesitant to give out this information without written authorization. The form may then be submitted to the official business clerk who processes it through a purchasing agent.
3. Prepare a production schedule that lists the dates when business activities are to be handled: payments for royalties and scripts; advertising deadlines; schedule of cast publicity pictures and production photographs; date when tickets and programs must be ordered, etc. While the student business manager may not initiate this schedule directly, contact can be made to remind those who are responsible.
4. Most theatre operations rely on a petty cash fund for small emergency purchases, usually less than $10. The business manager should keep an account of such purchases, itemizing each purchase receipt as to firm, items, cost, who made the purchase and for which crew. A copy of the itemized list and the original receipts can then be submitted to the business clerk for processing through approved channels. When the reimbursement is received, the business

manager can distribute the proper amounts to crew heads or individuals who made the purchases.

5. Entries should be posted in the ledger daily and totalled weekly. Where each crew may have a limit on the amount spent for production, the business manager should inform the crew head and the technical director of working balances. At the end of each production, the business manager should file a detailed report of all business matters with the directors.

6. The business manager may be responsible for ticket sales at the box office. This can involve the handling of a considerable amount of money. In such cases, record keeping is more complicated because it will include banking receipts, recording the number of tickets issued, and the actual number of seats occupied for each performance. A careful record of complementary tickets issued should be kept and included in the report.

There are those who say that a theatre that cannot meet the cost of production at the box office is not worth its salt. This is, of course, not always true. Commercial theatres must show a profit or close down. There are very few educational theatres or community theatres that are financially independent. Nevertheless, sound management practices and handling of funds can be a great asset when seeking subscribers and contributors to support theatre programs.

CONCLUSION

To summarize very briefly, the intent of this book has been to introduce the materials of the scene. To do so without also presenting the methods and techniques of using them would be meaningless. Although at times it has been difficult to avoid becoming overly technical, no topic has been pursued further than what a beginning technician should know to participate effectively in activity in the theatre.

The content should not be ranked in the category of a "how to do it" book. Any book that is devoted to the methods of doing something has a way of stimulating the unimaginative to be even less imaginative, and seldom produces good theatre. Thus, the sections dealing with construction are laced with the word "may," in hopes the reader will discover other possible ways of building things and new materials to use.

The "must" statements will be found mainly in the last chapter which deals with technical organization. Theatre is a highly disciplined art which is the result of creative output of artists and technicians with talents in many expressive media. Devotion, hard work, and a keen sense of responsibility, with perfection as the goal, are the "must" ingredients of a good theatre.

SUGGESTED READINGS

Gillette, A. S. *Stage Scenery: Its Construction and Rigging*. New York: Harper & Row, 1972.

Gruver, Bert, revised by Frank Hamilton. *The Stage Managers Handbook*. New York: Drama Book, 1972.

Plummer, Gail. *The Business of Show Business*. New York: Harper & Row, 1961.

INDEX